The Practices of Global Citizenship

The Practices of Global Citizenship

Hans Schattle

ROWMAN & LITTLEFIELD PUBLISHERS, INC.
Lanham • Boulder • New York • Toronto • Plymouth, UK

ROWMAN & LITTLEFIELD PUBLISHERS, INC.

Published in the United States of America
by Rowman & Littlefield Publishers, Inc.
A wholly owned subsidary of The Rowman & Littlefield Publishing Group, Inc.
4501 Forbes Boulevard, Suite 200, Lanham, Maryland 20706
www.rowmanlittlefield.com

Estover Road, Plymouth PL6 7PY, United Kingdom

British Library Cataloguing in Publication Information Available

Library of Congress Cataloging-in-Publication Data

Schattle, Hans.
  The practices of global citizenship / Hans Schattle.
    p. cm.
  Includes bibliographical references and index.
  ISBN-13: 978-0-7425-3898-6 (cloth : alk. paper)
  ISBN-10: 0-7425-3898-2 (cloth : alk. paper)
  ISBN-13: 978-0-7425-3899-3 (pbk. : alk. paper)
  ISBN-10: 0-7425-3899-0 (pbk. : alk. paper)
    1. World citizenship. 2. Globalization—Social aspects. 3. Civil society. I. Title.
JZ1320.4.S33 2008
323.6—dc22

                                                                2007021582

Printed in the United States of America

⊗™ The paper used in this publication meets the minimum requirements of
American National Standard for Information Sciences—Permanence of Paper
for Printed Library Materials, ANSI/NISO Z39.48-1992.

For my parents,
Arthur and Sheila Schattle

Contents

Acknowledgments

This book sees the light of day thanks to many years of support and encouragement from family, friends, mentors, colleagues, and self-described global citizens all around the world. The words on these pages are just a small measure of my deep gratitude. For starters, I wish to thank the individuals who contributed directly to this project by sharing their reflections and their life histories during interviews with me. My considerable debt to each person who granted me an interview—and agreed to be quoted by name in this book—is obvious in the pages that follow. Without the generosity and insights of these individuals, the study that produced this book never would have been feasible.

My inquiry into the idea of global citizenship dates back to my postgraduate research at the University of Oxford. I am indebted especially to David Marquand, my research supervisor at Oxford, and my examiners for the DPhil in political science, Stuart White and Anthony McGrew. Thanks also to numerous scholars who shared ideas and offered advice, especially Michael Freeden, Elizabeth Frazer, Randall Hansen, Kay Lehman Schlozman, Lance Bennett, and Sidney Tarrow. I also appreciated many comments from individuals at seminars and conferences at which I presented portions of this work.

Jennifer Knerr, formerly of Rowman & Littlefield, made the initial commitment to this book, and editor Jessica Gribble has been delightful to work with throughout the long process. I am also grateful to production editor Anna Schmöhe, copyeditor Elizabeth Yellen, and two anonymous reviewers of the manuscript. Of course, the many shortcomings remaining in this book are my own.

Portions of this book appeared in an article, "Communicating Global Citizenship: Multiple Discourses Beyond the Academy," published in the May 2005 issue of *Citizenship Studies* (vol. 9, no. 2, 119–33). I thank the journal's editors for their kind permission to include passages from the article in this book.

David Miles of Oxford University Computing Services helped me on many occasions as we created and then expanded my database of published references to global citizenship. Mansfield College, the University of Oxford Graduate Studies Office, the University of Oxford Vice-Chancellor's Fund, and the Babson College Board of Research provided me with grants along the way. Special thanks to the scores of secretaries and assistants around the world who helped me arrange interviews for this study, and also to Jane Buswell at Mansfield College, Esther Single at the University of Oxford, and Carol Fialkosky at Boston College. Additional thanks to my colleagues at Roger Williams University for their camaraderie and support as I wrote and revised the manuscript.

Most of all, heartfelt thanks to my extended families and friends, especially my spouse, YunKyung Choi; our little girl, Louise Marie; and my parents, Arthur and Sheila Schattle, to whom this book is dedicated, for their wholehearted encouragement of this endeavor and their steadfast love and kindness.

Hans Schattle
Bristol, Rhode Island
March 2007

Introduction

The idea of global citizenship, in recent years, has become all the more visible and varied around the world. From Grayslake, Illinois, to Invercargill, New Zealand, elementary and secondary schools are trying to inspire youngsters to grow into morally responsible, intellectually competent, and culturally perceptive global citizens. Within the political arena, alongside the perennial conferences of international institutions that hopscotch from Seattle to Prague to Hong Kong, activists on behalf of a wide range of causes—labor rights, poverty eradication, environmental protection—have proclaimed themselves as members of a global citizens movement struggling, for the good of all humanity, to bring social justice and democratic accountability into the world economy. At the same time, multinational corporations are increasingly crafting global citizenship strategies in an effort to project more socially responsible public images. Global citizenship is also resonant for some of the most highly achieving, affluent, and mobile individuals in the international marketplace. From a venture capitalist in Tel Aviv to a management consultant in Johannesburg, many highly sought-after professionals, enriched by graduate degrees from premier universities outside their countries of origin and networks of contacts literally around the world, regard themselves as global citizens.

Global citizenship might strike some individuals as a new and experimental idea. In reality, however, the many images and practices of global citizenship reflect an ancient tradition—the cosmopolitan tradition—that dates back at least as far as ancient Greece and has languished in the margins of political thought for more than twenty-five hundred years. The term "cosmopolitan" is a composite of the Greek words for "order," "universe" and "citizen." According to the cosmopolitan ideal, it is possible and desirable for individuals and institutions to regard each human person as worthy of equal respect and concern,[1] regardless of the legal and political boundaries of any existing government jurisdictions.[2] As this book will show, not all versions of contemporary global citizenship echo this moral aspiration—one of many competing approaches to cosmopolitanism in the present day.[3] Still, ever since Socrates and Diogenes both identified themselves as citizens of the universe, numerous thinkers and writers throughout history have advocated various forms of global membership and belonging as well as solidarity across humanity.[4]

Global citizenship, therefore, extends from a much older tradition than national citizenship,[5] which coincided especially with the American and French revolutions of the late eighteenth century and expanded the scale of democratic citizenship from ancient and medieval city-states. However, even as public recognition of global interdependence continues to increase, global citizenship is often dismissed by intellectuals and political actors as impracticable, especially in the absence of an overarching world government or a cohesive set of global governing institutions. Skeptics of global citizenship often argue that the nation-state remains the exclusive basis of political membership and allegiance—as well as legal jurisdiction over borders and passports—and that meaningful participation in politics can be found only within small-scale communities in which motivated and responsible citizens know and trust each other enough to identify and promote common interests through sustained public deliberation.[6] Those who doubt the feasibility of global citizenship continue to carry much weight in academic and public debate, especially within the realms of politics and political science, which tend to privilege more precise definitions of citizenship centered on the authority of national governments. Even among those heralding recent developments such as the growth of political activism across borders, the onset of global platforms of digital communication, and the inability of any nation-state to control its own destiny in today's interdependent world, much of the conventional wisdom continues to situate citizenship squarely within the nation-state and dismiss global citizenship as "blithe nonsense."[7]

This book provides a response to the skeptics by illustrating how many practices of global citizenship now flourish in the present day. Rarely does global citizenship at the dawn of the twenty-first century carry any direct implications for the institution of national citizenship or amount to advocacy for centralized worldwide government institutions. The legal institution of national citizenship might well remain firmly in the hands of nation-states, and nation-states might well remain a principal (but not exclusive) basis of political membership and allegiance, but these realities no longer keep global citizenship from flourishing in other ways. Like it or not, individuals all over the world are choosing to think of themselves as global citizens and to shape their lives as members and participants in communities reaching out to all humanity. Meanwhile, educational institutions, multinational corporations, advocacy groups, community service organizations, and even some national governments are embracing the idea of global citizenship. Indeed, as this book will illustrate, the term "global citizenship" is often used as a lever in public debate to evaluate the actions and policies of nation-states. For the most part, today's understandings of global citizenship now percolating in public life do not advocate a centralized world government or undermine national patriotism. Instead, they often extend notions of political participation and belonging not only outward into the international arena but also inward within the most immediate spheres of domestic politics and local civic life. For many of today's self-described global citizens, the popular adage "think globally, act locally" has evolved into something more comprehensive: "Think and act locally and globally."[8] These days, you don't have to leave home to be a global citizen, or to put it more modestly, to see yourself as a global citizen in continual formation.

Rather than emerging as a noun indicating fixed membership status or permanent transfers of authority and allegiance from the nation-state to the world, global citizenship now emerges frequently as a verb, a concept of action signifying ways of thinking and living within multiple cross-cutting communities—cities, regions, states, nations, and international collectives— as well as network-based communities such as neighborhood groups, service organizations, and professional associations. Global citizenship in public discourse typically evokes far more dynamic forms of belonging and participation than precisely defined models of national citizenship that emphasize passport controls and legal standing. Just as the term "globalization" is often defined as a series of processes that gradually and continuously strengthen sources of global interconnectedness with ever-increasing speed and intensity,[9] global citizenship is often depicted as a progression continuing in stages throughout the course of a lifetime.[10]

To be sure, self-described global citizens and organizations advocating global citizenship do not necessarily represent the prevailing sentiments of humanity. Nationalism is the most powerful basis of political allegiance and commitment in the world today. Even in the world's more affluent and technologically sophisticated countries, the idea of global citizenship has yet to strike a chord with the majority of the population.[11] The "tipping point" for global citizenship—an event or catalyst that would catapult this idea into the mainstream of public opinion—has yet to arrive. However, the ways in which the practices of global citizenship are now unfolding give us an early indication of how the long-enduring and long-sidelined cosmopolitan tradition is finally beginning to catch on. We have reached a pivotal moment in history: for centuries, philosophers and visionaries have been dreaming of global citizenship, and now the dream is beginning to turn into reality, not because of any changes in the authority of nation-states, but because everyday people are finding ways to take global citizenship for themselves.

While scholars in recent years have advanced and debated various theories of global citizenship, we know comparatively little about the practices of global citizenship from the points of view of individuals around the world who now think of themselves as global citizens, as well as organizations that have linked the idea of global citizenship to their activities, programs, and strategies. This book aims to help close such gaps in our knowledge by allowing numerous self-described global citizens and advocates of global citizenship to speak directly to us about how they have chosen to think about this idea. Through their personal narratives and insights, we are left with a detailed rendering of the many ways in which the idea of global citizenship actually finds meaningful and deliberate expression in the present day. The practices of global citizenship now encompass numerous strains of thinking, some of which are compatible with enduring ideals of citizenship and political community and some of which are not. This book provides a forum for these competing perspectives and invites further debate about which understandings of global citizenship might be more convincing than others. The concept of "citizenship" has a long and distinguished history of disagreement over its appropriate meaning,[12] and the practices of "global citizenship" open up new lines of contestation.

The study presented in this book amounts to the results of nearly a decade's worth of research and analysis. In order to identify how the practices of global citizenship have actually emerged in recent years, I put together a database[13] of news articles, public speeches, press releases, and similar documents that all share one key attribute: a published or spoken reference to "global citizenship" or one of its equivalent terms, such as "global citizen," "global citizens," and "global citizenry."[14] I coded these media references into dozens of categories for content analysis and identified from them a good representation of people who could be interviewed.

The purpose of the interviews was to clarify what the individuals mentioned in the news sources had been thinking when they made their respective public statements regarding global citizenship.[15] I did not impose any particular view of global citizenship on the respondents, nor did I ask hypothetical questions that would redeploy the more familiar aspects of national citizenship—such as voting rights, taxation, and border controls—into a model of world citizenship. Instead, I made every effort during conversations to focus on what these individuals had been thinking anyway—independently of being approached for this study—and to give the respondents the time to elaborate freely on their views.[16] Although each interview was tailored to the individual circumstances, several questions related to the broader research agenda were asked repeatedly, as appropriate:

- When did the idea of global citizenship (or a global citizen) first come into your vocabulary or enter your thinking?
- Was your usage of this term just an accident? Or just an eloquent turn of phrase? Or a metaphor? Did you really mean it?
- Taking away the term "global," what does it mean to you to be a citizen?
- What informed your thinking in using "global citizenship" that didn't necessarily show up in print?
- How do you think about your own identity as a citizen? In which community or communities do you consider yourself a citizen?
- What other ideas figured into your thinking when you turned to "global citizenship"?
- Instead of "global citizenship," why not use terms such as "global awareness," or "global person," or "member of the human family"? What does "global citizenship" bring to the table that other terms do not?
- Some people argue that citizenship necessarily must be restrained within state and national borders. How would you respond?
- Are persons global citizens from birth? Is everyone a global citizen by default, or by virtue of living in an interdependent world? Or do individuals become "global citizens" through life experience?

Thanks to the generosity of the people who shared their life histories and reflections with me during interviews for this study, we have a vivid and detailed portrait of myriad practices of global citizenship in the present day. And yet, any canvas of global citizenship inevitably must be incomplete. My decision to limit this study almost entirely to individuals and organizations that have chosen to identify with the specific term "global citizenship" meant that countless other persons and groups around the world with similar outlooks, endeavors, and qualities remained outside the boundaries of my analysis. As this study is also limited to usage of "global citizenship" in the English language, the vast majority of respondents came from English-speaking countries: 48 percent from the United States; 15 percent from the United Kingdom; 11 percent from Canada; 9 percent from Australia and New Zealand; and the remaining 17 percent from countries such as South Africa, Malaysia, Singapore, the Philippines, South Korea, and Japan. Unlike many studies in the social sciences, the names of the persons quoted in this book are real. No interviews conducted for this project were anonymous or confidential, as all the respondents had landed in my database through media references to global citizenship.[17]

First, this book explores the many sorts of formative experiences that have prompted individuals to consider themselves global citizens (chapter 1). Next the book examines how the term "global citizenship" encompasses various concepts—some of which emphasize global awareness, moral responsibility, and participation in politics and society (chapter 2), and others that emphasize achievement, cross-cultural empathy, and freedom of movement, at least for the world's most affluent and privileged individuals (chapter 3). The book then examines how the idea of global citizenship has been interpreted and applied in a variety of arenas, such as civil society organizations and activist groups (chapter 4); schools, colleges, and universities (chapter 5); multinational corporations (chapter 6); and governing institutions (chapter 7). The conclusion argues that the global citizenship, in the present day, is rich, complex, and tangible. In this new millennium, global citizenship has become much more than an abstract ideal espoused mainly by philosophers and visionaries. Now, more than ever, the practices of global citizenship are upon us.

CHAPTER ONE

Pathways of Global Citizens

What sorts of life experiences lead individuals to regard themselves as global citizens or to take the idea of global citizenship seriously? Global citizenship carries multiple origins in the lives of everyday people. For each self-described global citizen who refers to international travel as a starting point of global citizenship, another global citizen refers to an experience close to home, such as growing up in an unusually diverse or close-knit local community. For some individuals, global citizenship emerges through a career decision or a study abroad program and often finds expression in civic engagement within local communities overseas. For others, global citizenship originates as a state of mind or as an aspiration—even in dreams of moving beyond seemingly mundane surroundings and discovering other countries and cultures. Some view global citizenship primarily in the context of political activism, while others think mainly in terms of expanding cultural horizons, while still others relate global citizenship primarily to their professions and credit the helpful influences of mentors who encouraged them to overcome potential or perceived roadblocks. The pathways presented in this chapter serve to illustrate how global citizenship can be cultivated through a willingness to modify, enlarge, or at least look more carefully at the communities to which they belong.

The Impact of the Childhood Years

From the end of World War II to the collapse of communism—when three generations of today's self-described global citizens came of age—the term "global citizenship" remained almost entirely absent from public debate.[1] However, many individuals who now consider themselves global citizens remember building relationships, as youngsters, with people from backgrounds other than their own, as well as thinking about their lives as extending well beyond the borders of their native countries. With the benefit of clear hindsight, childhood memories often are identified as the first pathways of global citizenship. Many advocates of global citizenship come from families with international experiences or broad cultural outlooks. For instance, Don Will, a professor at Chapman University who has taught a course in global citizenship, is the son of a pacifist (who chose to work in a hospital during World War II rather than join the military) and the grandson of missionaries who built schools and churches across South America. Raised in a communal housing development in suburban Chicago—at a time when Chicago's many ethnic groups remained quite separate from one another in neighborhood enclaves—Will grew up in a remarkable melting pot: "We had African American families; we had mixed families; we had Jewish families; we'd go to Hanukkah parties; we would do all kinds of different things."[2]

A different sort of communal spirit influenced the thinking of Nelly Ukpokodu, who was born in Nigeria into the cultural group Etsako, composed of approximately 40,000 people living together within Edo State (now Bendel State). Now an associate professor of education at the University of Missouri in Kansas City, Ukpokodu regards herself as a global citizen and encourages her students to consider themselves global citizens. Ukpokodu traces her global citizen identity to a strong sense of local solidarity instilled during her upbringing: "Right from day one, when I was growing up, I recognized the interdependence of people and the human family . . . and every person from one end of the community knew the other people at the other end of the community."[3] Ukpokodu learned from her cultural group that "your family is not the only family that you have, that when you are born, you descend into a human family, and this human family involves so many people. One may be related by blood or not to you." Presented in this light, global citizenship begins by fostering ties with one's closest neighbors.

Still other self-described global citizens look back on their childhood days as motivating forces, but in a different sense: a sense of yearning for experiences that would broaden horizons and move them beyond small and seemingly isolated communities. Janet Sipple, professor and chair of St. Luke's Hospital School of Nursing at Moravian College in Bethlehem, Pennsylvania, traced the roots of her fascination with the outside world to her upbringing on a small tobacco plantation in the aptly named town of Farmville, North Carolina. As a youngster, Sipple read voraciously to pass the time and became especially fascinated with the Australian outbacks. About thirty-five years later, in 1989, Sipple took a sabbatical to Australia and taught for a year as a visiting professor at the University of Queensland while also touring the country and giving speeches to professional nursing associations. This experience prompted Sipple to launch an exchange program for professional nurses in the United States and Australia that continues to this day. More recently, Sipple has launched programs that place her nursing students in Australia and Honduras.

Sipple began to consider herself a "citizen of the world," in exactly those words, when she participated in a European exchange program in the summer of 1965, immediately after finishing her undergraduate education. Sipple's motivation came from what she did *not* hear her classmates at West Virginia University saying about their experiences abroad: "All I'd hear about were buildings, and I'd say well, what about the people? How could you be in another country and not know something about the people?" In order to learn about the people overseas, Sipple lived for a month with a family in the heart of Amsterdam and then traveled for a month around Europe. The discovery of "the breadth of this world," in her words, changed her life:

> I felt like I had sort of been brought up out of the earth like a seed that's blooming . . . in terms of my knowledge, in terms of understanding what it meant to be a foreigner. I'll never forget when I went on that plane, it dawned on me: I'm the foreigner; I'm the foreigner. I kept saying all summer, "I'm the foreigner." And that was such a strange feeling—that you didn't have this instant protection or support or even language, money, nothing. The familiar was taken away.[4]

While some individuals find that the experience of being "the foreigner" advances a sense of global citizenship, other individuals find global citizenship in helping visitors from abroad feel less like foreigners. Rosie Brown, for example, began to think of herself as a global citizen when she and her husband, Charlie Brown, began hosting international students at their home in Tulsa, Oklahoma. Brown traces her global citizenship to her upbringing on the U.S.-Canada border in Warroad, Minnesota—a town with an ironic name for someone with Brown's view of the world. When Brown was about ten years old, her elementary school class performed a musical skit about the Netherlands, complete with costumes such as wooden shoes and pointed hats: "And I just said to myself, I'm going there someday, and I think that was really my beginning when the world expanded to me."[5] At the tender age of sixty-three, Rosie Brown finally visited the Netherlands when she and her husband stopped in Amsterdam on their way to Zelenograd, Russia, one of

Tulsa's five sister cities, where they lived for a year as community volunteers. Brown's experiences at home and abroad speak to global citizenship as engagement across cultures.

The Power of Immigration

Short of clear quantitative evidence, it would be far too bold to make a sweeping claim that immigrants generally are more inclined than their counterparts in the general population to think of themselves as global citizens. Nevertheless, themes of immigration certainly figure as powerful formative experiences in the lives of many self-identifying global citizens. In particular, growing up in an immigrant family or in an immigrant community can profoundly influence how a person thinks about the communities to which she or he belongs, and many self-described global citizens say they have been shaped by such experiences. For instance, artist Christian Eckart, the son of German immigrants to Canada, grew up in a German community in Calgary and as a youngster spent Saturdays in German language classes; today, Eckart credits those surroundings in shaping his outlook as a global citizen.[6] Similarly, Washington SyCip, the founder of one of Asia's largest accounting and consulting firms and a former adviser to several international-development organizations, grew up in Manila, where his Chinese immigrant parents immersed the family in a Chinese community and enrolled SyCip and his siblings in Chinese language classes that met each weekday afternoon following their regular schooling. These cross-cultural encounters encouraged SyCip to study at Columbia University, where he earned a master's degree in economics and began a doctorate but set aside his thesis to volunteer for the United States military after the Japanese military imprisoned his father during the World War II.[7] Meanwhile, Michael Szabo, who left his native England to work in New Zealand as a Greenpeace campaigner for several years, said that having a father who had emigrated from Hungary influenced his life. Meeting his Hungarian relatives as a youngster and visiting Hungary as a young adult left Szabo feeling as if he belonged to something larger than the United Kingdom: "If your family is dispersed across borders, then the borders don't really get in the way of how you feel about your family."[8]

Retracing one's family history and ethnic heritage through visits to family homelands also serves to facilitate global citizenship as cross-cultural empathy. Consider how a two-month stay in the rural village of Kilkelly, Ireland, still quite poor and hardly developed in 1967, changed the mind-set of Robert Harper, who was raised, like millions of children of immigrants to the United States, in Brooklyn, New York:

We lived with relatives who probably lived in basically the same way as people from two hundred or three hundred years ago. They had the peat bogs out behind the house, and we went out and cut the squares of peat and put them on the fire, and we gathered the eggs and made the bread and so forth. I was eleven at the time, thinking that this was very different from going to the grocery store and buying things. It really opened my eyes to understand that there are a lot of different ways to live, and what we have and what we think is important is not necessarily important for other people.[9]

Besides learning how life could be much simpler outside Brooklyn, the personal ties that Harper and his family formed with the locals in Kilkelly had a lasting impact. One elderly man, who was not a relative of the family, shed tears when the family departed and pressed a five-pound note into Harper's hand. The summer in Ireland taught Harper that "the world was a little bit bigger" than Brooklyn. When Harper traces the origins of his interest in other civilizations and cultures, it is the childhood trip to Ireland that started a lifelong progression that has taken both Robert Harper and his wife, Catherine Harper, to Japan on separate Fulbright awards and inspired them to adopt a village in Malawi.

Political and Social Activism

Just as local surroundings have as much potential as international experiences to place people on pathways of global citizenship, the roots of active civic involvement among global citizens generally tend to be within domestic politics—even among those who have become transnational activists. Several global citizen activists interviewed for this research reported that their first experiences of political activity were linked with domestic causes and campaigns, illustrating yet again how global citizenship can originate at home. Activist and author Hazel Henderson first became an active participant in New York City politics during the mid-1960s, when she founded the group Citizens for Clean Air and took to the streets to protest industrial pollution. A young mother and housewife at the time, Henderson then worked with Ralph Nader to fight for environmental reforms within General Motors and won a seat for her organization on the corporation's board of directors. She helped organize the first Earth Day in 1970 and wrote a *Harvard Business Review* article on corporate responsibility, which yielded invitations from business schools worldwide to speak on what then was a new line of inquiry: business ethics. This led to what Henderson considers her international breakthrough as a citizen: her decision to attend the first United Nations environmental conference, which was held in 1972 in Sweden and which in

Henderson's mind brought together the global environmental movement: "The kinds of citizen activists who were there were Margaret Mead and Barry Commoner and all the greats, and I ended up in a group there where we had dinner together every night."[10] Her experiences at the conference and the acquaintances she made left Henderson thinking she was a "planetary pilgrim," which she came to regard as a forerunner of the idea of a global citizen: "We were almost, as Jonas Salk had written at about the same time, he said that this was a completely new breed in the world. He said these are the people who for the first time in history, in the human species, are taking responsibility for the whole human family on the planet. This was unprecedented. And so, I immediately self-identified. I thought, OK, that's a good enough image to work off."

For Maude Barlow, volunteer chair of the Council of Canadians, the trajectory of global citizenship started with the women's movement within Canada. In the early 1980s, after working as the city of Ottawa's first director of its Office of Equal Opportunities for Women, she left to join Prime Minister Pierre Trudeau as his senior adviser on women's issues. From here, Barlow found herself drawn into a groundswell of protest against "trade without rules," in her words, amid concern about the future of national health insurance and other Canadian social services especially relied on by unmarried women. The Council of Canadians operated at first entirely within the domestic arena to fight for Canadian social programs but entered international policy debates during the 1990s. After an unsuccessful battle against the predecessor to the North American Free Trade Agreement (NAFTA), and then against NAFTA itself, by 1997 Barlow's attention turned to the proposed Multilateral Agreement on Investment (MAI), which the Canadian government at the time was supporting. Barlow and numerous other activists around the world launched a media campaign against the MAI, which they criticized as giving multinational corporations global rights without corresponding global responsibilities: "And I guess it was in that period that I stopped seeing this as simply me, as a Canadian, fighting this, but me, as part of a global citizens' movement, fighting economic globalization as it is now characterized."[11] In this particular international battle, Barlow and her colleagues prevailed, at least for the near term. In the face of mounting resistance, the Organization for Economic Cooperation and Development (OECD) backed away from the MAI in late 1998. Barlow says she thinks of herself as both an "unrepentant Canadian" and a global citizen and considers her involvement in the transnational protest movement challenging economic globalization as essential in the struggle for retaining a distinctively Canadian way of life: "We couldn't fight it on a country basis alone, especially a middle power like Canada. . . . It just became clear to me (that as) transnational corporations were established that had basically outgrown nation-states, that our movement had to go global as well." Contrary to objections that global citizenship signifies remoteness from or indifference toward one's country of origin, Maude Barlow believes that global citizenship feeds into a strategy of articulating and protecting distinctly national interests and social programs, not subordinating them. Indeed, for Barlow, global citizenship amounts to a vigorous defense of Canadian public space within the international arena.

For Pat Montandon, a former San Francisco television personality and newspaper columnist well known in California for organizing charity fundraisers, the progression of global citizenship began in the heat of the arms race between the United States and the former Soviet Union. The nuclear threat had propelled itself into Montandon's consciousness when she experienced a terrifying vision of a nuclear holocaust, complete with an image of two children carried away to safety. Shortly after that vision, in 1982, Montandon helped organize a visit to California by Jehan Sadat, the widow of assassinated Egyptian president Anwar Sadat, for a conference on nuclear disarmament, with the focus on children as prospective teachers of peace. This left Montandon wondering about the potential for an international children's movement to reach heads of state. Using her media contacts and her social skills, Montandon organized a vigil in San Francisco's Union Square in which local children brought letters for President Ronald Reagan and the leader of the Soviet Union at the time, Yuri Andropov. The local vigil instantly snowballed into a movement with global reach when youngsters asked how these letters would be delivered. Montandon answered that question by organizing a trip to Washington, D.C., and Moscow, where she and several children were received in the Kremlin. Over the course of the next few years, Montandon led children on a total of thirty-four trips around the world, having private audiences with twenty-six world leaders, including Pope John Paul II and the Israeli prime minister, Menachem Begin. As Montandon recalled during an interview: "When I began Children as the Peacemakers in 1982, I had no idea what I was doing. I just knew I had to do it. And as it began to evolve, and became a foundation, and I went every place in the world, virtually, with children, I really realized that we were heading toward global citizenship, even twenty years ago. And of course, as time has passed, it's becoming more and more evident, I think."[12]

Similarly, respondents who participated in international volunteer programs also spoke about how settling into *local* communal life abroad proved important in shaping their qualities as global citizens. During their year of volunteer service in Zelenograd, Russia, Rosie and Charlie Brown were not directly involved in local politics, but they were engaged wholeheartedly in the local community. They taught English to local schoolchildren, studied Russian literature with other visiting adults, and served meals each day to approximately three hundred elderly women at a food pantry. Rosie Brown joined the International Women's Club of Moscow, while Charlie Brown volunteered at an orphanage. And yet, the most powerful way in which they came to feel like citizens of Zelenograd was quite routine: on many evenings, neighbors would stop by unannounced at their ground-floor apartment: "We had no shades on the windows, so when our lights were on, it meant we were home, and people would just come and knock on the window, and they would come in, and we'd make a pot of tea. And they loved to practice their English, and we loved to learn all we could about Russia."[13]

Becoming truly part of the neighborhood in a faraway country corresponds with Rosie Brown's general idea of being a citizen: to "belong somewhere" not necessarily in one's hometown. As she said, "I felt a sense of belonging in Russia . . . and I think anybody can do that anyplace." Indeed, Rosie and Charlie Brown found themselves creating a sense of belonging not only for themselves in Russia, but for the women at the food pantry:

> Part of their meal was soup, cabbage soup, and it gets spilled so easily, and so I decided to take a cloth, and my husband and I would take cloths, and we'd wipe the tables off. Such a simple thing. And then I'd take the cloths home with me and bleach them and bring them back the next week. Those people, you cannot imagine the smiles and the "thank you," in Russian, that we got. And that was so simple to do, but it wasn't being done—respecting those people enough to think that they should have a clean table to eat off of. Anyway, that's all part of being a citizen of the world.

This recollection serves to illustrate how a "foreigner," by carefully observing one's surroundings and responding affirmatively to them, can take on the qualities of a global citizen of a locality, even if only for a limited period of time. Moreover, Rosie Brown's yearlong cultural and social immersion in Russia during 1994 and 1995 propelled her into further political initiatives. She returned to Russia in 1997 to participate in a grassroots democracy workshop run by the League of Women Voters, working with about 125 Russian women. In 1999, Brown participated in a similar series of workshops in Mexico, one year in advance of the landmark election in which voters ousted the political party that had ruled Mexico for most of the twentieth century. More recently, Brown helped run workshops in Croatia. Just as local forms of involvement can lead to activity in the international arena, cultural immersion and political action also emerge as mutually reinforcing pathways of global citizenship.

Educational Programs

As Jean-Jacques Rousseau noted in *Émile*, the classic political philosophy text on citizen education: "We are born weak, we need strength; we are born totally unprovided, we need aid; we are born stupid, we need judgment. Everything we do not have at our birth and which we need when we are grown is given to us by education."[14] The importance of civic education has received abundant attention in scholarship as well as in government educational ministries and voluntary organizations. Indeed, some of the individuals interviewed for this research said that their first memory of the word "citizenship" entering their vocabulary came when they were graded for "citizenship" behavior during their primary-school years.[15]

While hardly any of the people interviewed for this study credited their formal education in grade school as helping shape them into *global* citizens,[16] traveling abroad to participate in educational programs has served a pivotal step in the lives of many self-described global citizens. In separate interviews for this study, two former university students who participated in overseas immersion programs in Africa reflected on how deeply their experiences abroad had affected them. Both women pursued higher education in Texas—one at Baylor University, the other at Mountain View College in the Dallas County Community College District—and both traveled to western Europe during their secondary-school years but had never previously traveled elsewhere internationally. In addition, the programs in which they took part—one in Kenya, the other in Senegal—both were sponsored by faculty members who articulated their hopes (in news articles prior to the journeys) that the students would become global citizens as a result of their experiences. Moreover, both women indicated in their interviews that they now view themselves as something more than American—that they feel interconnected with communities well beyond the shores of the United States. They also are considering career options that had not occurred to them before participating in their respective programs. However, both women stopped short of unequivocally declaring themselves global citizens and emphasized how their respective African immersion experiences reinforced their American citizen identities.

Sarah Willcox, who traveled to Senegal as a student at Mountain View College in the summer of 2000, did not even know where Senegal was located before she began to study French. She became inspired to participate in the Senegal trip immediately after her French instructor, Sherry Dean, promoted it on the first day of French class the previous autumn. The score of students who joined the trip spent a year watching videos, reading articles, and holding group discussions to prepare themselves. And yet, Willcox said nothing could have prepared her for the culture shock she experienced upon landing in Dakar and receiving two marriage proposals in the airport, just moments after landing. "I didn't know whether to take them seriously, but they were not going to leave me alone," she recalled.[17] Moments later, when the group of students crammed themselves and their luggage into a tiny bus to drive to the hotel, Willcox felt as if she were watching a UNICEF (United Nations Children's Fund) television commercial unfold before her eyes.

Before arriving in Senegal, the group from Mountain View had stopped in Paris and basked in the glory of monumental boulevards, elegant cafés, the grandeur of the Eiffel Tower, and the vibrant atmosphere on the streets. The students had been told that Dakar was the Paris of Senegal. From the vantage point of the bus in Dakar, however, the ramshackle, often half-finished houses made Paris seem very far away. The next morning, upon leaving their hotel, with its familiar Western creature comforts, the students experienced their second bit of culture shock: peddlers waiting especially for them and following the students as they traveled about town, as if knowing their exact itinerary. Seeing people living with severe poverty and disadvantages—children lacking ample food, a polio victim walking on his hands and knees—left Willcox feeling overwhelmed: "It's all that you can do not to empty out all your pockets and give it to them right there. I wanted to drain every bank account that I ever had and just give it out, just hand it all out, because it didn't matter. When you see things like that, you don't ever think about money the same way ever again."

By the end of their two-week stay in Senegal, the students began to feel more attached to the residents of Dakar. One factor in this attachment was that each student had been paired with a French-speaking conversation partner learning English at a local university. Especially memorable was a day trip to a small village, Darou Alfa, about sixty miles north of Dakar. The students were introduced to the village by two missionaries working to preserve an indigenous oral language by translating it into a written form. The students brought a gift of US$500 for the village, which they had raised mostly through bake sales during the previous year at Mountain View College. The local villagers treated the students like dignitaries. They dressed in their very best clothes and slaughtered a goat to cook a special feast. Even the act of eating broadened the cultural horizons of the American students, for everyone was served food in communal bowls shared by five or six people. Verbal communication with the local residents was impossible, as the villagers did not speak French. When the group presented their gift, Sherry Dean, the accompanying faculty member and program director, spoke in French to the missionaries, the missionaries then spoke the local dialect to the residents, and nonverbal communication took over as the villagers burst into emotional applause. Indeed, Willcox remembers that several of the residents standing behind her kissed her upon hearing about the gift, which was used by the village to buy malaria medication as well as to fund an educational initiative for mothers of newborn children.

The sense of being part of a global community, though not of being a global citizen, entered into Willcox's thinking during the trip and in the months that followed back in Texas. When the group held a reception to thank their donors, Willcox gave a speech in which she explained how the trip had changed the way she thinks about her role in the world:

> Before, I was just going about my business and was living my life, but now I see myself as a very small part of a very big picture. And you realize how the world kind of fits together, if that makes sense. I'm just a small part of all of that, and there's so many other things. It's so hard to explain. It's like I'm just this little bitty piece of the puzzle and there's just so much more to it, and I'm appreciative of that now, and I never was before. And my previous trips to England and to France didn't make me realize that. Those cultures are too much like my own.

Although Sherry Dean specifically thinks of the Senegal experience as helping students become global citizens, Willcox does not remember terms such as "global citizen" or "citizen of the world" being discussed during the trip or leading up to the trip. She does, however, recall talking with other students, some of whom had never left Texas before, about "how we fit into the world." Willcox added that she no longer views herself as strictly an American: "After you've experienced something like this, you can't, because if I felt that way, it would be like I was dismissing everything that I experienced, if that makes sense. . . . And I think just by virtue of being there, you get more of an understanding about how you really are a citizen of the world, not just the place where you live." Several Mountain View students who went on the trip continued raising money for Darou Alfa after they returned to Texas. At the time of her interview, in September 2000, Willcox was considering a return to Africa as a U.S. Peace Corps volunteer, an option she had never thought of before going to Senegal. Following her interview, Willcox lived in France for a year, teaching English to schoolchildren, and has since decided to become an elementary school teacher.

When Laura Seay of Baylor University arrived in Nairobi in the autumn of 1998, she truly experienced everyday life in the Kenyan capital. For starters, Seay depended on the Matatu, the no-frills public transportation system, to commute to her internship placement at Pride Africa, where she joined a team of professionals coordinating loans to small businesses just getting off the ground. During her internship, Seay processed grant applications, wrote articles for Pride Africa's newsletter, and helped prepare a strategic plan for the next five years. Seay also adapted to the severe poverty in Nairobi that confronted her every day and came to realize that just about everyone in Kenya personally knows someone lost to AIDS.

The Baylor program in Kenya places students in homes across the country for brief cultural-immersion experiences, and Seay said these opportunities were essential in enabling her to view Kenya from within. During her second week in Kenya, Seay stayed with a family in a rural village in the western part of the country, living in a makeshift house with clay walls, a corrugated iron roof, a dirt floor, and no electricity or water. About ten people were living there, and they were supported by one person's income. The village experience immersed the students in the customs of daily life, and included a funeral that comprised a mixture of Christian and tribal rituals, with drums beating into the early hours of the morning. Seay also lived for two weeks in Nairobi with a much wealthier couple who fell on the opposite end of the Kenyan socioeconomic spectrum; the husband worked as a building contractor and the wife as a university professor. "They had this wonderful house, nicer than my apartment [in Texas]. They had a brand new Land Rover, and a brand new BMW and a brand new Mercedes and all these things, cooks and housekeepers and guards and things."[18]

When Seay returned to Texas just one week before Christmas, she found the frenzied materialism of American life very unsettling:

> Coming from this place where things are relatively calm, and being dropped right in the middle of commercial season—everything is crazy; the world is swirling around you, and everyone's rushing and shopping—I was just sort of in shock for a couple of weeks. And then I went back to Baylor, a place where a lot of people are pretty wealthy and drive nice cars—I have a car; I had an apartment that was nice—it was really difficult for me to get used to living that way again. You feel kind of guilty. You think, "Well, do I really deserve to spend $10 on this thing or $30 on this shirt, when I know that that could pay tuition for a kid in Kenya to go to school?" So it was really difficult. It probably took me about six months to get used to American culture again.

Following her immersion in Kenya, Seay's academic focus shifted toward questions of social justice and democratization as well as broader theological questions of good and evil: "Why does God allow this kind of suffering? How do we justify our lifestyle when we have so much frivolity and other people are really suffering? I was spiritually asking myself, What are you going to do about what you now know, what you have seen?" This motivated Seay to take a class and write an undergraduate thesis on the Holocaust. After graduation from Baylor, Seay earned a master's degree in African studies at Yale University and then began doctoral work in political science at the University of Texas at Austin, with a focus on African politics.

Although her view of the world has changed, Seay does not think of "global citizen" as a term that would apply straightforwardly to her. In the summer of 1999, after she went to Kenya and before her final year at Baylor, Seay worked as an intern in the U.S. State Department headquarters in Washington, D.C., where she learned about another internship at the U.S. embassy in Cameroon. With her Kenyan immersion experience qualifying her as an emerging African expert in the eyes of the State Department, Seay was offered a placement. Immediately following her graduation from Baylor in May 2000, Seay worked in Yaoundé, Cameroon for the summer, writing speeches for the American ambassador, selecting Fulbright scholars, and liaising with universities. On this diplomatic internship, Seay found herself far more insulated from what she considered everyday African life than during her Baylor experience in Kenya. "I was living in this huge house. I had a cook and a maid and all these things for me, and drivers. It was really difficult—it was almost more difficult trying to get used to being in Africa and living sort of an upper-tier lifestyle."

The Baylor program in Kenya is intended, in part, to promote global citizenship. As Blake Burleson, a lecturer in Baylor's religion department and director of the African studies program, told a newspaper reporter: "We know that most of those who go become global citizens and are able to see the world with global eyes and learn not only about African culture but about themselves and America."[19] Laura Seay said she vaguely remembers her classmates in Kenya talking about being global citizens or citizens of the world, and she thinks of herself "as kind of being in the middle" between a sixth-generation Texan, an American, and a global citizen.

Alongside undergraduate educational programs, postgraduate and professional education programs abroad were cited repeatedly by people interviewed for this study as especially powerful formative experiences. The international professional networks cultivated in these cosmopolitan settings often channeled the future directions of the lives of respondents. Nava Swersky Sofer, a venture capitalist based in Tel Aviv, chose to attend the International Institute for Management Development (IMD) in Switzerland in order to establish a global career network. Sofer worked in Europe and in the United States before returning to Israel in 1999 after a decade abroad. Most of the sixty-two students in her IMD cohort—from more than seventy different countries—lived abroad after business school, though many of them, like herself, have since returned home. Sofer's experiences overseas convinced her that she operates more on an international basis than as an Israeli: "No, I'm not wholly Israeli. In some respects I feel more foreign here than in many other places. As a business person, yes, I'm probably more global than anything else. Sometimes I don't really know what I am anymore," she added with a smile.[20]

The international educational and career path of Imogen Mkhize, the first black South African to earn an MBA from Harvard Business School, provides a dramatic illustration of how self-confidence and mentoring can instill the necessary qualities to overcome limitations imposed by one's national citizenship. When Mkhize finished secondary school in 1981, the South African government would allow a black student to attend a white university only with special permission from the education ministry. Moreover, the education ministry would issue its consent only if the white university offered a degree that was unavailable at any of the South African black universities and if the white university had not reached its quota of black students. None of this stopped Mkhize from following her dream. She navigated the bureaucracy, made her way to Rhodes University in Grahamstown, and became the first black South African to earn a degree from Rhodes in an interdisciplinary program combining computer science and accounting.

A pivotal stage in Mkhize's career came in 1991, when she left a consulting job with Andersen to become executive director of the South African chapter of the Association for the Advancement of Black Accountants. She found a mentor in Thomas Watson, who led a similar association in Massachusetts and encouraged Mkhize to apply to Harvard. And yet, as Mkhize liberated herself from the impediments of apartheid and began to think of herself as a global citizen—a term that she and Watson both used in their conversations—she remembered where she came from. Mkhize was at Harvard during the 1994 South African presidential election, the first election in which South African blacks were allowed to vote. On the day of the election, which Mkhize remembers as "an emotional process," she joined several hundred South Africans at the polling station on Boston Common. "So I was a South African—you don't lose that. I was identified as a South African student, and in an environment like that [Harvard Business School], you just don't forget that you are, especially if you are the only black South African on campus."[21]

Earning an undergraduate degree abroad, while perhaps not as facilitative of high-powered networks as prestigious graduate programs in business or law, also was credited by several self-described global citizens interviewed for this research as shaping capacities to live and work in a multiplicity of settings. Al Dizon, an Internet content developer based in Singapore, was born in the Philippines and pointed to his university education in Singapore, particularly his concentration in economics, as helping him to recognize more adequately the nature of global economic interdependence. Studying in Singapore also shifted his ideological leanings toward free-market capitalism: "From then on, I wasn't just a Filipino. I also became a citizen of the world once I learned how to correlate events between countries. Twenty years ago, I couldn't have cared what happened to Indonesia. Today, I know that if Indonesia collapses, the whole of Southeast Asia would also collapse."[22]

Another respondent, Francis Woong-il Lee, former director of investment banking at Hana Bank in Korea, regarded his four years at Roanoke College in Virginia as an essential formative period of global citizenship. When Lee returned to Roanoke in 1998 to give the commencement speech—speaking at the dean's request about global citizenship—Lee combined themes of cross-cultural immersion and political activity. As student government president during his senior year, Lee had "embarked on a valiant mission to bring alcohol back to campus" after the school had prohibited all campus drinking. Although this issue might appear frivolous, Lee expended much energy and diplomacy while brokering a compromise with numerous constituencies around campus. In his commencement speech, Lee related his idea of a global citizen to this episode:

> I learned more about the democratic process in those eight months than in the previous eight years, during which I thought I'd learned all there was to know. This, I think, may be the true mark of the global citizen—the willingness to discover that you were ignorant and to resolve to gain true understanding through as direct an experience as possible. My experiences have taught me— as my grandfather's taught him—that it is dangerous to presume to know or judge the culture, customs, religion, politics, or morality of any person or persons, particularly those in or from other nations, without understanding firsthand what it means to practice and participate in those beliefs.[23]

Professional Opportunities

For some individuals, global citizenship has its origins in civic engagement, cultural immersion, or educational programs. For others, the pathways converge with careers in international business. Journalists often employ the term "global citizen" to describe corporate executives who either are based overseas or who travel abroad regularly; such references to global citizens tend to convey that the individuals in question are successful and sophisticated, but not necessarily active politically. One such journalistic reference stated: "The worldly sense you get from spending time with Novartis senior executive Cynthia Hogan isn't your imagination—she truly is a global citizen."[24] Although Hogan did not come up with this term to describe herself, during an interview she said it was a fitting description given her four-year tenure at the corporate headquarters of Novartis AG in Basel, Switzerland. The roots of Hogan's global citizenship reach back to her love for traveling as a teenager. Growing up in New York City, Hogan and a classmate saved their pocket money in order to travel to France for an entire summer. Immediately after finishing secondary school, Hogan returned to France for a year, living with a family and attending a local school: "Ever since then, I've just been very comfortable living abroad. I knew when I spent the year abroad, when I was sixteen, that I could live in Europe."[25]

As a university student, Hogan returned to Europe for another year to study French and German. After earning an MBA in finance and international business and teaching English for a summer in China, Hogan pursued a career in pharmaceutical sales and marketing specifically because it enabled her to travel across Asia and Europe. For Hogan, global citizenship did not depend so much on working abroad as on living abroad and becoming socially active in Basel. She served on the board of her daughter's elementary school and volunteered in a community health program as well as a program that helped English-speaking newcomers settle into town. Hogan said she sees no trade-off whatsoever between global citizenship and U.S. citizenship. In fact, living in Switzerland reinforced her identity as a citizen of the United States, and each July 4 she celebrated Independence Day with other Americans: "You become more patriotic—things that you really wouldn't care about when you're [in the United States], the symbolism becomes more important."

In contrast, the international career of Miles Colebrook, now retired from his position as group president of the advertising agency JWT International in London, left him increasingly with a sense of detachment from the United Kingdom, his native country. Having started work as a mailroom clerk directly after secondary school, Colebrook gradually moved up in the ranks and went to the University of Michigan in the mid-1970s to learn more about corporate finance. He refers to his four months of executive education in Ann Arbor as "my first proper international experience," and the impact of the program on Colebrook's personal outlook was much greater than its role in strengthening his grasp of finance: "It had a huge effect on me, because it was the first time I had been to the States, and at that time the UK (then beset with considerable economic instability and labor unrest) was in a terrible state, and I was quite despairing of the UK."[26] When Colebrook returned to the United Kingdom, he was promoted to group account director of JWT, ranking one notch below the chief executive of the London office. Rolex and Baccardi were among his accounts, and this prompted regular travel to Switzerland and Bermuda.

By the mid-1980s, as head of JWT's operations across Europe, Colebrook traveled routinely across continental Europe and was spending progressively less time in London. This shift in his center of gravity appealed very much to Colebrook: "I very quickly then distanced myself from the UK and felt very European, very easy moving from country to country, and felt that I belonged to the world rather than any particular part of it." Colebrook said that he regards himself much more as a global citizen and a European citizen than as a British citizen, though he also believes that part of being a global citizen is not worrying about such matters. At the time of his interview, in June 2000, Colebrook was responsible for JWT in Asia and in Europe and commonly spent weekends socializing with friends and colleagues in Shanghai or in Spain, his spouse's homeland: "I personally find the phrase 'global citizen' perfectly comfortable. For me, it means that an individual feels they belong to a much bigger kind of global church and feels not just comfortable, but they feel pleasant about it and find the concept of moving effortlessly around the globe extremely easy to deal with." The pathways of respondents within the burgeoning global professional class further illustrate how global citizenship unfolds, in the minds of some internationally mobile and engaged individuals, across a multiplicity of public spaces, irrespective of the state of global governing institutions.

Conclusion

Those who have embraced the idea of global citizenship tend to think about citizenship in much more expansive terms than formal membership in a nation-state or participation only within small-scale political communities. Rather, global citizenship commonly is portrayed by these individuals as ways of thinking and living that unfold gradually and progress over time. The life histories of self-described global citizens therefore provide a substantial reply to skeptics who have suggested, at times, that everyday people might not be capable of practicing global citizenship without distancing themselves from political and social life. As political philosopher Benjamin Barber once argued: "Diogenes may have regarded himself as a citizen of the world, but global citizenship demands of its patriots levels of abstraction and disembodiment most women and men will be unable or unwilling to muster, at least in the first instance."[27] On the contrary, however, many patriots of global citizenship who were interviewed for this study seemed to associate global citizenship with tangible and meaningful life experiences within face-to-face communities. In this regard, the findings presented in this chapter also show how meaningful "real-world" discourses pertaining to global citizenship have emerged beyond academic debates in political philosophy and social science.[28]

The pathways described in this chapter demonstrate how many self-described global citizens indeed display the qualities of motivation and responsibility so cherished in the civic republican tradition, with its ancient ideals of citizenship as self-rule and immersion in public life. Numerous individuals whose life histories have been shared here traced their global citizenship to political activism or social interaction within particular communities, from Kilkelly, Ireland, to the Etsako clan in Nigeria. Even if these individuals are not representative of how most people today shape their identities as citizens, their formative experiences help begin to illustrate how many self-described global citizens indeed carry out sustained political action and accept at least a partial responsibility for promoting a global common good. Even Benjamin Barber has come to recognize that global citizenship is worth pursuing. His recently formed advocacy organization, CivWorld: Citizens Campaign For Democracy, proclaims: "Our mission is to increase the awareness of our interdependence and create a new vision of what it means to be a global citizen in this interdependent world."[29]

In addition, the pathways of global citizenship—ranging from family histories and communal solidarity to political action campaigns and professional and educational opportunities —begin to uncover the multifaceted concepts of global citizenship now emerging in public discourse. Just as businesspeople such as Miles Colebrook and Imogen Mkhize have practiced different versions of global citizenship from activists Maude Barlow and Hazel Henderson, how the idea of global citizenship is understood depends very much on one's perspective. Some pathways of global citizenship hearken to moral visions of global awareness, responsibility, and participation, as well as cross-cultural empathy. Other pathways focus mainly on competitiveness in the global economy and freedom of movement across international borders. As shown in the next two chapters, the sorts of individuals who find global citizenship meaningful in their lives are motivated by multiple concepts that operate within this idea.

CHAPTER TWO

Primary Concepts of Global Citizenship

Now that the sorts of life experiences that inspire individuals to embrace the identity of a global citizen are in focus, it is helpful to look more deeply into the realm of ideas. What are the main patterns of thinking that operate within global citizenship? This chapter explores how awareness, responsibility, and participation amount to three primary concepts of global citizenship as this idea is now practiced beyond the academy. The next chapter explains how ideas of cross-cultural empathy, international mobility, and personal achievement also figure heavily as secondary concepts in contemporary understandings of global citizenship.

My analysis in these chapters is a specific interpretation based on the interview transcripts and published references to global citizenship examined for this study. It aims to open a debate about the meanings of global citizenship in practice. Other researchers examining the same data—or collecting their own data—might well come up with different orderings of concepts, and a larger research study casting wider nets across space and time would yield its own conceptual map. Therefore, I should briefly explain how three key considerations were taken into account in identifying and ordering the concepts presented in these two chapters. First, to what extent did each concept emerge as central, especially in the reflections of the persons interviewed for this study, as far as what global citizenship requires and why the term is seen as worth using? Second, to what extent, if at all, did each concept correspond with how the respondents thought about the meaning of citizenship more generally? Third, how did each concept relate—either positively or negatively—with the remaining concepts identified in the data?

The first two questions address the issue of whether each concept is central, even indispensable, in understanding the meaning of global citizenship. The third question ventures into the issue of coherence: If linkages and relationships can be observed across the concepts, then the body of thought under the umbrella of global citizenship takes on a greater level of coherence than if the concepts were to remain in isolation from each other. Therefore, each primary concept needed to play a central role in understanding global citizenship while also contributing to a coherent account of global citizenship. The threshold for a concept to qualify as secondary was somewhat lower. The concept needed to be prominent in the published references and interview transcripts but not necessarily central in the minds of the respondents. Nor did a secondary concept of global citizenship need to illustrate how the persons interviewed for this study thought about citizenship more generally. In addition, it was not necessary for a secondary concept to fit together with other concepts, provided that each concept, in itself, was indeed an important and distinct strain of global citizenship in contemporary public discourse.

Awareness, responsibility, and participation deserve special attention as primary concepts of global citizenship for three reasons: First, these three concepts commonly emerged as central in the thinking of those interviewed as far as what global citizenship requires and why the idea of global citizenship is seen as worthwhile. Second, ideas of awareness, responsibility, and participation often corresponded with how the respondents thought about the meaning of citizenship—not only global citizenship but also citizenship of any kind. Third, the respondents often portrayed ideas of awareness, responsibility, and participation as intertwined with one another. These three concepts can be viewed as a trajectory in which progressions of global citizenship emerge in the lives of individuals, with awareness of one's role in the world instilling a sense of responsibility that in turn inspires participation in politics or civil society. The trajectory does not necessarily flow in a single direction; participation can instill a heightened sense of responsibility, and both participation and responsibility serve to amplify awareness. As much as these three concepts are interconnected, awareness came across as the clearest identifiable starting point for global citizenship.

Global Citizenship as Awareness

More so than any other concept, the persons interviewed for this study framed global citizenship as dependent on awareness of oneself and the outside world. Especially when individuals were asked challenging questions about how anyone could possibly be a global citizen without a centralized world government, without recognized world passports, or without national and ethnic identities giving way to a widely acknowledged civic identity shared across humanity, a common reply in the interviews was that anyone can be a global citizen through awareness or a state of mind. In fact, several respondents brought up a related word: consciousness. A California political activist, when asked how the term "global citizenship" had entered her vocabulary, replied: "I think it's a word that we have tried to put to a growing consciousness" in pursuit of greater democratic empowerment in the global economy.[1] A former representative in the U.S. Congress stressed that global citizenship is "part of my consciousness," particularly with regard to the use of natural resources: "What I waste is someone else's survival."[2] A peace activist who circled the globe with a group of children during the latter years of the Cold War, meeting with numerous world leaders, noted that the youngsters gained "a global consciousness, which is where global citizenship has to start."[3] A university dean explained how his institution tries to raise global citizenship "in the consciousness of our students and say, look, when you leave here, you have some obligations not just in a local way of thinking but in a global way of thinking."[4] The chairman of a huge multinational corporation said he aims for his employees to "develop a consciousness that they are also citizens of the world, and that while we're implanted and living in one place, what we do and don't do may impact much larger areas."[5] Such comments illustrate not only the centrality of awareness in their minds of the respondents with regard to global citizenship, but also how awareness feeds into related ideas of responsibility and participation.

The emphasis placed on consciousness by the respondents converges, in fact, with interpretations from the academic literature that emphasize consciousness as vital to what it means to be a citizen of any kind. As Benjamin Barber has noted: "Citizenship is a dynamic relationship among strangers who are transformed into neighbors, whose commonality derives from expanding consciousness rather than geographical proximity."[6] Likewise, although David Held does not define citizenship per se specifically in terms of consciousness, he has argued that "cosmopolitan citizens" must be "capable of mediating between national traditions, communities of fate and alternative styles of life" and also be able to reason from others' points of view.[7] Even T. H. Marshall, best remembered for his definition of citizenship as a trilogy of civil, political, and social rights upheld within a nation-state, also emphasized that "modern national consciousness" accompanied the advent of modern civil rights, and that citizenship depends on "a direct sense of community membership based on loyalty to a civilisation which is a common possession."[8] Such passages serve to illustrate how various understandings of citizenship, more generally defined, are also resonant within interpretations of global citizenship.

In addition, the meanings of "global" and "globalization," in the minds of some scholars, correspond with understandings of human consciousness. As Roland Robertson and Habib Haque Khondker have written, "In its most basic sense globalization involves the compression of the entire world, on the one hand, and a rapid increase in consciousness of the whole world, on the other."[9] Martin Shaw, meanwhile, has argued that the meaning of "global" hinges on "the development of *a common consciousness of human society on a world scale*."[10] These sociological definitions of "global" or "globalization" rely on human awareness that develops over time rather than on any sort of end state in which the world is unified. Such definitions of globalization that emphasize intensifying economic, social, and cultural linkages across the planet also commonly suggest that multiple sources of fragmentation and differentiation will persist—and can even be regarded as integral to globalization itself. James Rosenau has coined the term "fragmegration" in an effort to articulate how the world is simultaneously becoming more global and more local.[11] Both the terms "global" and "citizen," then, standing on their own, have been closely associated with "consciousness" in the academic literature.

Some advocates of global citizenship worry that the sort of consciousness needed for individuals to practice global citizenship is in very short supply. Oscar Arias, the president of Costa Rica, lamented during an interview for this study: "I don't think people are ready to accept the term of a global citizen. People are not aware that we live in a more interdependent and interconnected world, a globalized world. Some of us can use it, because we are much more aware. But not the average individual in any particular society."[12] In the present day, the nation-state retains its place as an epicenter of common political consciousness and loyalty, and nationalism is also defined frequently in terms of consciousness. Nationalism as consciousness, though, tends to emphasize conformity and homogeneity, and defenders of the nation-state as the exclusive basis for political community maintain that a shared consciousness cannot develop beyond the nation-state.[13] In contrast, for those thinking and talking about global citizenship, the "civilisation which is a common possession" does not correspond evenly with the borders of the nation-state. What global citizenship as awareness seems to involve for individual persons can be explored first with regard to self-awareness and then with respect to outward awareness of one's surroundings and the world.

Self-Awareness

At first glance, global citizenship might strike some as implying an absence of place. However, many individuals who find meaning in the term maintain that it depends on strong and well-defined roots, not only within a particular community but also with respect to one's own individuality. For instance, a novelist from New Mexico eloquently defines a global citizen as "somebody that can move between different worlds, what one perceives as these invisible membranes that separate culture and landscape and environment and people from different backgrounds." This author also notes that the individuals she has known with this sense of fluidity share an essential personal quality: "No matter where they were, they were at home; they were comfortable in the universe of their own skin, and consequently that made them available and fresh whenever they met other people in any sort of situation."[14] Self-awareness, then, can be considered an initial step of global citizenship and the lens through which further experiences and insights are perceived. As noted by a French-language teacher who has led her students on immersion experiences in Africa: "The thing that I say to my students is becoming a global citizen is not something that happens overnight; it's a process of self-awareness and as you become self-aware, you become more aware of others."[15]

Self-awareness also extends into questions of national identity, as some people who think of themselves as global citizens flatly rejected the notion that one's sources of national identity should be seen as restricted. As one woman noted during an interview: "I was born in Korea, and I'm a U.S. citizen. That's a pretty finite state, right? But there's so many more interesting ways of life—and living and being—that's outside of just that finite state of being an immigrant Korean who's now a U.S. citizen. So why not be open to it?"[16] Likewise, an artist born in Calgary, who at the time of his interview was dividing his time mainly between New York City and Amsterdam, said he does not restrict his personal identity as a citizen to any particular country but rather identifies with a group of friends in North America and Europe who "basically share the same values and the same kind of sense of a pretty big global perspective."[17] Self-awareness as related to global citizenship, then, means avoiding clipping one's wings as well as remaining at ease in one's own skin.

Outward Awareness

Global citizenship as outward awareness entails such myriad personal qualities as understanding complex issues from multiple vantage points, recognizing sources of global interdependence and a "shared fate" implicating humanity and the planet, and looking beyond distinctions, at least in one's mind, between insiders and outsiders in order to view the human experience in more universal terms. For some, global citizenship amounts to playing down the significance of nations as imagined,[18] or at least as arbitrary. A board member of the Japanese affiliate of Earthwatch Institute maintained that geopolitical boundaries, however formidable in the eyes of many government officials and political scientists, should be dismissed as figments of the imagination: "There's no such real physical barriers; the barriers are only our minds. So if we can reach that state of identity of having global consciousness, all the conflict will be stopped."[19] For others, global citizenship involves awakening to new insights about one's native country or continent as one gains perspectives from other lands. One young woman from Ohio, who spent a year in the Netherlands on an exchange through the American Field Service (AFS)—an organization that itself includes "global citizenship" in its mission—said she began to change her position on the gun control debate in the United States after listening to the thoughts of her Dutch classmates following the 1999 massacre at Columbine High School in Littleton, Colorado.[20] An administrator for UNICEF Canada stressed that in her view, the essence of global citizenship is found in awareness, not actions such as making ethical purchases: "The action of consuming doesn't make the difference. The shift in attitude or the shift in awareness is what is required. That's the fundamental change."[21]

Such recognition of global interdependence leads into the moral vision of bridging divisions in one's mind between one's immediate kin and distant strangers. Consider this passage from an interview with the cofounder of Global Exchange, a human rights advocacy group, regarding the need for global employment standards, particularly in factories run in developing countries by multinational corporations:

> If it were your daughter working in that factory, what would you want the conditions to be? Would you want them to have bathroom breaks? Yeah, you would. I see it at the spiritual conceptual level, at the highest level of abstraction, as erasing the division between "us" and "them"—the ability to create "other" in the human mind, erasing that, so it's all "we." So if you approach policymaking as if it were your family that would be subjected to the policies, what would you want the policies to be?[22]

The policy prescription implied in this passage carries into global citizenship as responsibility, as in morally credible labor standards. However, the underlying principle—thinking of workers in distant factories with the same degree of respect and concern as a person would think of his or her offspring—stems from awareness. Perhaps not everyone in the most affluent countries can identify with the conditions of sweatshop workers in developing countries, but the vast majority of adults can identify with the intensity of parenting.

Indeed, recognition of universalities of the human experience (of which parenting would certainly qualify) was articulated by several persons interviewed for this study as an important element of global citizenship. Some respondents turned to spiritual language; a porcelain designer from New York City noted that for her, global citizenship requires "viewing other people as basically a good soul. . . . We basically start out as a human soul with a common essence. The clothes we put on, the cultural customs and all those things are like flavors. So I think it requires viewing mankind as people that are like you but not externally."[23] Likewise, a university professor born and raised in Nigeria and now living in Missouri noted that global citizenship, in her mind, has nothing to do with acquiring or giving up national citizenship but is "a mind-set that makes you aware of you as part of the human family, and going beyond your interests to recognize the needs and challenges in resolving some of the problems that the world is faced with."[24] Consider also this view of global citizenship as expressed by the principal of an all-girls secondary school located on the southern coast of New Zealand:

> I define "global citizen" as a girl from Southland, perhaps off a farm, being able to go and live and work in just about every country in the world and know that the universalities of human experience are going to be far greater in her modern world than the differences. And where the differences exist, she will be able to understand and respond to them.[25]

This passage blends ideas of achievement, professional accomplishment, and freedom of movement with the goal of looking beyond barriers that can separate human beings. Such aspirations of discovering commonalities with other human beings also emerged in accounts of experiences shared by respondents. A university professor from West Virginia who initiated a program to bring Internet access to elementary schools in rural Appalachia recalled how conversations between children in rural Appalachia and children in Mexico led quickly to the identification of common routines, however mundane, and helped form common bonds: "They began to see that, hey, their lives are similar to ours—they get up in the morning, and they have to go to school and they don't like school, and they like some of the same music . . . and so what they started seeing is instead of the differences between them and us, they began to see a lot of similarity between them and us."[26]

While communication in cyberspace certainly can facilitate greater recognition of the human experience and its common elements, others emphasized the importance of face-to-face dialogue. A young woman from Oregon, who came to regard herself as a global citizen after exploring Europe for six months, said the trip taught her that "young people are really a lot the same, no matter what country they come from. We all kind of have similar ideas and similar kinds of passions about life."[27] Similarly, a community volunteer from Oklahoma expressed how she had grown as a person, first by hosting dozens of visitors from overseas in her home and later through political activism and volunteer work in Mexico, Russia, and Croatia: "I have learned that people, for the most part, are really wonderful, and that most people, global citizens, want peace in the world; they want better things for their children; they want better health care, better living conditions, and it's shaped me . . . it has shaped everything about my life."[28] In short, awareness of the wider world provides the motivation for many self-described global citizens to embark on sustained involvement in society or politics and to begin to take responsibility for a global common good.

Global Citizenship as Responsibility

The terms "global citizenship" and "global responsibility" often seem interchangeable for people who describe themselves as global citizens or advocate global citizenship. This comes as no surprise, as the aspiration of shared moral obligations across humankind has endured through the ages as a central element of cosmopolitanism. In the eloquent words of Kwame Anthony Appiah, "The one thought that cosmopolitans share is that no local loyalty can ever justify forgetting that each human being has responsibilities to each other."[29]

Three key points underscore how responsibility emerged as central in the minds of numerous people interviewed for this study. First, several respondents turned to notions of responsibility as they answered questions that challenged whether the term "global citizenship" is worth using—such as whether global citizenship is unfeasible or a contradiction in terms, as well as what value, if any, is added by bringing terms such as "global citizenship" into public debate. Second, many individuals who defined global citizenship as responsibility seem to view responsibility mainly as an outgrowth of personal awareness and as voluntary in nature, rather than along the lines of such familiar compulsory responsibilities of national citizenship as conscription, taxation, and serving on juries, as well as the voluntary responsibility of voting.[30] Third, ideas of global citizenship as responsibility were raised largely by advocates of the term. Many of these individuals stopped short of making claims that global citizenship is already in place or that everyone is now a global citizen. Rather, they expressed a need for certain principles or suggested that more responsible global citizenship would amount to a favorable turn of events.

In reflecting on global citizenship as responsibility, some respondents specifically framed rights and responsibilities together as essential for any kind of citizenship, while the majority of respondents set aside, at least implicitly, the language of rights and focused instead on responsibilities accepted in light of increased awareness. For a perspective with an emphasis on rights, consider this passage from Georg Kell, the head of the United Nations Global Compact,[31] in response to an interview question asking if it might be counterproductive to use the term "global citizenship" if "global responsibility" is what he really meant:

> The beauty of the term [global citizenship] is it brings in the notion of rights that should be balanced with responsibilities . . . and maybe it is counterproductive, in political terms, to overuse the term because it would provoke all sorts of resistance arguing that there is no such territory beyond the nation-state. But then it offers all the strength of trying to come to grips with a broad definition of our rights and responsibilities in a space that is not yet defined.[32]

Similarly, the president of the American Field Service (AFS) turned to notions of rights and responsibilities in defending the usage of "global citizenship" in the organization's mission statement. As Paul Shay noted during an interview: "I think it's this combination of belonging to a community, having certain rights in that community but also certain responsibilities; it's that combination of factors together that seems to be captured by "global citizen" better than by some of the other terms that we could use to describe a similar set of values."[33] An Australian journalist, meanwhile, defended his self-identification as a global citizen by saying that the term signifies a combination of rights and responsibilities, as well as a sense of belonging to the entire planet: "Unfortunately, one of the things in most cultures is we claim rights but never, ever want to face our responsibilities, and they might be environmental, they might be human-rights responsibilities, and that's what I say as a citizen—I'm part of this bloody globe; I've got to do my bit."[34]

The Universal Declaration of Human Rights, signed in 1948 at the founding of the United Nations, is not binding in the same manner as national or state constitutions, but it nevertheless issues key imperatives for national governments, such as the duty to protect refugees and internally displaced persons, as well as any individuals abused or mistreated within their countries of residence. In an interview for this study, Louise Arbour, the United Nations high commissioner for human rights, framed the idea of global citizenship in terms of safeguarding the human rights of those no longer protected by their governments:

> In terms of crimes against humanity, and the personal criminal liability of leaders, I think the challenge that we're looking at is how to protect fundamental human rights of those [persons] whose kind of protector, the state, has completely failed . . . To the extent that there's been a complete inability or unwillingness of their government to protect their most basic fundamental universal human rights, I think they have a legitimate claim, for that purpose, to turn to the international community. So in that sense, they are the original global citizens. They have no other citizenship, in a sense, than their humanity.[35]

For all the power of rights-based interpretations of global citizenship, the majority of people interviewed seemed to link the idea of global citizenship more closely with awareness. A former vice president of Earthwatch Institute, who at first articulated an understanding of global citizenship as synonymous with global consciousness, when pressed on what value, if any, might be added by using the term "global citizenship," replied: "Global citizenship implies a responsibility to be a good citizen. Global consciousness merely implies that you've just got to be aware, that you don't have to do anything about it. That's why it's a better term."[36] Likewise, a cofounder of Global Citizens Network, an international volunteer service organization, said that "citizen" "conjured up responsibility" among those who started the organization: "We do have a responsibility to learn about the rest of the world and not become isolated, and that was certainly something we were thinking when we were developing our charter and using the words that we were using."[37] Note that responsibility, in this instance, is framed in connection with learning and voluntary participation, rather than as a coercive tie derived from formal membership within a country. What responsible global citizenship requires, in the minds of people thinking and talking about the concept, can be explored first in terms of principled decision making and then with regard to solidarity across humanity.

Principled Decision Making

Global citizenship as principled decision making applies every bit as much within local communities as in the international arena. Environmental issues were cited especially often as an area in which responsible—and aware—global citizens are concerned about the effects of government policies as well as their personal daily choices. For example, an information technology consultant from San Francisco, who defined a global citizen as "someone who makes decisions based on an awareness of the impact of those decisions on the planet," added in the next sentence that she never would buy a sport-utility vehicle.[38] Lester Brown, founder of both the Worldwatch Institute and the Earth Policy Institute in Washington, D.C., framed global citizenship as responsibility to the planet and to future generations:

> We have to recognize that given the advances in technology, given the growth in the global economy and the capacity we now have in this country [the United States]—for example, we can unilaterally change the world's climate—in fact, we're almost doing that—and so I think we have to recognize that we have a responsibility now that goes far beyond our boundaries. . . . Recognizing that the earth is an ecosystem almost automatically defines us as global citizens.[39]

In keeping with this ecological perspective, Brown defines "citizenship," generally speaking, as a way of life rather than as a legally binding tie to any particular country: "Citizenship means behaving in a way that recognizes the way in which we affect, through our daily lives, the rest of the people on the planet and the rest of life on the planet." Note that notions of legally protected rights or formal membership status are entirely absent from this definition, which instead focuses primarily on responsible behavior linked with recognition of global interdependence.

Another person interviewed for this study first thought about the idea of global citizenship while she was writing a letter to the editor of her local newspaper after traveling across Europe. During her journey, she came to believe that Americans, collectively speaking, need to become better global citizens, especially with regard to energy conservation:

> The United States makes up only 5 percent of the world's population but consumes 25 percent of the world's energy, generates 20 percent of the world's waste, has the highest consumption rate, and is one of the leading contributors to global warming (creating 23 percent of the world's carbon dioxide emissions). We are the most wasteful country in the world . . . we need to be more responsible global citizens.[40]

The author of the letter, a medical student at the time of her interview for this study, linked her usage of "global citizens" with global interdependence and responsibility:

> It was the phrase I wanted to use, because we talk about being citizens of America . . . and being a citizen of that country gives you certain privileges and

certain responsibilities, and certain rights, but I think that in today's world you can't just exist within your own country. We have global impact on what we do in this country, and what's happening in other countries affects us. I think that the world has become a much smaller place, and the environmental degradation that's happening in other countries is definitely affecting us. . . . We're the most powerful country and the richest country, and so it's our responsibility to lead the way and be responsible global citizens, because if we're not going to do it, why would anybody else do it?"[41]

Concern about principled decision making for the long-term benefit of the planet also emerged during interviews in which individuals framed entire countries, or national governments, as global citizens.[42] As noted by a former campaigner for Greenpeace in New Zealand:

To me, it [global citizenship] means in that context that the New Zealand government had a responsibility to the global environment and more than simply the environment within its own national boundaries. And my understanding of that concept is that—as with individual citizens—governments, corporations, and other entities also have global responsibilities that extend beyond their own immediate areas of jurisdiction and ownership or, I suppose, strictly speaking, formal obligations."[43]

The above passage emphasizes responsibility beyond one's immediate spheres of obligation and ownership, and in several other instances, respondents deployed the idea of ownership, at least figuratively, on a planetary scale. Here again, clear links emerged between ideas of awareness, responsibility, and participation. An administrator at an educational-travel company, for instance, noted that the "growing awareness about what kind of ripple effect our actions in the United States can have elsewhere" promises to foster greater "responsibility and ownership in various world problems."[44] Another respondent forcefully evoked a notion of planetary ownership during an interview, as she defended using global citizenship, rather than any alternative terms, on the grounds that citizenship means "each individual actually has ownership and entitlement but also incredible responsibility and obligation."[45] To illustrate her point, this person reflected on having recently learned about the melting ice cap at the peak of Mount Kilimanjaro: "And I was thinking to myself, you know, if I don't play my cards right and somehow help that, whether it's through money or making people more aware through information, that my daughter's never going to get to see the snow caps of Kilimanjaro." This person essentially cast herself as a stakeholder, if not a literal owner, in the global treasure of Mount Kilimanjaro: a stakeholder with the capacity—and the moral obligation—to participate and make a difference in some way, however indirectly. This underscores that global citizenship, for many respondents, entails being aware of responsibilities beyond one's immediate communities and perhaps making decisions to change one's behavior patterns accordingly.

Solidarity Across Humanity

The theme of thinking and acting in ways that extend beyond one's immediate spheres of obligation and ownership leads into yet another important element of responsible global citizenship: strengthening solidarity across all humanity. Solidarity and responsibility are very much intertwined. Indeed, the original French usage of *solidarité* signifies collective responsibility.[46] Although notions of solidarity often signify bonds of friendship and unity within limited groups with interests that appear to coincide,[47] the self-described global citizens interviewed for this book frequently joined together ideas of global solidarity and global responsibility. This was especially true among individuals who were preoccupied with resolving global problems such as endemic poverty.

One respondent, who worked for a Catholic international-development organization based in Canada, justified the usage of "global citizenship" rather than alternative terms because, in his words, global citizenship is synonymous with "global equality" and "the notion of solidarity with the poor, the preferential option of the poor. . . . It's not a question of just promoting love and friendship throughout the world; it's a question of redressing the enormous imbalances that exist."[48] While some who pour energy into promoting global justice are inspired by religious principles, others pursue such moral visions in secular terms. One activist (an avowed atheist), the former secretary-general for the Paris-based International Federation of Human Rights, emphasized that for her, global citizenship revolved around a sense of proximity to global problems and the people affected by them:

> I wouldn't say, "Oh, I feel at home everywhere." I don't. I just got back from China, and clearly there are cultural differences; or indeed, when I'm in Syria [home to her father's side of the family], and I'm supposed to wear the veil; or in Afghanistan—I definitely wouldn't feel at home in Afghanistan. But I would say I feel [like] a planetary citizen in the sense that I feel concerned about what's happening everywhere. I feel planetary in the sense that I don't feel closer to the problems of France than I do to the problems of Burma . . . proximity is not defined by geography. So it's in that sense that I feel planetary: the proximity that I feel and the closeness that I feel to people is not at all defined by culture or geography or citizenship."[49]

These sorts of individuals came across during interviews as living examples of moral philosopher Martha Nussbaum's ideal of a "world citizen"—one who places at least as much priority on the well-being of distant strangers as one's next-door neighbors[50]—as well as Benjamin Barber's idea of citizenship that places "expanding consciousness," rather than geographical proximity, as the source of common bonds.[51]

In contrast, other activists who think about global citizenship in the context of addressing problems facing humanity use the term primarily as a lofty moral vision of the future, rather than as any sort of description of present circumstances or personal identities. In the eyes of two activists interviewed for this book (on opposite sides of the Atlantic), the persistence of global poverty and the threat of nuclear weapons foreclose the fulfillment of global citizenship. A British peace activist, when asked if it is possible for anyone to attain global citizenship as long as nuclear weapons remain on the planet, replied: "I think you can't; you can't possibly call yourself a citizen while you're busy threatening to annihilate someone across the street."[52] Similarly, the cofounder of the advocacy group Global Exchange, one of the organizations that mobilized the November 1999 demonstrations outside the World Trade Organization meeting in Seattle, said that "as long as there's a child starving somewhere in the world, I can't really be a global citizen."[53] Perhaps modesty is a virtue in any perspective on global citizenship, a term potentially more liable than most to pretensions. On the other hand, if full citizenship in any community were to require, as a precondition, the resolution to any and all significant problems facing the community, no one ever would attain full citizenship.

Some of those interviewed provided vivid illustrations of how they have chosen to live in solidarity as "global neighbors." For example, Robert and Catherine Harper, both elementary school teachers from Long Island, New York, have forged strong personal connections with Thyolo, a village in Malawi, through a long-lasting correspondence with a missionary Catholic priest that started when Catherine Harper responded to a request from the village for rosary beads. As the priest kept them informed of resources needed by the villagers, the Harpers continued to respond. During the past several years, the Harpers have donated funds for an orchard and a flock of chickens, in hopes of helping the village achieve greater self-sufficiency. More recently, the Harpers provided emergency funds to Thyolo to replace maize after the entire country was stricken by crop failure. The couple's involvement stretches beyond their shared sense of moral obligation and extends into notions of belonging and community. As Catherine Harper put it: "We're villagers in Malawi, even though we're geographically removed."[54]

The qualities of responsible global citizens emphasize both moral accountability and solidarity toward all life on the planet. Responsible global citizens, be they individuals acting largely on their own or public officials acting on behalf of entire countries, make decisions that account for likely impacts on wider constituencies than any particular country of origin. Having a sense of proximity to global problems that might be dismissed by others as remote also gives expression to the moral visions of obligation and ownership beyond one's immediate communities. What is more, many self-identifying global citizens believe that the fulfillment of moral responsibilities to humanity requires the advancement of a global institutional framework and democratically accountable public spaces to establish fair systems of rules and reach principled decisions when it comes to international policymaking. Such global citizens tend to live out their respective ethics of responsibility by working for such an evolution of public space.

Global Citizenship as Participation

Global citizenship as participation corresponds, on a grand scale, with the classical civic republican ideal of citizenship as self-rule. As written by Aristotle, who held up participation in the public forum of ancient Athens as "the most choiceworthy way of life" in *The Politics*: "The good citizen should know and have the capacity both to be ruled and to rule, and this very thing is the virtue of a citizen—knowledge of rule over free persons from both [points of view]."[55] Among the self-described global citizens interviewed for this study—and especially among transnational activists who had invoked the term "global citizenship" in public statements—ideals of democratic empowerment and participation among everyday people, often alongside quests for greater public accountability within international institutions, figured prominently in understandings of citizenship of any kind.[56] Other respondents associated global citizenship more closely with community involvement rather than expressly political action or campaigns aimed at directly influencing government.

For example, a corporate executive who spent several years living in Switzerland and enthusiastically became involved in her local community defined a citizen primarily in social terms, as a member of a community "who participates more than just living there—participates in the school, participates in local events, probably goes to a local church, the local grocery. It's the social life context."[57] Another respondent defined citizenship as "participating in the affairs of the community, and actually influencing the people who you are exposed to in what you believe is good and right—and educating, having the chance to educate others, whether it's philosophical or humanitarian or even technical."[58] Yet another respondent said that she believes that citizenship is "just how we live from day to day and how we treat people."[59] Other individuals focused on civic engagement and face-to-face interaction as important criteria for citizenship; indeed, a market research study in New Zealand classified two contrasting segments of the population as "global citizens" and "provincial hermits"—the former seen as dynamic and engaged in domestic civic life, while also internationally outward looking; the latter seen as stagnant, lethargic, and apathetic.[60] A technology writer and advocate of global citizenship framed a similar contrast between citizens who are "interacting with other people in society, as opposed to the person who has no interest in dealing with people."[61]

What global citizenship as participation requires can be subdivided into two principal (and overlapping) strains of thinking: voice and activity, on the one hand, and quests for reform, on the other. Participation classified within voice and activity revolves mainly around the idea of having a say in public life—sustained community involvement that is not necessarily political in nature, and also not necessarily in pursuit of sweeping reforms in international institutions (or domestic political institutions, for that matter). Reform-seeking global citizens, meanwhile, often aim to expand channels in which public debate can proceed, hold international institutions accountable to stakeholders, and, in some cases, redefine values sought in the economy and society. In some instances, the reformist strain of participation also encompasses goals such as greater global equality and social welfare.

Voice and Activity

The most basic version of global citizenship as participation involves simply contributing to the political or social life of a community, even if one is not necessarily legally a citizen of the country in question. Several self-described global citizens who had lived abroad emphasized that participating in a local community away from home translated, at least in their minds, into global citizenship. One individual who spent several years living overseas made it clear that he regarded himself a global citizen even while lacking the right to vote in his country of residence. When asked, in an interview, if the lack of voting rights impaired his sense of belonging to the various communities in which he lived, he responded that he felt very much a part of political life nevertheless:

> While I was disenfranchised, I still was able to get actively involved in debate, in getting information about the political situation in each country. The very fact that I was involved in university and educational projects meant that in-

variably I came across quite a bit of political debate—people interested in politics, people moving in and out of politics. I certainly didn't feel a great sense of loss not being able to vote, because I was still able to engage in debate and conversation with people who were voting and was able to get my ideas across anyway.[62]

For this individual, being deprived of voting rights in his adopted country did not leave him feeling deprived of a public voice in his community.

The scale of global citizenship as participation, similar to the primary concepts of awareness and responsibility, can be domestic as well as international. Some large corporations have linked the idea of global citizenship with contributions to local civic life in the communities in which they do business, regardless of the country in question. A multinational insurance company based in Canada, for example, brought the term "global citizenship" into its lexicon when it shifted the emphasis of its worldwide corporate philanthropy from donations to the active involvement of corporate staff on volunteer projects. Rather than simply handing over checks to community groups, employees around the world now collaborate with volunteer organizations, particularly in promoting health education.[63] Likewise, a pharmaceutical corporation repeatedly referred to by its chairman as a global citizen has initiated a universally implemented community service program, in which all employees worldwide have been encouraged to take the same day off once a year for volunteer activities.[64]

Such local contributions are just one form of participatory global citizenship, and these sorts of initiatives would not necessarily qualify as global citizenship in the minds of those respondents who had much more internationally oriented criteria as to what sort of participation would qualify, in their minds, as genuine global citizenship. For example, a leader of a Catholic international-development organization based in Canada argued that global citizens are individuals whose "primary interest," in his words, is the well-being of people in developing countries: "So my point is that if we have somebody here who is very much a local activist—in antipoverty, or in food, or in any social justice issue locally—that person will not tend to be perceived as a global citizen, unless they have that international issue."[65]

Politically active global citizens focus on directly influencing the practices and decisions of governing institutions—demanding responsible policies from domestic political institutions and subjecting international institutions to public scrutiny. One transnational activist interviewed for this book said that global citizenship has to do with "the idea of where should we have, over what institution should we have democratic control, and what are the institutions that really decide over people's lives and against whom we should organize some form of counterpower."[66] For this individual, legally a citizen of France, organizing a teach-in outside the September 2000 meeting in Prague of the International Monetary Fund and World Bank amounted to global citizenship by virtue of trying to hold these powerful institutions accountable. Similarly, with regard to challenging power, the former leader of a transnational advocacy group promoting a human right to food emphasized that the internationalization of corporate power "means the counterbalancing power on the citizen side has to be transnational movements, based on national and regional movements that link globally."[67]

Although political participation in this regard is aimed at promoting responsible decisions by governing institutions, many activists also believe that participation in itself fulfills the moral responsibilities of global citizenship. As an environmental campaigner for the World Council of Churches put it, American church leaders who in early 2001 opposed the United States government's withdrawal from the Kyoto Protocol on climate change were "exercising their responsibility as global citizens within their country to try and change those decisions."[68] Global citizenship, as deployed here within the arena of domestic policy, is presented as a fusion of responsibility, participation, and awareness of global environmental issues. In addition, the goals of changing the policies of national governments and counterbalancing the powers of corporations and international governing institutions lead into global citizenship as quests for reform.

Calls for Accountability and Reform

Global citizen activists seeking reforms within governing institutions are motivated by the goal of democratic empowerment as well as idealistic aspirations for human flourishing. Many transnational activists do seem to burn with desire to change the world for the benefit of the least advantaged. The cofounder of the advocacy group Global Exchange recalled how his experiences traveling in impoverished countries and encountering children facing death left him determined to "get at the causal roots, the institutional causality" of poverty by challenging government and corporate power.[69] Reformers, then, do not merely seek to secure greater democratic control over the institutions they hold under scrutiny; they raise the stakes and strive for change. Maude Barlow, the chair of the Council of Canadians, who led the successful campaign against the Multilateral Agreement on Investment (MAI) and also has participated in numerous demonstrations outside meetings of international economic institutions, said that in her view, the goal of the "global citizens movement,"[70] as she called it, is twofold: first, to amplify the role of politics in the global economy and reclaim political space that has been lost to remote and unaccountable processes of decision making; second, to change the rules in the global economy, particularly with regard to international trade regulations that critics believe are stacked in favor of corporate interests: "I don't believe in a global economy with footloose transnational corporations and transnational capital that is not governed in any way by laws at any level. I [also] don't believe it's enough anymore to do it at the nation-state level. We have to bring the rule of law to global institutions."[71]

The desire to bring the rule of law to international economic institutions signals how numerous critics of economic globalization are seeking more globalization, not less, in order to tame the capricious forces of unchecked global capitalism. It is especially noteworthy that although relatively few respondents equated or linked global citizenship with universal human rights,[72] reform-seeking transnational activists in the interview population were somewhat more inclined than other respondents to claim that each human person is a global citizen by virtue of human rights. As a leading campaigner to alleviate world hunger put it: "For me, every human being is a global citizen, but some of their rights of citizenship are being denied to them if they're going hungry."[73] Another activist compared his work to "putting flesh on the bones of those basic principles" of both the U.S. Declaration of Independence and the United Nations Declaration on Human Rights.[74]

By no means must reform-seeking global citizens be transnational activists—in many instances, self-described global citizens carry out quests for reform in their neighborhoods and homes. The organizer of an environmentally innovative cohousing initiative in Cambridge, Massachusetts, noted that many of the participating residents—global citizens, in her mind—could have afforded larger, more expensive houses, but that the community is "the embodiment of a philosophy that there's a higher standard of living, both socially and spiritually, that can be achieved if we are willing to pull together and invest some time and effort into what the community needs and how we live. And I think that has global ramifications, because if we demonstrate that, then it's there for other people to notice. That's a statement of faith."[75] Making such a statement of faith, while planted literally in one's own backyard, serves as an interesting counterweight to more overtly political and transnational versions of global citizenship as participation. As noted throughout this book, global citizenship often signifies forms of civic engagement that are mainly domestic and cross-cultural rather than international and political. Not only does global citizenship involve reclaiming transnational space for the public, but global citizenship also thrives within local public space.

Conclusion

This chapter has illustrated the centrality of awareness, responsibility, and participation in the practices of global citizenship as well as the extent to which these three concepts are interwoven in the minds of the people interviewed for this study. The trajectory or circular flow that can be identified among notions of awareness, responsibility, and participation is worth unpacking in further detail, as the relationships among them reinforce their standing as primary concepts of global citizenship. Taken together, the concepts of awareness, responsibility, and participation also emphasize the recognition of global interdependence, a key consolidating idea within global citizenship discourse in its own right.

Global citizenship as awareness involves thinking beyond one's imagined physical boundaries and recognizing interdependence among countries, cultures, economies, ecosystems, and all life on the planet; global citizenship as consciousness implies an understanding of not only how human beings and their respective communities and habitats are interconnected but also how issues such as human rights, poverty, trade, and environmental sustainability intersect. What is more, global citizenship as awareness involves thinking about decisions and policies with the same degree of care and sensitivity that one would expect if the fates of immediate family members or one's children or grandchildren were at stake. Consequently, some self-described global citizens regard awareness as a fundamental early stage of global citizenship, with political action, ethical purchases, or other choices or habits motivated by concern for humanity or the planet as outward manifestations of global awareness.

Responsibility often serves as the ethical fulcrum between awareness and participation. Principled decision making derives from reflection on how one's actions leave an impact on the planet; it also entails consideration of the interests of communities outside one's immediate purview. This applies to individuals as well as national governments and multinational corporations. Responsibility also involves being proactive, and taking the initiative to "do my bit,"[76] as one respondent put it, rather than waiting for others to take the first steps; this underscores the link between responsibility and participation. Both responsibility and participation within the practices of global citizenship almost always are related to voluntary initiatives rather than legally binding obligations, even as these actions are motivated by strong senses of duty intertwined with moral aspirations of solidarity, such as the decision of a couple from the United States to adopt a village in Malawi and hence to think of themselves as fellow villagers from afar in a global neighborhood. Participation, in turn, entails having a voice within communities and governments at home and abroad, and in many cases, mounting pressure for democratic reforms and improvements in public policy.

In reiterating how the primary concepts are related, it is helpful to illustrate a few instances in which the people interviewed for this study seemed to articulate progressions in their thinking about global citizenship across ideas of awareness, responsibility, and participation. Consider, for starters, the definition of a "global citizen" offered by an advocacy manager for the Australian affiliate of Oxfam:

> It would be an individual who has an understanding of the way a society operates at a global level, and having that understanding, that they interpret, for whatever reason, that they have some responsibility as an individual to take action to achieve social justice or equity or environmental sustainability. Somebody who is motivated for whatever reason to take action as opportunities arise on those sorts of issues.[77]

This definition of a global citizen combines notions of awareness, responsibility, and motivation for action as essential ingredients of global citizenship. Consider also this similarly encompassing definition, from a vice president at Earthwatch Institute, which emphasizes responsible actions that originate from heightened awareness:

> To me, one of the definitions, I think, is understanding what you do in life is connected and produces a reaction that may be right on the other side of the world. I'll give you an example: when you switch on an electrical light, you don't think about the energy requirement in a power station to burn a fossil fuel that produces gas into the atmosphere. Your simple action of turning on the light produces a connection, which results in global warming. Understanding those connections is, to me, what global citizenship is about . . . I think global citizens are people who understand those kinds of connections and ideally, act on them to produce good outcomes rather than bad outcomes.[78]

The ethos of making decisions and taking specific actions, with the good of the planet in mind, also emerged among respondents engaged in the most immediate of public spheres, such as the cohousing community in Cambridge, Massachusetts. When one of the community's leaders, a self-described global citizen, was asked during an interview how she could possibly be a citizen of an entity beyond one's country, she replied with another question that bears a close resemblance to the logic of the above passage: "Don't you think that if you believe that what you do has an effect regardless of political boundaries, that it is incumbent upon you to think beyond those boundaries about what's happening and try to act in such a way that the consequences are not deleterious? We're faced with decisions every day that have a global impact, and so how can we not think of ourselves as global citizens?"[79] This point serves to illustrate, once again, how global citizenship can derive from recognition of global interdependence as it unfolds within local public space. It also demonstrates how global citizenship in practice often works across altruism and pragmatism.

Similarly, another respondent defined global citizenship as understanding global interdependence and therefore living responsibly: "I think it [global citizenship] means being aware of and living in a way that's consciously friendly to people around the world. I think it means voting in a conscientious way. I think it means being aware of what it is that we're supporting through purchases that we make. I think that the way that we treat our environment here in Oxford, Ohio, affects the environment in Oxford, England."[80] Once again, all three primary concepts are interwoven across this interpretation of global citizenship. Likewise, the head of a regional government foundation in Japan combined awareness, responsibility, and participation by defining a global citizen, at the most basic level, as a person who is knowledgeable of issues of international significance, and, at a more advanced level, as a person who will "change your daily life in response to what you acknowledge to be the issue," possibly through involvement with an international non-governmental organization.[81]

Such passages illustrate how awareness, responsibility, and participation, taken together, are at the heart of what global citizenship means to individuals who have embraced the term. These three primary concepts were central in the minds of the respondents in their understandings of global citizenship, notably convergent with their definitions of both global citizenship and citizenship, and also mutually dependent on each other for their full power. If any of the three primary concepts were to be removed from this analysis, then the composite of global citizenship left behind would be impoverished, especially considering that the removal of any one of the primary concepts would substantially weaken the power of the remaining two concepts in providing a response to skeptics of global citizenship. Only awareness, responsibility, and participation fit together so tightly as to render themselves greater than the sum of their parts in contemporary public discourses and practices of global citizenship.

CHAPTER THREE

Secondary Concepts of Global Citizenship

Concepts of awareness, responsibility, and participation together contribute to a robust and coherent image of global citizenship. However, the richness and complexity of contemporary global citizenship discourse lead us to other key strains of thinking that also need to be examined in order to provide a full account of how global citizenship is now interpreted and practiced. Concepts of cross-cultural empathy, personal achievement, and international mobility stop short of operating as central organizing principles in the body of thought surrounding the term "global citizenship." Nevertheless, these three secondary concepts of global citizenship are essential in exploring comprehensively how the term "global citizenship" has been applied beyond the spheres of political philosophy and social science—and not always in ways that signal senses of belonging, obligation, or solidarity within a prospective global community. Global citizenship as cross-cultural empathy—which in some respects derives from the concept of awareness—focuses primarily on human relationships and social interaction, often within local communities. Global citizenship as international mobility represents, in some cases, sheer disengagement from civic life within any political community. Meanwhile, global citizenship as achievement emphasizes academic and professional competence as well as economic competitiveness.

Global Citizenship as Cross-Cultural Empathy

The cross-cultural aspects of global citizenship spring to life in human relationships across many sources of difference, such as ethnicity, language, religion, and social class. For individuals who consider themselves global citizens in a cross-cultural sense, global citizenship has little, if anything, to do with where a person votes, or from which country one holds a passport, and everything to do with how an individual interacts with others and fits in wherever he or she should happen to be planted at any moment in time, even if only temporarily. Global citizenship, in this context, implies a readiness to cross intangible borders that others might consider all too formidable. As novelist Denise Chávez noted during an interview as she reflected on her experiences of immersion in other countries and cultures, global citizenship means that one can be the "outsider" and still nurture strong ties within a community and acquire a sense of comfort:

> I have my passport, but culture, global culture has more to do than your passport. It's how you perceive yourself in the world, as somebody who is comfortable in the world and can befriend and identify with and connect on some kind of heart level with other people in other environments. When I was in Russia, some years back, I felt very much at home—I felt very Russian and very comfortable, and people told me they felt that I was kin in a certain kind of way; there was this certain kind of an honest emotionalism to the people. When I go to Mexico, I feel very Mexican, and I am Mexican-American, but something happens to me: there's a certain kind of freedom to be whatever it is that you need to be at that time.[1]

Note that "global culture" in this passage emerges not at all in an amorphous global ocean[2] but in particular identities. Being a global citizen, for Chávez, involves immersion into the fabric of the places that she visits; it encompasses a notion of liberty to set herself inside other communities and cultures and feel as kin, at least for the moment. In many respects, Chávez embodies the Latin American notion of *mestize* in light of her ability to absorb multiple cultural traditions harmoniously. As Gloria Anzaldúa has written:

> The new *mestize* copes by developing a tolerance for contradictions. She learns to be Indian in Mexican culture, to be Mexican from an Anglo point of view. She learns to juggle cultures. She has a plural personality, she operates in a pluralistic mode . . . nothing rejected, nothing abandoned. Not only does she sustain contradictions, she turns the ambivalence into something else.[3]

Moreover, not only did Chávez feel at home in Russia as an outsider, but she and the local Russians she met seemed like close kin to one another. In this regard, cross-cultural empathy entails an element of reciprocity, at least temporarily, between insiders and outsiders.

Two closely related classifications were culled from the interviews for this study regarding what is meant by global citizenship as cross-cultural empathy. The broader classification is engagement across cultures, as in reaching out across different cultural groups and traditions, regardless of whether one belongs to the dominant group or a minority group within any given community. Embedded within this is the classification of being the outsider, as in immersing oneself into an unfamiliar culture.[4]

Engagement Across Cultures

Whether one is an outsider in unfamiliar surroundings or fully entrenched in one's place of birth, global citizenship as cross-cultural empathy depends heavily on a willingness to build personal relationships with those from other backgrounds. Although an easy acceptance of people from different ethnic and cultural backgrounds might seem largely beyond the sphere of politics, cross-cultural empathy in many circumstances also takes on political significance. An Australian journalist who defined citizenship in terms of rights and responsibilities said that global citizenship, in his view, means not fearing other cultures—both in terms of traveling overseas and welcoming immigrants into Australia. Just one day before this person was interviewed, he participated (as a citizen, not as a reporter) in a mass demonstration in Melbourne in which an estimated 300,000 people called for reconciliation with Australia's aboriginal population: "We are a migrant culture, and there are enormous numbers of people with different faces and different colored skins and different accents. I don't feel that they're a threat. That's my concept if you talk about a global citizen: it's someone who doesn't feel threatened by other cultures and who sort of feels his own culture is robust enough to stand up amongst them, that that culture itself is a product of diversity."[5]

In keeping with this view of diversity as enriching, a parent from California put her moral vision of global citizenship into practice by enrolling her daughter in a bilingual school that conducts classes in Spanish as well as in English and enrolls a cross-section of youngsters from Anglo and Latino backgrounds. This dual-language experience, in the parent's eyes, lends itself to more than language learning: "She can share with them [the classmates] what she's learning about being Jewish. They can share with her what they know about their parents and grandparents perhaps being raised in Argentina or Mexico. That's where global citizenship starts. It's how you think of your community . . . To be a global citizen, all you have to do is think about somebody else."[6] Global citizenship, then, not only involves thinking about someone else and absorbing the cultural traditions of others but also involves sharing one's heritage. In this regard, engagement across cultures entails perspective-sharing as well as perspective-taking.

This links back to global citizenship as awareness: as a state of mind, as consciously thinking from the perspective of another person—and identifying common goals and attributes. For instance, investment banker Francis Woong-il Lee, a Korean who earned his undergraduate degree in the United States, said in an interview for this study that he began to move beyond his initial "cultural discomfort," in his words, when he looked at his classmates not in terms of their ethnic or cultural identities but in terms of their more essential personal qualities. As he noted in a commencement speech he delivered more than thirty years after his graduation from Roanoke College in Virginia, "It was not, I decided, the things that separated us that mattered— it was the things we admired in each other despite—or even because of—our differences. What was important was that we tried to overcome cultural differences and to like—or dislike—each other on the basis of who we were, not because we were Korean or American."[7] In other words, looking at another person through his or her inner qualities as a human being amounts, in itself, to a personal quality of a global citizen.[8]

By no means are such ideals necessarily easy to achieve in practice. Potentially intimidating aspects of global citizenship, in many cases, are everyday challenges close to home, such as confronting bigotry in one's own backyard. As noted by a London journalist with a local view of global citizenship as engagement across cultures: "I don't think you necessarily have to step out of your village to be a global citizen. It just means things, like, if someone's making a horrible racist or bigoted comment in the playground, just saying something about it. To me, those fairly small steps, they all make a world."[9] These insights with respect to engagement across cultures underscore how global citizenship often carries forth through encounters and relationships within local communities.

Being the "Outsider"
Global citizenship as cross-cultural empathy, for many individuals, blossoms especially after they walk in the shoes of an outsider and still cultivate a genuine sense of belonging. Some of the self-described global citizens interviewed for this study conveyed how they felt very much at home while living in communities in which they were legally classified as aliens. For example, David Fuller, an Australian educational administrator with considerable experience living abroad, summarized his perspective on what it means to be a global citizen as "not feeling threatened, not feeling an alien, but being able to function in other cultures and reasonably quickly; not hav-

ing this sort of traumatic period of having to sort of settle in and take a long time to find your feet but to be able to move in fairly quickly and be able to operate and see the differences and compensate for the differences."[10]

It is ironic that Fuller found his own ideal of global citizenship elusive upon returning to his native Australia, after eleven years overseas, with his Malaysian spouse and their small children with mixed ethnic identities. Fuller and his family first attempted to settle in Brisbane, but they found that in public places, ranging from shopping centers to city buses, racist comments repeatedly were directed at them, leaving Fuller feeling like an outsider of sorts in his country of origin. After five months, Fuller found a different job and the family moved to Wollongong, a city near Sydney, in New South Wales, that boasts nearly one hundred nationalities among its residents. Here the multicultural environment allowed Fuller and his family to feel truly at home:

> It's a city that cut its teeth dealing with different cultures and new people, so the attitude here is quite different. We found it a lot easier, because the children weren't coffee-colored children in a white environment. They were coffee-colored amongst other coffee-coloreds. There were a lot of people from Mediterranean backgrounds, from mixed marriages, from all sorts of different backgrounds, and our kids didn't stand out.

Fuller came to regard himself as a global citizen while overseas, when he found it increasingly difficult to relate with the Australians he happened to meet in his travels. Indeed, he was unique among this study's respondents to conceive of the general idea of citizenship mainly in terms of cross-cultural empathy:

> To me, it [citizenship] is more of a mental construct than a legal thing. The legality of it, the ability to travel on a passport from a different country to me doesn't matter. It matters a lot to other people, I realize, particularly political scientists. But to myself, it is really, I suppose, it's a freedom to be able to operate and a feeling of comfort in other cultures and moving from one culture to another, and a sense of belonging.

This corresponds with some recently emerging academic interpretations of citizenship that are expansively oriented toward cultural affinities that emphasize informal channels of membership and senses of belonging, rather than legal membership standing or participation in politics. As Stephen Frosh has written, from the vantage point of psychology, citizenship has to do with "the investments which human subjects accrue toward their social world. . . . To be a citizen, one not only has to formally belong somewhere;

one has also to feel that this belonging is real."[11] Achieving such a sense of belonging requires open-mindedness from the outsiders transplanting themselves into other cultures as well as the insiders receiving them. Clearly, global citizenship as cross-cultural empathy will not necessarily emerge just anywhere, just as it did not emerge for Fuller and his family in Brisbane. One can belong to a polity officially as a full citizen, with full legal rights and no obvious discrimination, and still feel like an alien if the environment proves inhospitable. Despite Fuller's Australian citizenship, the feeling of being treated like an alien in Brisbane prompted a decision to take refuge in a more welcoming community.

Short-term immersion experiences, rather than living abroad for years at a time, were far more common ways in which people interviewed for this study gained the opportunity to become outsiders. Some respondents shared experiences of how they had transcended seemingly formidable barriers while living outside their familiar surroundings. For example, a music teacher from the United States, who went to Japan on a Fulbright fellowship, found himself a complete outsider there, discovering in railroad stations and retail stores "what it felt to be illiterate, totally illiterate, and communicating to people with hand gestures and pointing and smiles,"[12] such as one instance in which a Japanese person drew a picture of a chair and crossed it out in order to convey to him that no seats were available on a train. But when this person walked into a choir rehearsal at a junior high school, he became the first and only teacher in his group of visitors to communicate directly with the Japanese students—through the universal language of music—as he accompanied the choir on the piano.

A different sort of adaptation process was conveyed by a self-described global citizen—the first black South African to earn an MBA at Harvard Business School—who discovered, approximately four months into the program, that she had not blended into her environment as much as she had thought. In fact, her fellow students and professors had difficulty relating to her and were treating her with extreme caution, especially in classroom settings:

> That really came as a surprise, in fact, as a shock, when I realized what was going on. And then, I started the process of putting people at ease. On the one hand, while, for me, I just blended in well and I did not really focus on the differences that much; they, on the other hand, saw a lot of differences, and hence their treatment of me was not in a normal way that they treated each other. But that changed over time. It had to. And I had to go through a process of making people feel comfortable, that, you know, I'm comfortable, I'm normal, just relate to me the way you relate to others.[13]

This student initiated a "serious talk," in her words, with one professor who seemed unusually hesitant, during class discussions, to challenge her remarks, apparently out of fear of how she might react. After they talked, the relationship changed, and the two continued to correspond for years afterward. This episode serves to illustrate that even if an outsider is beginning to feel comfortable outside his or her home culture, further steps of engagement often are required to put the insiders at ease; once again, global citizenship as cross-cultural empathy entails overcoming fear. The steps that outsiders must be prepared to take in order to adapt successfully into a different culture relate back to broader questions of awareness and participation—as in having enough knowledge of oneself and of one's circumstances to help smooth the way for successful adaptation.

All in all, being the outsider entails crossing cultural boundaries with grace and verve; it requires the willingness to nurture a sense of belonging in an unfamiliar setting. Engagement across cultures, meanwhile, requires levels of interest and sensitivity, as well as the willingness to absorb and contribute to communal life and include people who might otherwise feel left at the margins. The concept of cross-cultural empathy further illustrates how global citizenship emerges, in many cases, through human relationships that individuals build in the course of their lives.

Global Citizenship as Achievement

Media references to global citizenship occasionally read like a who's who list of celebrities. Journalists around the world have discovered that "global citizen" works as a convenient catchphrase to describe illustrious individuals—especially those who are world renowned, maintain residences in more than one country, and are also active in various global humanitarian causes. Scores of famous actors, athletes, entrepreneurs, musicians, scientists, spiritual leaders, and writers have been extolled as global citizens in glowing press accounts: Muhammad Ali, Bill Gates, Jane Goodall, Emmylou Harris, Angelina Jolie, the Dalai Lama, Rupert Murdoch, V. S. Naipaul, Yoko Ono, Mary Robinson, Ted Turner, Dionne Warwick, and the late Isaac Stern and Sir Peter Ustinov.

Not everybody called a global citizen by virtue of their achievement agrees with the label, however. Several distinguished people declared "global citizens" by dignitaries, journalists, or awards committees were quite modest during interviews for this study, and, at times, were reluctant to classify themselves as global citizens. Louise Arbour, the current United Nations high commissioner for human rights, was labeled a global citizen by *Châtelaine*, a women's magazine in Quebec, during her tenure as a justice on the Supreme Court of Canada. In an interview for this study, Arbour discounted the label as a badge of identity and (as noted in chapter 2) talked at length about how global citizenship for her, a self-described French Canadian, meant protecting the human rights of refugees and displaced persons around the world: "It's much more attractive to me to think of 'global citizens' as those who have no state to turn to to seek protection than to think of 'global citizen' the way I think many people would, in terms of international stardom."[14] Likewise, David Rockefeller—the retired president of Chase Manhattan Bank and one of the founders of both the Trilateral Commission and the International Executive Service Corps—politely took exception to being declared "an exemplary global citizen"[15] by President Bill Clinton upon receiving the Medal of Freedom at the White House in January 1998. A veteran of World War II who served for two and a half years in North Africa and France, Rockefeller said that he considers himself as "an American who has broad interests in other parts of the world." Moreover, when these sorts of individuals did say that they either regarded themselves as global citizens or found some redeeming value in the term, generally they did not place emphasis on personal achievement and instead seemed to focus on the concepts of awareness, responsibility, and participation, as discussed in chapter 2.

Notions of global citizenship as achievement were articulated most frequently during interviews with educators who aspire to develop a new generation of competent and competitive global citizens. The articulation of global citizenship as achievement was particularly apparent in secondary education, as secondary-school principals espousing global citizenship seemed acutely concerned that their students would advance to universities and reach sufficient academic and technological proficiency to compete in the global marketplace. For example, Father Bressani Catholic High School, located near Toronto, reconfigured its cooperative program that had long placed its students in jobs with local businesses. Traditional co-op placements had been in lumberyards, restaurants, and retail stores and generally had not attracted the school's brightest students. More recently, however, the program has reached out to more academically motivated students and placed them into international law firms, international agencies (such as UNICEF), and high-tech corporations. At times, the students assigned to these organizations have learned startling lessons about the volatility of the global economy. One student, who went on to pursue a university degree in engineering, lost both of his supervisors at Bombardier when the aerospace corporation suddenly restructured its operations and immediately reassigned the engineers working with the student to offices in Montreal and in Wichita, Kansas.[16] As former principal Brian O'Sullivan recalled:

> Here was a student seeing a major global aerospace company doing some restructuring, and from a relatively safe position on his part. . . . One of the sort of interesting notes, too, was the student's reaction. You almost forget, you have to sort of second guess a teenager. His reaction, initially, was, "Well, this is annoying, I've got a new person [for a supervisor]." Our reaction was, "Stand back and watch this. You might be annoyed, but people's careers are being shifted internationally here. Enjoy the view."

Preparing students for the global economy is just one slice of the global education program at Father Bressani Catholic High School. Faculty and staff work to shape the social consciences of students as much as they emphasize academic achievement. The school curriculum includes a service component that requires each student to spend ten hours each year working in places such as Toronto food banks, soup kitchens, and distribution centers for parcels of food during the Christmas season. The activities are local, though O'Sullivan considers the lessons learned about human life universal.

From the opposite corner of the world, at Southland Girls High School in Invercargill, New Zealand, former principal Linda Braun said that the term "global citizenship" entered her vocabulary around 1997, as the school began successfully recruiting Asian students from overseas, leading to a much more internationally mobile and culturally diverse student body. Alongside the cultural transformation of the school, Braun associated global citizenship mainly with notions of competence and competitiveness. Upon returning from an international conference for secondary-school principals held in 1998 in Helsinki, Finland, Braun told a local news reporter: "The message that is coming through very clearly is that technology, literacy and numeracy are the keys to global citizenship. We might be relatively isolated in New Zealand, but, through communication, through learning languages and through having an international outlook, we can keep pace with developments in places like Europe."[17]

To help translate this international outlook into daily life, the school invested NZ$300,000 in a computer network and placed computer terminals in open public spaces rather than in enclosed classrooms. The school provided each student with unlimited Internet access and an e-mail account—an amenity more common at universities than secondary schools and a move that at the time placed Southland Girls technologically ahead of every other secondary school in the surrounding region. Braun also placed an emphasis on four extracurricular "quadrants"—sports, cultural activities, leadership, and service. These four "quadrants" encompass numerous clubs dedicated to local service projects, such as a swimming program that assists children with disabilities, as well as global issues, such as a chapter of Amnesty International. The strategy focused on civic competence and professional competitiveness is working: More than 90 percent of Southland Girls High School graduates go on to university education, and half of them become the first university graduates in their families.

The concept of achievement, on the surface, might appear to focus primarily on personal qualities related to competitiveness for its own sake, rather than personal qualities related to motivation and responsibility within a political community. However, in many respects, the qualities that educators are concerned about instilling in their students—being widely knowledgeable and well rounded, taking on leadership roles, having good analytical skills, and so forth—can be viewed as precursors to meaningful citizen commitments in political life. Moreover, although ancient philosophers considered the public forum the locus of civic virtue, with citizen competence defined mainly as the ability to make decisions in harmony with the public good,[18] contemporary normative interpretations of citizenship—particularly in conservative political thinking—have expanded the realm of competence into society at large, the marketplace included.[19] As Herman van Gunsteren has observed:

> Individual competence also is essential for the exercise of citizenship. A chairman who does not break the rules but is otherwise incompetent in presiding over and guiding a meeting can be a disaster. . . . Goodwill and a consensus on norms and values, which have a central place in many discourses on "feelings" of citizenship, are not enough. They are neither a necessary nor sufficient condition for transforming a community of fate into a republic of citizens. Of course, tolerance and respect—the wish not to humiliate and not to be humiliated—are important; but without competence—the ability, inventiveness, and good judgment—to actually organize differences, they come to naught.[20]

Therefore, educational initiatives that are not overtly political can be regarded, nevertheless, as contributing to the development of intellectually and culturally astute global citizens. Indeed, educational programs that emphasize leadership qualities and the early acquisition of professional skills can be regarded as valuable in producing citizens with high levels of motivation for sustained political involvement as well as senses of responsibility for the common good, globally as well as nationally. Just as the less overtly political concepts of awareness and cross-cultural empathy both encompass numerous personal qualities that serve as important precursors for civic engagement, the same can be said for global citizenship as achievement.

Global Citizenship as International Mobility

The secondary concept of international mobility amounts to a curious blend of predictability and discontinuity. It is predictable in that a term as sweeping as "global citizenship" inevitably would be expected to signify, at times, the unimpeded movement of individual people around the world—even if in reality, the legal restrictions of national citizenship keep the vast majority of the world's population contained within their countries of origin. It is discontinuous in that notions of global citizenship attached to international mobility tend to be divorced, at times, from the primary concepts of awareness, responsibility, and participation. Global citizenship as international mobility often tends to be more about professional opportunities and lifestyle options than about political or social responsibility and engagement, and the experiences of self-described global citizens who approach this term from the concept of mobility tend to reflect an especially privileged view of the world.

The individuals who fit into this classification tend to mirror Bryan Turner's description of "postmodern citizens" as "characterised by cool loyalties and thin patterns of solidarity" and oriented toward "disloyalty and ironic distance."[21] This strain of global citizenship also parallels what Aihwa Ong, from the vantage point of cultural anthropology, has called "flexible citizenship" among an elite segment of professionals who spread their careers across multiple continents and disperse their families, sending their "parachute kids" to schools overseas. These "outwardly mobile" individuals, in Ong's words, are "aligned more by world market conditions than the moral meaning of citizenship in a particular nation."[22] In addition, global citizenship as international mobility is sometimes framed as severing ties from one's native country, in some instances for the sake of financial gain. Hence global citizenship as international mobility rubs shoulders, in an odd sort of way, with more conventional notions of citizenship as legal standing within the nation-state.

Internationally mobile global citizens often mirror the sorts of individuals that political economist Robert Reich has called "symbolic analysts," as in intellectually sophisticated professionals with expertise commanding maximum market value in a borderless economy.[23] It is interesting that Reich has used the term "global citizenship" in articulating his concern that the new global elites seem to lack the qualities necessary for robust citizenship:

> The cosmopolitan man or woman with a sense of global citizenship is thus able to maintain an appropriate perspective on the world's problems and possibilities. But will the cosmopolitan with a global perspective choose to act fairly and compassionately? . . . For without strong attachments and loyalties extending

beyond families and friends, symbolic analysts may never develop the habits and attitudes of social responsibility. They will be world citizens, but without accepting or even acknowledging any of the obligations that citizenship in a polity normally implies.[24]

Despite such concerns, global citizenship as international mobility did converge with ideals of civic engagement for some of the individuals interviewed for this study, particularly activists and volunteers who travel abroad. In many other cases, however, international mobility seemed to correlate with detachment from citizenship of any kind. While civic engagement versus civic detachment amounts to one prominent fault line within global citizenship as international mobility, one important dividing line is this: International mobility independent of citizenship status often centered around how individuals adapt to their surroundings when living and working abroad. International mobility *with* implications for citizenship status touched more closely on themes related to immigration, border controls, and, in rare cases, renouncing citizenship ties to one's country of origin.

Mobility Independent of Citizenship Status

The majority of internationally mobile persons interviewed for this study had relocated not as immigrants but for professional or educational opportunities, or, in some cases, volunteer service programs. For the most part, these mobile individuals seemed to take their national citizenship as given, even as they immersed themselves, albeit partially and temporarily, in unfamiliar territory. In this regard, internationally mobile global citizens engaged in communal life abroad often spoke of being good neighbors while away from home. This did *not* entail, for these individuals, regarding everyone in the world as a "global neighbor." Rather, it meant settling into a new community and becoming part of that community, at least in some modest way.

Therefore, when international mobility involves becoming a de facto citizen at least within the social life of a local community abroad, it can strengthen a person's civic engagement and communal attachments rather than weaken them. Moreover, the sorts of mobile individuals who nurtured civic ties away from home usually also were the types of people who would simultaneously maintain strong senses of attachment within their countries of origin—and resettle at home eventually. For these sorts of individuals, the sense of belonging that accompanies domestic forms of citizenship is not necessarily diminished by international experiences. Instead, the sense of belonging is transplanted into communities that the expatriates call home for a temporary period of time. For example, Rick Ellis, chief executive of TV

New Zealand, said that his family went about "nesting" in local communities abroad while Ellis worked for several years in the United Kingdom and in Australia:

> When we live and work in the UK, particularly in London, which I prefer, we feel like we're part of the UK. We pay our taxes; our kids go to school; we make friends; we have family there that we can visit on a weekend. When I'm there, I feel like I'm part of the place, so I guess once again, it's an attitude of mind: that when you are in a location other than where you were originally born and brought up, if you feel like a citizen, then consider yourself a citizen.[25]

Note that nesting requires neither a passport nor voting rights—two classic elements of national citizenship—though interestingly enough, Ellis referred to the mundane duty of paying taxes as one aspect of nesting. Mainly Ellis thinks of nesting in terms of immersing his family within the civic life of the community. While living abroad, Ellis has volunteered with fund-raising efforts at his children's schools, and he has made a point of sending the children to schools serving local families rather than schools geared toward expatriates.

Now back in their native New Zealand, Ellis and his family stay in contact with many of the friends they have made overseas. Indeed, Ellis said he frequently tells his three children that they are global citizens, allows them to travel overseas on their own to visit their friends, and has encouraged them to consider going to a university either in the United Kingdom or the United States. Ellis said he thinks about global citizenship not in terms of a worldwide allegiance, but in terms of shifting national allegiances within the various countries in which his family has lived, all of which happen to be English speaking: "When I'm in the UK, I have a tax file number, I have a national health number, and when I go to Twickenham to watch rugby, I cheer for England. And when I'm in Australia, and I go to the Melbourne cricket ground to watch Australia play whoever, I'm cheering for Australia. . . . I'm also a royalist, I have to confess: I salute the queen when the flag's up at Buckingham Palace!"

For other individuals interviewed, international mobility was strongly associated with a sense of distance from one's country of origin. It is difficult to make any cause-and-effect claim in this regard: it is not entirely clear whether a lack of belonging usually prompts international migration or whether international migration erodes one's sense of belonging. Perhaps the relationship between migration and detachment, for some individuals, is mutually reinforcing. In any case, several respondents who think of themselves as global citizens articulated how they came to perceive themselves as being removed from their respective home countries during experiences overseas. A London advertising executive, for instance, began to feel disengaged from the United Kingdom, first after spending a year in the United States on a management education program, and even more so after his corporate role expanded to include jurisdiction for continental Europe and, eventually, Asia. Although this person had always been based, at least officially, in London, he explained how he quite literally did not have a strong sense of place. He noted that when he traveled on business (60–70 percent of the time), "frequently I'll wake up somewhere, and it takes me five minutes to work out . . . to remember where I am, and I don't find that at all odd."[26] This person added about flying into Heathrow Airport: "I don't regard it as flying home. I regard it as flying into London."

Barbara Moses, a psychologist and career expert based in Canada who often works with internationally mobile professionals, said that the term "global citizenship" often implies an absence of place: "It's really more that 'I am not defined by city, state, or country; I really have no sense of definition, but if I must have a sense of definition, then it would be citizen of the world.' It's not so much opting to be a global citizen. It's that 'I have no sense of belonging to my own community.'"[27] Lacking a clear sense of belonging, upwardly mobile professionals fill the void by forming allegiances to incomes and career prospects. These sorts of individuals have no plans to trade in their national passports, but national citizenship is not at all salient in how they go about their lives. What is more, global citizenship, for them, is a way of acknowledging a diminished sense of attachment to their respective countries of origin. They are practicing a strikingly different version of global citizenship from the sorts of individuals who think about global citizenship mainly in terms of awareness, responsibility, and participation, and in relation to engagement in politics and society.

In other cases, internationally mobile respondents appeared to think about global citizenship neither in terms of engagement nor in terms of disengagement but rather as an expression that simply conveys enthusiasm for international travel and a feeling, in some cases, that they could live anywhere, provided that they are able to maintain high living standards. These individuals did not necessarily show an interest in transnational political activism or feel a sense of kinship with humankind; nor were they looking to change their country of citizenship. On the contrary, most of these individuals seemed to recognize the privileges associated with holding passports from countries such as Canada, the United Kingdom, and the United States. This particular strain of global citizenship has little, if anything, to do with political or social engagement and just about everything to do with lifestyle: the term describes an affluent subset of individuals with the means and the will to live on just about any continent, especially if they have reached a point in their lives where residency need not be dictated by employment or other professional considerations.[28]

For example, Linda Braun, who promoted the idea of global citizenship in the secondary school that she led on the south coast of New Zealand, said during an interview in September 2000 that she and her husband were seriously considering taking early retirement to live abroad—in multiple locations, according to season—with New South Wales, Italy, and France the likely choices: "I would have [once] said we were dyed-in-the-wool New Zealanders [but] I think we feel least like New Zealanders now. We're very keen to go and live overseas."[29] And they did—now retired, Braun and her husband live in China for several months each year while Braun consults for a variety of organizations, including the United Nations Development Programme and the Chinese Ministry of Commerce in Beijing. Investment banker Francis Woong-il Lee, meanwhile, noted that although he considers Korea his home, he plans to retire to Connecticut, where he still owns a house from his years in New York City: "I feel Korea's an exciting place to work in, but after I'm retired, I think I'll enjoy a little nature that the U.S. has to offer."[30] Global citizenship as retirement abroad is by no means exclusive to the wealthier classes; the published references also turned up a news account of a growing number of Japanese pensioners building modest retirement houses in Australia. As the article noted:

> This new category of owner is drawn from the working classes of Japan; retirees who are dependent on modest, fixed incomes. It conveys a new image of the global citizen. People with no access to status, privilege or wealth are making a commitment to spending the rest of their lives as tourists, literally and officially. Their motivation is to gain access to low-cost housing on foreign soil, offering a quality of life they cannot afford in the country in which they officially reside.[31]

For those too young to spend the remainder of their lives as tourists, global citizenship as experienced through international mobility yields the benefit of professional recognition abroad. Cynthia Hogan, the pharmaceutical executive profiled in chapter 1, often found herself conducting meetings in French while based in Switzerland, and she said that one sign of her global citizenship, in her mind, was not so much being called a global citizen in a news article published in the United States but rather being quoted in French and in German by European news sources: "To me, that's more of being a global player than having an American paper write about you saying you're global."[32] Furthermore, professional recognition in the international arena need not entail working abroad, as important as that might be, but rather can emerge simply by being plugged into professional networks worldwide. A management consultant and self-described global citizen noted that regardless of where she might choose to live, "I'll still be accessing a whole lot of markets in different ways for whatever purpose."[33]

Mobility with Implications for Citizenship Status

Although most self-described global citizens interviewed for this study seemed to think about global citizenship entirely outside the context of national citizenship status, some respondents did think about global citizenship at least partly in terms of moving across international borders, and, in a few cases, overcoming restrictions imposed by nation-states on people's movement. Rosie Brown, the community volunteer from Oklahoma profiled in chapter 1, helped an Ethiopian man, whom she and her husband had met on a service trip abroad, secure political asylum in the United States.[34] Another self-identifying global citizen expressed discomfort with the United States border patrols, the enforcement mechanisms of bounded national citizenship, that operate in her native New Mexico even as local farmers depend on the labor of undocumented immigrant workers.[35] Such moral objections echo a well-known summation from political theorist Joseph Carens: "Citizenship in Western liberal democracies is the modern equivalent of feudal privilege—an inherited status that greatly enhances one's life chances."[36]

In addition to arguing in favor of less restrictive national borders, some respondents said that they derived their thinking about global citizenship from their respective life experiences either as immigrants or as children of immigrants. A Toronto journalist, himself an immigrant from India, noted that contemporary immigrants to Canada—thanks largely to communications advances such as inexpensive overseas phone calls, television programs beamed via satellite from abroad, and newspapers available worldwide on the Internet—maintain a far more active interest in the countries in which their families have roots than did earlier generations that more commonly developed "amnesia" with regard to their homelands.[37]

Such perspectives on international mobility and immigration do converge with moral visions that emphasize solidarity and engagement across borders. However, other perspectives in this regard include disengagement from civic life and, in some cases, outright withdrawal from one's country of citizenship. One very dramatic example of this can be found in the writing of Canadian financial journalist Jonathan Chevreau, who has argued that global citizenship involves uprooting national stakes primarily for the sake of monetary gain:

> For those would-be wealthy international citizens of the world, the phrase "off-shore" has almost magical power. Usually, the term is used in the context of taxes, as in offshore tax havens or offshore trusts. But offshore also is used to describe the unshackled investments of the new global citizen. In parallel with the explosive growth of onshore mutual funds, offshore investment funds have also been exploding at the rate of three new ones a day—with more than 14,000 worldwide.[38]

This statement, written in 1999 at the peak of a stock market bubble in North America and much of Europe, suggests that wealthy global citizens ought to take responsibility for their investment portfolios but not necessarily for their fellow Canadians. Global citizenship as offshore investing is symptomatic of a stark divide, at least in libertarian thinking, between the affluent individual's pursuit of economic self-interest and the public good within any country.

During an interview, Chevreau made it clear that his view of global citizenship entails not only investing offshore, but also moving offshore to escape domestic taxation. In other words, global citizens break away from their homelands for the purpose of getting the most from their money elsewhere. Chevreau described his outlook as substituting the role of a customer for that of a citizen. He also compared the Canadian government to a robber and likened offshore tax havens to businesses preoccupied with customer satisfaction:

> So rather than the Canadian model of the IRS [the Internal Revenue Service, in the United States] which is basically, "Stick 'em up, hands up, hand over your money," the concept is that you can choose what jurisdiction you go to, and you should be negotiating a rate of taxation in exchange for certain services, just like a business. The government should be in the business of providing services: it could be customer protection services; it could be roads, medical care, whatever. . . . They should act like businesses and negotiate with their customers, and if the customers don't get the rate they want of taxation, then they go to another jurisdiction and negotiate with them.[39]

Following the idea of a "sovereign individual," as advanced by libertarians James Davidson and William Rees-Mogg,[40] Chevreau discards as archaic and burdensome the idea of citizenship as a permanent tie linking fellow members of a political community in favor of a radically individualistic model of unimpeded consumer choice. The implications for citizenship status, in this case, come into play when a wealthy Canadian closes out his or her retirement savings plan, takes the cash, pays an early-withdrawal tax penalty to

Canada, sells the house, and then, in Chevreau's words, "basically disowns the country."[41] Chevreau said that these so-called global citizens, in his view, usually spend summers in Canada and winters in their new legal domicile, typically in Florida, Mexico, or the Caribbean: "They have a cottage in Canada and their grandchildren and the whole bit. So they still have their ties to Canada, mostly. But as far as the tax man's concerned and their physical assets, they have severed their connection with their home country. They have become a global citizen." In reality, though, these sorts of individuals are living out a dual arrangement within two political jurisdictions, rather than situating themselves in the world as a whole, and ultimately the practice of severing ties to one's home country amounts to an allegiance primarily to one's personal income and assets rather than to any sort of political community.[42]

Global citizenship as international mobility often hearkens mainly to global consumerism, and the sentiments of detachment and disengagement advocated by some individuals in this regard fuel the suspicions of political theorists and social scientists who doubt that global citizenship can withstand critical scrutiny as a valid model of citizenship. In the eyes of some critics, the ascendancy of the new cosmopolitan elite class has imperiled the very essence of democratic citizenship. As the late Christopher Lasch lamented: "The new elites are home only in transit, en route to a high-level conference, to the grand opening of a new franchise, to an international film festival or an undiscovered resort. Theirs is essentially a tourist's view of the world—not a perspective likely to encourage a passionate devotion to democracy."[43] Even scholars who find some promise in the idea of global citizenship often argue that no one should be classified as a global citizen based on factors such as mobility and wealth. As an anonymous reviewer for this book objected: "It is not sensible to call global entrepreneurs global citizens, just because they travel a lot. . . . No sophisticated writer in the field would accept that these are global citizens."

Despite such objections, to ignore this notable strain of thinking within contemporary public understandings and practices of global citizenship would be to paint an unfinished picture of how this term is now interpreted and communicated. As noted earlier, this study presents evidence of myriad concepts and practices now associated with the idea of global citizenship, as they have actually emerged beyond academic debates, and thereby invites further debate as to whether or not these concepts and practices truly count as global citizenship. What is more, as illustrated above, many internationally mobile individuals who have lived overseas, often on professional assignments, perceive themselves as global citizens in a way that speaks thoughtfully to ideals of civic engagement. For some people in this privileged bracket of the population, global citizenship derives not only from mobility but also from participation in local community life abroad. By no means does global citizenship as international mobility always operate in isolation from other, more politically and socially grounded concepts and practices.

Conclusion

Taken together, the primary and secondary concepts of global citizenship illustrate the rich and multifaceted practices of global citizenship in the present day. The concepts of awareness and participation, for starters, show how numerous self-described global citizens do indeed display motivation for sustained political involvement, and the concept of awareness further reveals how global citizens are able to look at issues from a multiplicity of vantage points and perspectives. The concept of responsibility shows how principled decision making and notions of solidarity across humanity both factor into moral accountability that many global citizens accept personally for themselves, regardless of the evolution of global governing institutions.

The concept of cross-cultural empathy contributes uniquely to this study by illustrating how mutual recognition and social trust can emerge powerfully by means of engagement across lines of nationality, ethnicity, language, and religion. The concept of achievement reminds us how educational programs, even those that are not expressly political in nature, are fertile seedbeds for students to become politically involved later in life. The concept of mobility, in contrast, illustrates vividly how some self-proclaimed global citizens remove themselves from political engagement of any kind. And yet, many self-described global citizens with jet-set lifestyles did come across as being actively involved in local communities while living and working abroad.

The idea of global citizenship contains vast internal divisions, especially with regard to articulations of collective responsibility, on the one hand, and assertions of individual privilege on the other.[44] Admittedly, when we look at the entire range of individuals who describe themselves as global citizens, we end up with some strange bedfellows. As such scholars as Richard Falk and John Urry have observed, many global citizens who fit the profile of "global activists" working for such goals as world peace or environmental sustainability have an entirely different set of priorities and perspectives from "global capitalists" concerned with the performances of their enterprises and investment portfolios or, in turn, "global cosmopolitans" who might feel at ease traveling around the world but lack vigorous and ongoing political and moral commitments.[45] And yet, such a multitude of approaches—compatible or incompatible, morally credible or morally dubious—serves to illustrate how the idea of global citizenship is becoming all the more tangible for everyday people, and in ways that vary according to their individual aptitudes, agendas, and interests: whether through accessing markets around the world, cultivating a sense of belonging outside one's comfort zone, or communicating through the universal language of music. Rarely is global citizenship conceived as an end state that would require extraordinary developments such as worldwide political unification or the resolution of the world's most daunting problems. Instead, global citizenship now emerges in our world, as we know it, gradually and progressively through voluntary choices and actions. With these multiple concepts of global citizenship entered into the analysis, the next section of this book looks further at how the term "global citizenship" springs to life, in practice, within numerous civil society organizations, schools and universities, multinational corporations, and governing institutions.

CHAPTER FOUR

Global Citizenship in Civil Society

Global citizenship today flourishes through the outlooks and activities of individuals and institutions. Lacking any enforceable version of a global passport, and lacking a cohesive and developed worldwide political system that would shift authority and allegiances away from nation-states, global citizenship emerges as an entirely different phenomenon from the more familiar model of national citizenship and its emphasis on legal status and formal membership. While national citizenship ultimately amounts to a binding set of rights and duties among individuals within the polity, the ties that hold together global citizens are freely chosen and work across conventional geo-political boundaries. Therefore, voluntary organizations—advocacy groups, community associations, church groups, and so forth, and the informal networks that hold together participants from these groups, dispersed around the world—are among the most visible hubs of global citizenship today.

Civil society is the realm in which global citizenship especially thrives, and the many ways of defining "civil society" could occupy a study in itself. Michael Walzer has offered a helpfully concise, albeit broad definition of civil society as "the space of uncoerced human association and also the set of relational networks—formed for the sake of family, faith, interest, and ideology—that fill this space."[1] This definition opens the door for businesses and other economic actors, as well as schools, colleges, and universities, to be classified as agents within civil society (although much debate continues as to whether profit-making organizations should count as civil society actors). In this book,

educational institutions and multinational corporations are examined sepa-
rately, in chapters 5 and 6, while the discussion here on civil society will focus mainly on political advocacy groups and service organizations.

The power of civil society in transforming public life in local, national,
and international communities has generated much scholarly interest as well
as public attention in recent years. The pivotal roles played by civic groups
in some of the most historic periods of the twentieth century—such as the
civil rights era in the United States, the struggle against apartheid in South
Africa, and the collapse of communism in central and eastern Europe—as
well as the explosion in international communication among networks of activists brought together, in part, by advances in digital communication, suggest strong linkages between transnational activism and global citizenship.
The advances within transnational activist networks became most visible in
November 1999, when protesters from all over the world converged on Seattle and marched outside the stalled negotiations of the World Trade Organization.

However, are transnational activists necessarily global citizens? The academic literature demonstrates no consensus on this question. Scholars in
some instances have classified transnational activists as global citizens[2]—and
as shown in chapter 1, many such activists agree with the label. However, it
is rare for international-relations scholars to claim that the proliferation of
international nongovernmental organizations provides evidence of an
emerging global citizenry. In one leading monograph tracing the evolution of
transnational civil society, Margaret Keck and Kathryn Sikkink document a
so-called boomerang effect in which domestic grassroots organizations form
alliances with international organizations in order to mount both internal
and external pressure on state and national governments, especially repressive political authorities that are in violation of international human rights
standards. However, although the authors believe that such nonstate actors
in the international arena carry implications for state sovereignty, they do
not claim that these transnational advocacy networks feed into any sort of
cosmopolitan citizenship or global citizenry.[3] This is generally the rule in recent international relations scholarship on transnational activism. One
prominent exception is the recent volume by Michael Edwards and John
Gaventa, which specifically links citizen action on an international scale
with the term "global citizenship." As Gaventa has written:

> Global citizenship is the exercise of the right to participate in decision making
> in social, economic, cultural and political life, within and across the local, na-
> tional and global arenas. This is true especially at the global level: Where the

institutions and authority of global governance are not so clear, the rights of citizenship are made real not only through legal instruments but through the process of citizen action.[4]

In short, some scholars regard transnational activism as a form of global citizenship, but transnational activists are not necessarily self-identifying global citizens or advocates of global citizenship. As this chapter shows, voluntary organizations oriented toward service often seem more eager than political advocacy groups to gravitate toward the term "global citizenship."

Global Activists or Global Citizens?

The idea of global citizenship has been marshaled on both sides of the great divide between supporters and critics of economic globalization. In early 2001, when the global protest movement targeting international economic institutions had reached its peak in visibility, notions of global citizenship were invoked in passing not only by some members of the World Social Forum assembled in Porto Alegre, Brazil, but also by the then president of the World Bank James D. Wolfensohn during a speech at the German Bundestag and by World Economic Forum founder Klaus Schwab at the yearly summit of business and government elites in Davos, Switzerland.

For years, activists who have campaigned either to reform or abolish the World Bank, the International Monetary Fund (IMF), and the World Trade Organization (WTO) have referred to themselves publicly as global citizens or part of a global citizens movement. As Anne-Christine Habbard, the then secretary-general of the Paris-based International Federation of Human Rights, told a news reporter in Prague outside the September 2000 meeting of the International Monetary Fund and World Bank: "Ours is a new planetary citizenship, reflecting the fact that decisions have migrated from state level. Voting for national representatives, an old expression of citizenship, achieves nothing, because they have scant power."[5] Similarly, the group of activists who collaborated on the volume *Alternatives to Economic Globalization* call for actively engaged practices of local, national, and global citizenship, and they suggest that global citizenship involves confronting the big international economic institutions and multinational corporations "while simultaneously embodying alternatives through community empowerment, democratic decision making and equality in organizing."[6] However, such arguments about the viability of global citizenship are by no means the norm in the protest movement. Another widely circulated volume entitled *We Are Everywhere*, which was recently published by a group of activists critical of economic globalization, makes absolutely no mention of global citizenship.[7] In order to account more thoroughly for the varying perspectives of today's transnational activists, interviews for this study were conducted with six individuals who participated in demonstrations in Prague in September 2000 outside the IMF and World Bank meetings.

During their interviews, the individuals were asked to elaborate first on their experiences as activists, and later, toward the end of the interview, on their thoughts about citizenship. Typically the interviews began with a general discussion about how the individuals had become involved in a particular cause or advocacy group and what had led them to Prague. Only after the conversation progressed was the idea of citizenship brought into the discussion. At this point, respondents were *not* initially asked whether or not they thought of themselves as global citizens but instead were asked in which communities they considered themselves to be citizens and whether the idea of citizenship was meaningful to them. The more specific term "global citizen" was introduced only after this ground was covered. In some cases, as it turned out, the respondents brought up "global citizen" or similar terms, such as "citizen of the world," without being asked.[8]

Predictably enough, all six individuals expressed strong reservations about economic globalization and usually had participated in multiple protests within the two years prior to being interviewed. However, they did not necessarily see eye-to-eye on questions such as what sorts of protest strategies are appropriate or effective or what alternatives to the present systems of international trade and finance would be preferable. During their interviews, the activists also offered very different perspectives on whether or not they regarded themselves as global citizens. On this question, the group was split straight down the middle: three individuals perceived themselves as either a global citizen or a citizen of the world, and three did not. One interesting pattern emerged: the individuals who did *not* regard themselves as global citizens tended to think of citizenship as synonymous with national enforcement of border controls or as participation within a political community small in scale, whereas the individuals who accepted the term "global citizen" tended to view citizenship in more expansive terms. The skeptics of global citizenship are profiled here first, followed by the three respondents who did consider themselves global citizens.

Global Activists but Not Global Citizens
For millions of television viewers worldwide, Chelsea Mozen became the face of the September 2000 Prague protests. A U.S. citizen originally from Atlanta, Georgia, Mozen served as a spokesperson for the Initiative Against

Economic Globalisation, a Czech group that coordinated protesters at the summit. Similar to those of the activists in the main interview population who considered themselves global citizens, the roots of Mozen's civic engagement trace back to domestic politics and society. During her years in secondary school, Mozen organized a school fund to help build a Habitat for Humanity house and volunteered in an after-school program for urban Atlanta children. After earning a university degree, Mozen moved to Washington, D.C., and worked for nearly two years in the city government's social services bureau before leaving for Prague and joining INPEG (Initiative Against Economic Globalisation) as a volunteer.

After the September 2000 protests, Mozen remained in Prague and helped to launch Krtkova Kolona, a library and café that now serves as a gathering place for Czech political and social activists. After three years in Prague, Mozen moved to New York to earn a master's degree in economics from the New School for Social Research. Although Mozen regards herself as a player in a global movement, she never has thought of herself as a global citizen or as a world citizen. Asked in the most general of terms about what it means to her to be a citizen, Mozen initially was unsure how to respond:

> Goodness, I don't know that I think about it so much. No one's ever hounded into me the idea of what it means to be a citizen. I know that I'm a citizen of the United States, but I certainly don't feel an affinity toward that. In terms of being a citizen of the world, the word "citizen" to me kind of strikes me as national allegiance and nationalism and I don't feel that. I don't pledge "allegiance." I don't want to sing, "I'm proud to be an American."[9] And I don't want to do the same with Czech [Republic], either, or any other place that I might live.[10]

Mozen added that she feels a sense of responsibility to people living outside the United States—but as someone resigned to United States citizenship: "I don't feel responsible to a government or a national boundary so much, but I feel responsible to people around the world. I feel responsible that my citizenship, the place that I'm from, is causing so much poverty and death around the world." For Mozen, citizenship ultimately has to do with the country that she is from, the United States, and her disillusionment with the U.S. government discourages Mozen from thinking of herself as a citizen of any kind even as she is active in transnational political and social causes: "There are so many connotations of the word 'citizen.' There's definitely tons and tons of connotations of passports and boundaries and being let in and out of countries because of your citizenship. So I think my natural inclination is to not claim that word and to not want to be part of that type of nationalism."

This objection—that citizenship is unavoidably associated with nationalism—was echoed by another respondent who campaigned in both Prague and Seattle. Similar to Mozen, Jeff Ferguson, an undergraduate student at Bard College at the time of his interview, associated citizenship mainly with state and national boundaries and the enforcement of border controls: "I don't know if I reject the term outright, but I don't really think in terms of citizenship. I'm definitely aware of the privilege of my legal status as a citizen of the United States. . . . Most of my awareness of citizenship is in terms of the struggles of undocumented workers and so on."[11] Although Ferguson said that he avoids the idea of citizenship, in relation to his own political identity and activity, Ferguson spoke passionately about having a sense of responsibility for humanity: "The fundamental moral ground for social engagement, for me, is consciously identifying as a human. It's identifying as part of the species, as living on this planet and having a fundamental responsibility involved in that. I think that's related to the idea of a citizen of the world but not exactly identical." In essence, Ferguson believes it is possible, and preferable, to have a global identity, as a human being, without drawing on the identity of a global citizen—and without carrying whatever conceptual or ethical baggage that "citizenship" or "global citizenship" might entail.

While Mozen and Ferguson thought about citizenship mainly in terms of legal status, one of their fellow campaigners skeptical of global citizenship focused on the issue of democratic participation. Arthur Foelsche took part in protests in Prague, Quebec City, and Seattle while earning a master's degree from the Institute for Social Ecology in the close-knit village of Plainfield, Vermont. During an interview for this study, Foelsche said that he considered himself a citizen of Plainfield but that he believes that the term "citizenship" has been "polluted" by an emphasis on border controls. Asked if he considers himself a citizen of any communities beyond Plainfield, Foelsche immediately ruled out Vermont, despite his strong affinity for Vermont's progressive political climate, especially the state's civil union legislation that since 2000 has upheld marriage rights for same-sex couples: "I'm very much behind that, and I very much believe in that spirit of Vermont. But I don't really call myself a Vermonter."[12] (This disclaimer, Foelsche noted, is somewhat tongue-in-cheek: many Vermont residents hesitate to call themselves Vermonters if their families have not lived in Vermont for generations!)

Foelsche also ruled out the United States as a meaningful basis for his citizenship, saying that the institution of national citizenship does not square with his belief in localized self-government, though Foelsche did acknowledge the benefits of holding a U.S. passport. Asked at this point if he would turn to a U.S. embassy abroad if he were arrested in a protest, Foelsche replied that he has, in fact, been arrested twice at demonstrations in Canada—once outside a meeting of the Organization of American States and again outside a meeting of the proposed Free Trade Association of the Americas: "Obviously, if I get in trouble, I'm going to use the embassy. Just because I'm against the concept of nation-states doesn't mean that I deny that we live in a world full of them. I could rescind my American citizenship. I could even claim German citizenship [his family's roots trace back to Germany]. But I don't see that as an end. I don't think that either of those kinds of options are very effective."

Just as Foelsche resisted the idea of national citizenship, he also dismissed the idea of global citizenship as too remote from meaningful political relationships and everyday social life. In his mind, global citizenship is linked too closely with world government supporters and the very international institutions that he has targeted in protests. Note how local community again takes precedence in Foelsche's comments:

> The reason I don't identify as a citizen of the world, although obviously that's sort of implicit in what I'm suggesting, is because I see the importance of maintaining community-level autonomy—autonomy with a sense of obligation and indeed an ethic. And I don't think that internationalism, as an institutional concept, is going to be effective for changing the world. My interest is structuring power so that individuals have access to it. And by structuring power in terms of having global institutions like the UN or the WTO, we erode the individual's ability to participate in them. While I think it is absolutely important that we think of ourselves in terms of the rest of the world, the mechanism through which we do that is not one gigantic global institution but rather a network and a confederation of local communities which can communicate to each other.

All in all, Foelsche said that he regards himself not as a global citizen, but as a citizen of Plainfield who is engaged in the world. Reflecting the view of philosopher Murray Bookchin, who in 1974 cofounded the Institute for Social Ecology,[13] Foelsche's understanding of political community as dependent on face-to-face interaction is accompanied by a belief that genuine citizenship is possible only on a truly small scale.

Global Activists and Global Citizens

The activists who went to Prague and *did* think of themselves as global citizens tended to think of citizenship in more flexible terms than state authority or national allegiance. Similar to their counterparts profiled above, they generally backed away from thinking of themselves as enthusiastic citizens of their respective countries. However, they were far more optimistic about prospects for global citizenship and much more willing to describe themselves as global citizens. Tomasz Terlecki, executive director of CEE Bankwatch Network,[14] collaborated in Prague with Friends of the Earth and the anti-debt coalition Jubilee 2000 (now known as Jubilee Research) to sponsor a public forum on international debt relief and the environmental impacts of projects sponsored by the IMF and World Bank. Terlecki also attended a panel discussion at Prague Castle, organized by Czech Republic president Václav Havel, during which activists from nongovernmental organizations debated with officials from the IMF and World Bank. When asked during an interview what it means to be a citizen, Terlecki responded that he sees himself primarily as belonging to Kraków, his hometown, and that he defines citizenship as having a visible stake in public decision making. Terlecki made it clear that he departs from an understanding of citizenship as associated with any predetermined government authority or nation-state:

> I'm an anarchist myself, so I take a citizen as a part of a community and I take my own responsibility for defining what kind of a community I'm a citizen of. Of course I am a citizen of Poland, but I feel much more a citizen of my hometown, Kraków. Poland is much more abstracted than a citizen of Kraków. The country [of Poland] that we have now is very different from other countries that we had back into history, and I don't really take states as such that seriously.[15]

Terlecki added that he also views himself, to a lesser degree, as a "citizen of the world," in his words, given his efforts to shape decisions made by international economic institutions: "I think I've achieved a situation that I know what kinds of actions are required for me, as a citizen of the world, to have a say in decision making about my future and the future of the world. . . . I already have been given a chance to talk with decision makers. Now we can go one step further and try to have influence on who is a decision maker."[16] Terlecki emerges as an interesting contrast to Arthur Foelsche, profiled in the previous section. Both men conceive of citizenship in terms of democratic empowerment, but Terlecki emerges as much more willing than Foelsche to deploy the idea of citizenship in the context of trying to influence international institutions.

Among the six people interviewed within this group of activists, Tomasz Terlecki and Evan Henshaw-Plath, creator of the website www.protest.net, emerged as the closest examples of citizens choosing to situate themselves within multiple political communities, as advocated by political philosophers such as David Held and Michael Sandel, thus mediating potentially conflicting senses of loyalty and obligation. During an interview in November 2000, Henshaw-Plath said he regarded himself as a citizen of three communities: the world, the United States, and his hometown of Arcata, California. He said it would be difficult to choose between being primarily a local citizen or a world citizen, but that U.S. citizenship, for him, definitely ranked last in the trio and that he is "not very proud" to be an American. And yet, Henshaw-Plath emphasized that he considers himself an American in the sense of "cultural continuity."[17]

After Henshaw-Plath described in detail how he was arrested in Prague during a protest outside the IMF and World Bank meetings and was deported from the Czech Republic, he was asked in general terms what it meant to him to be a citizen. His lengthy response, an excerpt of which appears below, was filled with reservations about the term, particularly in national and legal contexts. Ultimately, Henshaw-Plath fell back on the idea of a world citizen. It is important to note that the terms "world citizen" and "global citizen" had not been discussed at all during the interview until Henshaw-Plath described himself as such:

> The term "citizen" is a really interesting one because it has both really positive and negative connotations. "Citizen" involves being active and engaged in your society and having rights, which I support, but also I have problems with the term "citizen" because as I was going through the deportation process and getting kicked out of the Czech Republic, I realized how if you aren't a citizen and you don't get that sort of privilege, you lose so many rights. That all of a sudden I went from a person who had a country and had all these ties and support, to being sort of kicked around in immigration systems and not having any rights and much freedom. And so, I think that my sort of feeling is that what I identify with now is sort of being a world citizen. That I work with all these people all over the world and have these connections and I'll continue to have these connections. And I think citizenship can really be expanded to understand the responsibility to both your local and global communities.[18]

Henshaw-Plath added that he had come across the term "world citizen" before going to Prague but until his experiences in Prague, he never thought the term would apply to him. His view of the world first expanded beyond the United States, he said, when at the age of fifteen he traveled to India with his mother and worked with a Roman Catholic priest in Bombay.

Martin Shaw[19] was the veteran campaigner within this group of activists. An electrician by trade from the United Kingdom who turned environmental activist, Shaw was arrested repeatedly in Britain during the 1990s for his involvement with Genetix Snowball, a protest group known for occupying farmland, wrecking genetically modified crops, and planting organic flowers and vegetables in their place. He took part in the Seattle demonstrations, helped organize the Prague protests, and has been described in the news media not as a global citizen but rather as a "full-time international anarchist."[20] During an interview, Shaw said that he agrees with the anarchist label and that anarchism, to him, is "a belief in people to organize themselves and that the tyranny of government causes some of the greatest suffering in the world."[21]

Being an anarchist, at least in Shaw's mind, is not entirely incompatible with being a citizen: "To be honest, I haven't given it a great deal of thought, but I do regard myself as a citizen, and one actively engaged rather than passively allowing the government to dictate how the world is shaped." Likewise, Shaw does not consider himself a citizen of the United Kingdom, even after being reminded of that fact when deported from the United States in early 2000. Asked where he does consider himself a citizen, Shaw replied: "It sounds very cheesy, but the world. It really is. We are affected by global economic and environmental systems. Whatever happens anywhere affects us all."[22]

Shaw said that he does not view humanity-at-large as his community but rather sees himself as a member of a more specific transnational community: the international protest movement. When Shaw began protesting during the 1980s outside nuclear power facilities in the United Kingdom, he viewed his communities as strictly domestic—his work colleagues, classmates, and fellow protesters. Shaw said that his more recent travels have shown him how campaigners around the world are united by common concerns as well as a sense of solidarity. While traveling abroad, Shaw often has been given free accommodation by fellow campaigners (at the time of the interview he had just returned from The Hague, after protesting outside a negotiating session on the Kyoto Protocol) and he said that this experience added to his sense of being a citizen of the world. Shaw put it this way: "Surviving in the States on the goodwill of the campaigners there, moving from campaigning community to campaigning community, and realizing the joy of that—that reciprocal arrangement that carries on." It is interesting that this self-described citizen of the world turned specifically to the idea of reciprocity—the same concept invoked by political philosopher David Miller in his argument against the feasibility of cosmopolitan citizenship. While Miller believes that only fellow nationals within a "determinate" community truly can stand in reciprocity with one another as citizens,[23] Shaw perceives himself as standing in reciprocity with like-minded protesters across continents.

Citizenship and the Prague 2000 Activists

The insights shared by these participants in the September 2000 demonstrations in Prague illustrate how any scholarly claim that transnational activists are global citizens depends in part on the self-perceptions of the activists. Some activists agree that transnational activism corresponds with a new conception and practice of global citizenship, but others would vigorously challenge and deny this proposition. Especially striking is that the formative experiences of some of the transnational activists who do *not* find much value in the idea of global citizenship are remarkably similar to many of the self-described global citizens whose reflections are shared elsewhere in this book. For example, the domestic roots of Chelsea Mozen's political activism bear a resemblance to the trajectories of the transnational activists profiled in chapter 1, namely, Maude Barlow, Hazel Henderson, and Pat Montandon. Moreover, all three skeptics of global citizenship within this group of activists articulated strong personal ethics of global responsibility that closely parallel the sentiments of numerous respondents from the main interview population for this study. If these skeptical activists were not so reluctant to apply the term "global citizenship" to their experiences, they could be singled out as exemplifying global citizenship from the standpoint of scholars choosing to argue that transnational activists are global citizens.

An additional substantial difference between activists who choose to identity as global citizens and activists who do not relates to the question of public space. Self-described global citizen activists such as Tomasz Terlecki view the concept very much in terms of the pursuit of global public space, in which stakeholder concerns can be called to attention particularly in deliberations within international institutions. As Terlecki noted, his idea of global citizenship extends into the prospect of having a say in decision making within key international institutions. On the other hand, some of the skeptical activists with regard to global citizenship questioned the extent to which public-policy decisions should be made at all in the international arena and instead voiced a strong preference, as did Arthur Foelsche, for stronger channels of collaboration and power sharing among local communities. In this respect, the two groups of activists seemed to think differently about what counts as feasible public space or how much citizens can accomplish in different public spaces. Both sets of activists aim to structure power in ways that provide access for everyday citizens and allow the voices of the people to be heard, but they differ in their approaches: skeptical activists seem resigned to an impasse between local public space and global citizenship, while activists more hospitable to the idea of global citizenship seem to hold out more hope for everyday people to gain substantial access to power in the international arena. Such comparisons illustrate further how some transnational activists who might seem to exhibit the qualities of global citizens do not necessarily find the term salient in framing their political participation.

Service, Advocacy, and Global Citizenship

Because "global citizenship" is a loaded word within activist circles, the term has emerged far more commonly among organizations focused on service and education that are trying to articulate how participants shape and transform their lives through community involvement. One of the first service organizations to take up the mantle of global citizenship was Canada World Youth, which in 2000 incorporated the term "global citizenship" into one of its statements of purpose. The so-called Vision Statement declares: "Canada World Youth envisions a world of active, engaged global citizens who share responsibility for the well-being of all people and of the planet."[24] The global citizenship outlook from Canada World Youth operates across domestic and international public space, as its volunteers divide their service (usually lasting four to seven months) between a placement in a local community in Canada and a placement in Africa, Asia, the Caribbean, Latin America, or eastern Europe. Typical volunteer placements are with community organizations, but in some cases volunteers work in small businesses or in government offices. Matthew Pearce, the director of Canada World Youth, said that the term "global citizenship" encompasses the sorts of personal qualities that volunteers are seen as strengthening in the course of participating in the program:

> When we talk about global citizens, we're talking about people who have that capacity to confront a local issue and be mindful of its impact and be mindful of other options that may be out there that could be better than ones that might simply be generated by the local group. So it's seeing the other cultures and other circumstances far from oneself as containing a potential solution, or something that would be useful and constructive, and also being mindful of the impact of a decision or a course of action taken locally that inevitably has an impact on others.

This interplay between local and global circumstances is at the heart of Canada World Youth's vision of enabling global citizens. Indeed, volunteers in this program are every bit as engaged in Canadian civic life as in local communities overseas.

A local-global continuum holds true with numerous other service organizations across North America. Global Visionaries, based in Seattle and San Francisco, aims "to educate and empower youth to become active leaders and global citizens who promote social and environmental justice through community service at home and abroad."[25] Similar to Canada World Youth, Global Visionaries offers opportunities for both local and international service. Locally, students are placed in community organizations that assist recent immigrants, while international projects have included immersion trips to Guatemala and Costa Rica, where volunteers have built homes for families and supported the development of schools and health clinics. Similarly, New York City–based NetAid sponsors Global Citizen Corps, which enlists and trains high school students interested educating their peers and involving them in ongoing campaigns to end world poverty.[26]

Another California community organization, the Oakland-based World Bridges, sponsors a Young Ambassadors program in which young adults from low-income families combine local community service during the school year with a summer of international service projects. Participants in recent programs have worked with immigrant youth in Denmark and helped preserve the former site of a concentration camp in Germany as part of a planned memorial for victims of the Holocaust. In an interview, World Bridges co-founder Bettina Mok said that the program puts forward a "very deliberate" understanding of global citizenship, especially since many of the participants situate themselves almost exclusively within their local communities when they start the program: "It would be irresponsible to think of ourselves as separate from the world, so from the very beginning of our training program, our core program, we let people know that we define community as global community, and that every individual who goes through our program will be looking at their role both locally and globally."[27] Mok added that participants in local service projects also share reflections on the international significance of community issues: "For example, when we go to visit a toxic site or an environmental justice issue in San Francisco, we ask the question, Why is this important beyond just this neighborhood or the Bay Area in general, when we consume energy or pollute the air? How does this impact people in other parts of the world?"

Such initiatives from civil society organizations are expanding worldwide. In South Korea, for instance, Global Civic Sharing works to provide educational programs, medical support, agricultural development, and humanitarian aid in China, Mongolia, Vietnam, and Iraq. The organization also has taken stands on such controversial global policy issues as opposing North Korea's development of nuclear weapons and the March 2003 invasion of Iraq led by the United States. Even within service organizations that have not expressly adopted global citizenship into mission statements, participants often come away from their volunteer experiences with a strengthened sense of global citizenship. As teacher Yvette Gillespie reflected after four years of service in Namibia with the group Australian Volunteers International, which sends volunteers to more than forty countries: "You become more aware you are a global citizen. . . . It's also affirmed how much better it is to choose love and understanding over fear and uncertainty. Unless you challenge yourself to see and experience outside your own box, you limit your own potential and appreciation of the quality of life."[28]

Church organizations, especially those concerned with humanitarian relief, also have picked up the mantle of global citizenship in sponsoring outreach and education programs. When World Vision Australia in May 2004 sponsored 40 Hour Famine, in which participants gave up their e-mail and Internet access as well as their meals to raise money for Tanzania, program manager Ben Romeril called the project "a great way for Australians to act as global citizens and do something real to help people living in desperate poverty."[29] World Vision also sponsors a yearly Youth Leadership Convention that encourages young people to think as global citizens, looking especially at issues such as child trafficking and the global spread of HIV and AIDS. In 2003, World Vision began releasing a yearly report entitled *Island Nation or Global Citizen?* that examines the extent to which Australians have contributed to efforts to reduce global poverty. The studies have found that although Australians have increased private donations to humanitarian causes, contributions from the Australian government have declined.[30] And when World Vision released a CD entitled *War and Refugees*, director Tim Costello emphasized that he hoped the video would help students recognize their place as "future global citizens."[31] Similar to World Vision, in terms of encouraging global citizenship in the next generation, the Britain-based relief organization Christian Aid has launched the Global Gang website, which facilitates exchanges of ideas among children around the world and indirectly promotes global understanding.[32]

All in all, the arena of civil society provides fertile ground for understandings and practices of global citizenship to emerge within domestic and international public space. Within voluntary organizations, as illustrated by the examples that follow, global citizenship often serves as shorthand for describing how participants transform their lives through involvement in programs and campaigns sponsored by advocacy groups and community service organizations. What is more, the introduction of global citizenship into a civil society organization's agenda or mission statement tends to be accompanied by considerable soul-searching and, in some instances, prompts controversy.

Earthwatch Institute

Earthwatch Institute sponsors research expeditions worldwide that aim to build bridges between scientists and laypeople who assist in the field. Founded in 1971 in Boston, Massachusetts, on the principle of public participation in scientific research, Earthwatch gradually spread to three other continents. The organization now has affiliates in Australia, Japan, and the United Kingdom, while the international headquarters remain in the United States.[33] Volunteers on Earthwatch trips hold a wide variety of positions—doctors, administrators, teachers, techies, and so forth. Recognition of the powerful role filled by volunteers on its overseas activities prompted the organization's leadership to turn to the idea of global citizenship during a period of strategic change following Earthwatch's twenty-fifth anniversary in 1996.

The silver anniversary motivated Earthwatch to take stock of its successes and its shortcomings, and the most daunting obstacles, in the words of former vice president Andrew Mitchell, were that Earthwatch was "grossly undercapitalized" and that the organization lacked a clear sense of purpose, with each of the four affiliates operating on a different wavelength.[34] To rectify this Babel-like problem—and to begin projecting a coherent image of Earthwatch as a global organization to corporate foundations—the organization's leaders held meetings at each affiliate in an attempt to identify what exactly distinguished Earthwatch from other scientific and environmental organizations. In a sense, this signified the onset of an Earthwatch strategy to assert its reason for existence more clearly and forcefully across transnational public space. In the Tokyo office, a breakthrough seemed to emerge when a board member named Kikujiro Namba, a businessman who had lived in Paris for many years and also belonged to the Club of Rome,[35] proposed that Earthwatch ultimately was about global citizenship and that the volunteers, by virtue of their involvement in Earthwatch projects, were becoming global citizens.[36] The term "global citizenship," then, could be useful in explaining how Earthwatch, by placing everyday people in the front lines of scientific research, helped motivate the general public to care about science and the environment. For Mitchell, who in 1989 cofounded the British affiliate of Earthwatch, this idea of global citizenship was a major revelation. Earthwatch had long recognized the impact of its work on scientific knowledge. Namba seemed to suggest something more: Earthwatch made an even more powerful impact on the lives of its volunteers. This left Mitchell thinking that perhaps the volunteers, and the changes in their lives, were in fact the single most important legacy of Earthwatch: "And so this idea of global citizenship, we thought, was clearly a major result, and we had to start singing that from the rooftops."

Earthwatch's revamped mission statement, therefore, emphasized the importance of partnerships among teams of scientists, educators, and the general public, and put forward three main objectives that, according to Mitchell, were "designed to be the three legs of the Earthwatch stool in the future." The objectives were (1) scientific research, as in collecting data that casts light on environmental issues; (2) experiential learning, as in the participation of volunteers, teachers, and students in research projects; and (3) global citizenship. A manifesto entitled "Earthwatch Institute: The Next Twenty-five Years: Finding Solutions for a Sustainable Future," spelled out in detail exactly what Earthwatch meant by "global citizenship" and how the organization understood the transformative effects of its activities on participants:

> Joining an Earthwatch project uniquely brings participants face-to-face with nature's global web and inspires them to understand which strands they can pull themselves, from home. The experience can result in significant new leadership within their local communities. To date 50,000 Earthwatch volunteers have worked side by side with participants from other cultures, finding common concerns in global issues, experiencing other points of view, and together learning objective lessons that science teaches. On returning, some decide to manage their corporations differently, get involved in local nature centers or museums, work in labs or universities, or provide further support back in the field. In short, they return as working and involved ambassadors for the planet. This attitude change affects others around them and delivers results every bit as dramatic as those produced by our research teams. This program aims to raise public awareness, inspire personal responsibility, and promote a new way of thinking, thus contributing to the emerging culture of global citizenship.

Note that Earthwatch's understanding of global citizenship encompassed concepts of awareness, responsibility, and participation. Moreover, particular attention was given to volunteers' *local* activities upon returning to their home communities following the completion of Earthwatch projects. The "emerging culture of global citizenship," as portrayed by Earthwatch, has nothing to do with global governance, let alone world government. Instead, Earthwatch applied the term "global citizenship" to describe how individuals were able to integrate environmental awareness into their daily lives, beyond the realm of politics. Although volunteering overseas on an Earthwatch project essentially amounts to short-term transnational activism, the more lasting signs of global citizenship, as characterized by Earthwatch and as exemplified by volunteers who exhibit the qualities of motivated and responsible "ambassadors for the planet," emerged within domestic public space. This was true even in cases in which volunteers continued their service within local communities abroad—and within civil society rather than directly in the arenas of politics and government.

The Earthwatch manifesto lists several brief examples of individuals who channeled their energy in new directions as a result of volunteering. An electronics expert who studied bears in Nepal had returned there to set up a solar energy company providing electricity to four hundred remote villages. A group of volunteers from a project in New Guinea funded their native field assistant's university education and also hosted him in the United States. A volunteer on an archaeology project in Swaziland sold his tire dealership when he turned sixty and went to work in the inner city. When Earthwatch referred to "global citizenship," these were the sorts of individuals the organization had in mind. In an internal memorandum written in May 1997, Earthwatch's education director asked the question, How do we measure whether we are promoting Global Citizenship? and suggested that three stages of global citizenship could be identified: (1) awareness of world problems, cultural differences, and various points of view in decision making; (2) investigation of environmental and other global issues beyond the Earthwatch experience; and (3) taking action through additional volunteer and advocacy work.[37]

However, this sort of brainstorming did not last long, as Earthwatch's relaunched mission hit a snag that provides an instructive example of how usage of the term "global citizenship" can backfire within civil society organizations. Although the first two objectives of the revamped mission statement—scientific research and experiential learning—were accepted throughout the organization, Earthwatch ran into two major problems with its use of "global citizenship." The first problem emerged in Mitchell's former home base, the British affiliate. As Mitchell noted with biting irony:

> The British office said, "There's no way we're going to talk about global citizenship. That's a bunch of bullshit—typical Americans—all kinds of fancy words with no meaning. This doesn't sell in Britain." . . . They said, "Look, you can tell us to use 'global citizenship,' but it doesn't help us, because companies here don't understand what it means, and we will not be able to raise funding with that." So they were fiercely resistant to it. The British were much happier with the notion of environmental responsibility rather than global citizenship. Environmental responsibility or stewardship was something more focused, and

the air of responsibility to people is something very British, because we've had all these notions of colonialism and empire where we do feel responsible—we exploit, but we do it with responsibility, as well—and whether we did or we didn't, we think we've done it in a responsible way.

While the immediate manifestation of the problem with the term "global citizenship" was British resistance,[38] Mitchell soon realized that the underlying cause of the problem was that the four Earthwatch affiliates each had a different take on global citizenship. The objectives of scientific research and experiential learning were widely understood and accepted, but the objective of global citizenship revived concern that the four affiliates were operating on different wavelengths. The Babel problem persisted, as the idea of global citizenship failed to translate clearly across the different branches of Earthwatch.

Moreover, many Earthwatch personnel who harbored neither hostility toward nor prejudice against global citizenship began to question whether any substantial difference could be found between the terms "global citizenship" and "experiential learning." Within Earthwatch, at least, both terms seemed to signify volunteer education and public awareness. This apparent overlap vindicated, in a sense, the British critics who alleged that "global citizenship" failed to bring anything unique to the table. Mitchell and his colleagues raised this issue with a panel of scientists in the United States, "and they said, really, the problem is that whether you're a scientist, a teacher, or a CEO, you all get global citizenship out of this experience. In other words, it applies to all of us. And that what we really should be looking for is three different themes but with an overarching umbrella which is called 'global citizenship.'" Following this recommendation, Earthwatch's senior management team returned to the drawing board and presented the three objectives—the three legs of the Earthwatch stool—as research, education, and conservation. The research and education objectives were basically the same as the earlier objectives of scientific research and experiential learning, while the conservation objective essentially replaced the term "global citizenship." As these three objectives became widely established and clearly understood throughout Earthwatch, and the storm clouds of the earlier Babel problem gave way to a clear blue sky, the idea of global citizenship ended up on the sidelines.

Consequently, the term "global citizenship" fell out of favor at Earthwatch. Although Mitchell championed global citizenship within Earthwatch and suggested during an interview that perhaps the term had receded into the margins only temporarily, he also acknowledged that the idea had run into serious problems: "It's a difficult concept for people to grasp. The people in the trenches say, 'Aaah, it's just another title.' It's quite hard to get the whole institution to live and breathe these concepts." Part of the problem was that "global citizenship" never truly resonated below the upper management echelons of Earthwatch. What is more, the diminished profile of global citizenship can be seen in hindsight as a sound strategic decision. In November 2000, Earthwatch secured a US$5 million grant from Ford Motor Company for conservation research—the very objective that replaced "global citizenship." In theory, research, education, and conservation were supposed to be three legs of one Earthwatch stool regarded as global citizenship. But in practice, research, education, and conservation became three distinct stools, and the idea of global citizenship fell between them.

Global Citizens Network

The imposing name might suggest a massive organization with bureaus and staff operating literally across the planet, but Global Citizens Network is a tiny, nonprofit organization that sends teams of volunteers around the world to participate in local community development projects. Based in a one-room office rented from a church in St. Paul, Minnesota, Global Citizens Network promotes volunteer service trips similar to Earthwatch but with a different objective: local community development. Volunteers normally hail from affluent countries, most commonly the United States, and they live with host families and work in collaboration with village residents on projects such as construction work on schools or community centers. The experience usually includes training in language, social institutions, and traditions, and, depending on the location, focuses on themes such as agriculture, environmental protection, and the role of women in economic development. The first teams of volunteers traveled in 1993 to Guatemala, Kenya, and St. Vincent, and Global Citizens Network also has worked with Native American communities in Arizona, New Mexico, and South Dakota. Although Global Citizens Network programs aim to strengthen local public space, volunteers who travel abroad also can be considered short-term transnational activists.

Global Citizens Network was founded in 1992, when several staffers and board members from a similar organization, Global Volunteers, decided to create a separate organization more grassroots in character. As cofounder and former executive director Carol North recalled during an interview, Global Citizens Network's founders spent long hours debating "just the right words" for the name of the new entity. Their collective reasoning, as conveyed by

North, mirrored concepts of awareness, participation, and cross-cultural empathy:

> We obviously wanted to convey the sense of "global." That was a really important aspect of it, because we wanted our volunteers to be experiencing other cultures in many parts of the world. The "citizens" aspect came in from the standpoint that we wanted people to feel as if they were a citizen of the world and that we are interdependent and clearly depend on each other's cultures for our richness—that no-boundaries concept of citizenship, global citizenship. And then "network"—a network of people who share these ideals, who have had similar experiences and promote this kind of cross-cultural understanding.[39]

In this regard, North said that she sees the word "global" as describing both the citizens and the network; the organization is *not* a global network without global citizens. As North explained: "We liked the word 'citizen.' We liked what it meant and what it stood for, and putting it with 'global' is what was meaningful to us."[40]

Global Citizens Network emphasizes the human capabilities of the organization's volunteers as well as residents of the communities being served. The organization undertakes community projects in partnership *with* (rather than for) local residents, who are required to assume leadership roles in all projects and supervise Global Citizens Network volunteers. The organization's approach has come into conflict, at times, with prevailing assumptions in communities overseas. In Belize, for example, local officials expected Global Citizens Network to bring in resources worth thousands of dollars and build facilities on their own, without enlisting local residents. As North recalled: "They were used to kind of the British model where they would come in, sometimes in fatigues and helicopters from above, and basically say, OK, here's all the materials, here's all the money, we'll just build it for you, and then leave, and that wasn't a development model that we were comfortable with." After completing six trips to Belize, Global Citizens Network withdrew from the country because the organization's approach did not match local expectations, and local communities, meanwhile, seemed either unable or unwilling to mobilize enough volunteers to collaborate with Global Citizens Network representatives.

In this regard, Global Citizens Network requires what amounts to a preexisting *local* citizens network in its partner communities. Global Citizens Network also prefers to dispatch volunteers to projects initiated by local communities. In Kenya, for instance, Global Citizens Network works with a community that has its own fund-raiser. In Mexico, Global Citizens Network sends volunteers to a village that asks all residents, or at least all the men, to spend a certain number of hours per week in community service. As North noted:

> That's one of our criteria for deciding whether we can develop a partnership with a site. If they don't already have a sense of volunteerism in the community, then that's a red flag for us, and that was unfortunately a lesson we learned too late in Belize. It's been a challenge on the Navajo reservation for us, because again it's a model that they've seen where the government will come in and just provide handouts and do everything for them. The communities where it has worked are where they don't receive a regular handout, and they realize that if they want to get something done, they've got to do it themselves. And that was really a big part of our organization—we don't want to create dependence.

Global Citizens Network enters a local community with no strings attached. While the organization expects local collaboration on projects, the volunteers do not regard themselves as missionaries or as promoting anything other than mutual respect and understanding. If anything, Global Citizens Network aims to promote local self-sufficiency—and vibrant public space—in the communities it visits. This leads to another challenge for Global Citizens Network, related to the issue of not wanting to create dependence: deciding when a village partnership has lasted long enough and that the time has come to move elsewhere.

The emphasis on local self-sufficiency extends from how Global Citizens Network's founders equated citizenship with responsibility. Indeed, when North was asked what the idea of a citizen meant to her, she replied: "I think 'citizen' sort of conjures up responsibility, and perhaps that may be what we were thinking when we thought of 'citizen,' because we do have a responsibility to learn about the rest of the world and not become isolated." Asked when volunteers on Global Citizens Network projects become global citizens, at least in her thinking, North replied that it varies. In some cases, she finds that individuals become global citizens as a result of participating as volunteers and immersing themselves into local communities. In other cases, North believes that individuals come forward to volunteer precisely because they already are global citizens. In the end, North said that she considers global citizenship "an outlook that recognizes the value of learning about other cultures and the value of not creating dependence but rather developing friendships, developing partnerships with local people." The example of Global Citizens Network, then, provides an illustration of how global citizenship is conceived as voluntarily adopted by transnational civil society actors who build partnerships in local communities around the world.

Global Citizens Association

With its vision of a worldwide institutional framework for public deliberation, in contrast with the other voluntary organizations profiled in this section, the Global Citizens Association brings the world government perspective into this analysis. Based in Vancouver, Canada, the tiny group of world government supporters describes itself as "a nonprofit, non-partisan corresponding world network supporting the notion of planetary citizenship, the brotherhood and sisterhood of humankind, the Nation of Humanity."[41] In the view of association president Duncan Graham, a retired geography teacher, everyone is a citizen of the world simply by virtue of living on planet Earth, but the world lacks the necessary institutions to form a genuine political community. Hence the Global Citizens Association supports a worldwide democratically elected legislature, along with executive and judicial branches of world government. Essentially the Global Citizens Association supports the development of worldwide governing institutions that some international-relations theorists, including David Held and Richard Falk, believe would be necessary for cosmopolitan democracy to emerge in full force.[42]

Although the Global Citizens Association endorses a highly structured model of worldwide public space, its members do not exactly situate themselves within transnational activist networks as these networks have emerged in recent years—especially with regard to the protest movement that has targeted international economic institutions. Graham lives just two hours north of Seattle by car, but he stayed away from Seattle during the November 1999 meeting of the WTO. The agenda of the Global Citizens Association, which not only supports free trade but also endorses worldwide monetary union and a worldwide currency, does not exactly converge with the movement challenging economic globalization. Graham has called for the WTO to implement democratic reforms and develop stronger labor and environmental standards, but Graham showed no interest in joining the cacophony of voices in the globalization protest movement:

> We are critical of the present [global economic] structure, that it's inadequate, but there was a range of protest at Seattle and Prague, and some of them actually are nationalists. They are against the idea of any free trade. They're against the idea of the World Trade Organization having power over the natural resources. So in some ways they're the opposite of what we're saying. We're saying, yes, free trade and a global currency, but it must be fair to all sectors of the [global] community. We cannot have all the employment or jobs going to some third world country with inadequate safety standards just to get cheap goods.[43]

The Global Citizens Association advocates nuclear disarmament and takes heart in what Graham calls "incremental steps" toward world government. During his interview, for instance, Graham talked with enthusiasm about the formation of the International Criminal Court. Although Graham did not at all view global citizenship as a potential contradiction in terms, he said that he considers the United Nations "a misnamed organization" because the constituent members of the General Assembly often find themselves deadlocked according to clashing national interests.

Most interesting about the world government agenda of the Global Citizens Association is how it differs from the agendas of the other voluntary associations discussed in this chapter that focus instead on building up advocacy campaigns and service programs while influencing the lives of participants. The objective of world government appears to be completely off the radar screens of other voluntary organizations using the term "global citizenship." Supporters of world government have invoked notions of global citizenship for a longer period of time than have their counterparts in civil society, but the former now find themselves at the margins of contemporary global citizenship discourse. And yet, similar to respondents from other voluntary organizations, Graham eloquently articulated the concept of awareness in likening global citizenship to a growing "worldwide whisper," the phrase from Alfred Lord Tennyson's epic poem "Locksley Hall," which envisions a transition from international warfare to a world federation. From Graham's vantage point, global citizenship is a "whisper that's growing in our minds . . . we're becoming globally aware without even thinking about it or having to rationalize it." Although Graham supports global citizenship via world government, absent this development, the Global Citizens Association nevertheless exemplifies global citizenship as awareness and participation in its advocacy for such a transformation of public space.

Conclusion

The emphasis on global citizenship as emerging from voluntary actions and initiatives is especially clear when examining how the term has been interpreted within civil society organizations. Even the members of the Global Citizens Association, in the absence of world government, ultimately consider themselves global citizens through their own endeavors rather than through any sort of hypothetical standing in a worldwide polity. Moreover, organizations choosing to bring the term "global citizenship" into their mission statements, programs, and strategies tend to articulate this idea in the contexts of education and service—the transformative effects on participants—rather than through expressly political action. Global citizenship seems to be deployed in civil society mainly by groups that operate outside the political arena but find the term meaningful in expressing how their organizations help shape human minds, build human character, and strengthen local as well as transnational communal ties.

Given such fluid understandings, global citizenship often takes on a distinctly local flavor within civil society, consistent with the multilayered interpretations of citizenship and community held by transnational activists who believe that the term "global citizenship" is a meaningful way to frame their endeavors. This serves to illustrate how the evolution of global civil society is a far richer and more complex phenomenon than the extrapolation of civic engagement into the international arena, since the development of global civil society brings transformations of local civic life around the world, often motivated by forming and strengthening organizational partnerships across borders.

Global citizenship in civil society commonly unfolds within local public space and lends itself to more textured understandings of public space than might be assumed at first glance. The case studies presented in this chapter reinforce the writings of political philosophers and social theorists who have argued that a cosmopolitan public sphere should not be conceived primarily as an overarching, worldwide public space but rather as multiple public spaces that intersect at various levels and transcend distinctions between civil society and government institutions as epicenters of civic activity and public deliberation. The idea of a public sphere, as articulated by Jürgen Habermas and his followers, revolves around how public issues within any community are framed, debated, and interpreted rather than how authority is carried out by governments. This supple view of the public sphere lends elements of flexibility and feasibility to the cosmopolitan tradition.[44]

A key element of a cosmopolitan public sphere, as proposed by James Bohman, is the ability of "world citizens" to influence, on an ongoing basis, the myriad governing institutions across existing public spaces—local, national, and international. Indeed, Bohman echoes the thinking of numerous interview respondents quoted in this book who think about global citizenship as a continuous and dynamic process—or series of processes—rather than as an end state: "The cosmopolitan public sphere is not merely a structure but an ongoing process: the process by which emerging collective actors address the audience of world citizens and, in so doing, change the institutions that organize the public into majorities.[45] The agendas of the transnational activists and civil society organizations studied in this chapter fit into an image of global citizenship as an ongoing process of broadening public influence that unfolds across a variety of public spaces. Moreover, the activists and organizations show how agendas related to global citizenship aim not only to *widen* public space from domestic politics and society into the international arena but also to *deepen* public space, often within local communities, by bringing together individuals and groups from a variety of ethnic, cultural, and religious backgrounds in hopes of fostering mutual dialogue, understanding, and respect. Once again, this renders global citizenship all the more accessible to everyday people. As shown in the next chapter, educational institutions provide some of the most fertile ground for the practices of global citizenship to take root.

CHAPTER FIVE

Global Education and Global Citizenship

Global citizenship has reached a fascinating stage of evolution within the educational arena. Especially during the past decade, academic programs and extracurricular initiatives aiming to produce global citizens or promote global citizenship have proliferated among schools, universities, and allied educational organizations across the English-speaking world. How has the concept of global citizenship been defined, articulated, and pursued by schools, colleges, and universities? How has global citizenship been worked into academic programs as well as extracurricular offerings? What competing interpretations of global citizenship have emerged? What have been some of the biggest challenges in implementing global citizenship initiatives? This chapter brings together examples of schools, colleges, and universities that illustrate how educational strategies relating directly with the term "global citizenship" have taken shape in recent years.

While global citizenship education remains very much an emerging field,[1] educational programs encouraging citizenship within a global community are not a new phenomenon. Since the early 1970s, it appears, notions of global citizenship have been advocated within the educational arena, at least in the United States. As early as 1979, the curriculum guidelines of the National Council for the Social Studies (in the United States) stated that the purpose of social studies education is "to prepare students to be rational, humane, participating citizens in a world that is increasingly interdependent." In 1984, the council's president, Carole Hahn, placed global citizenship on the agenda of the professional organization with an impassioned argument in her annual presidential address that can be viewed as an early sign that interest in global citizenship would increase in the years to come:

> Just as the spread of nationalism since the eighteenth century caused people to rethink the meaning of "citizen," so now it is once again time to rethink that concept in light of our global interdependence. Like it or not, each of us riding on this planet is affected by one another's decisions and actions. We share a common destiny and, to an increasing extent, we share a common culture. Although most of us do not realize it, we are participants in a global society.[2]

The content of global citizenship education in the United States depends on the specific agendas of educators and their respective institutions. In some cases, global citizenship education emphasizes political concerns, such as awareness of international organizations and their roles in promoting human rights and tackling common problems.[3] In other cases, global citizenship education advocates a moral vision of treating the "human family" as interconnected and therefore aims to promote respect of ethnic and cultural diversity both at home and abroad.[4] Political geography is also a common overarching theme, encompassing such issues as world hunger and population growth.[5] Still others approach global citizenship education mainly from an environmental perspective that aims to help youngsters "understand their place in the natural world and their relationships to other living things."[6] Civic organizations also are sources of global citizenship education for adolescents across the English-speaking world. The Boy Scouts of America has a merit badge on "citizenship in the world" that focuses heavily on knowledge of international affairs and geography, while 4-H programs in the United States have encouraged teenagers to think as global citizens. Taken together, these varying educational interpretations of global citizenship straddle domestic and international public space.

The most eloquent and comprehensive case for global citizenship education at the university level has been made by moral philosopher Martha Nussbaum, who has argued forcefully for universities to apply the Socratic vision of the "examined life" by offering liberal arts courses that enable students to "cultivate their humanity" through critical inquiry and reflection into their personal backgrounds in relation to other traditions and perspectives. Nussbaum aspires for university students to situate themselves within concentric circles, not only in terms of overlapping political communities but "groups formed on the basis of ethnic, religious, linguistic, historical, professional, and gender identities." Nussbaum's ideal of "world citizenship" is evocative of both the widening and deepening of public space:

Beyond all these circles is the largest one, that of humanity as a whole. Our task as citizens of the world, and as educators who prepare people to be citizens of the world, will be to "draw the circles somehow toward the center," making all human beings like our fellow city-dwellers. In other words, we need not give up our special affections and identifications, whether national or ethnic or religious; but we should work to make all human beings part of our community of dialogue and concern.[7]

From elementary schools to universities, initiatives related to global citizenship face the challenge of building bridges across civic education and global education—two separate categories of educational initiatives that do not exactly share a history of compatibility.[8] While advocates of citizenship education historically have placed primary emphasis on raising levels of knowledge about domestic politics and national traditions as well as engendering public support and loyalty to nation-states, advocates of global education have placed emphasis primarily on raising awareness of global issues.[9] Because global education initiatives do not necessarily prescribe loyalty to a particular nation-state, advocates of citizenship education—at least as traditionally conceived—sometimes emerge as the most vociferous opponents of global education.[10] Initiatives related to multicultural education—aiming to facilitate mutual understanding and respect across ethnic, religious and cultural traditions—often fit more easily within global citizenship education.

When reviewing how the following schools, colleges, and universities have embarked on global citizenship education, it is important to keep in mind that educational programs for global citizenship work across education for democratic citizenship, education for global understanding, and education for cross-cultural empathy. Despite the dramatic growth of global education programs, the specific term "global citizenship" is used in a relatively small number of schools, colleges, and universities, especially within the United States. The educational initiatives discussed in this chapter do not amount to an exact representative sample of any kind, but together they provide a good representation of how the idea of global citizenship has been applied within the educational arena. The institutions examined here are on the vanguard of global citizenship education and provide early indicators of how education for global citizenship might continue to evolve. They also illustrate how the idea of global citizenship often enters into the minds of young children and adults within the very local and immediate public spaces of the classroom, the schoolyard, and the campus.

Prairie Crossing Charter School

Prairie Crossing Charter School, which opened in September 1999 in the community of Grayslake, Illinois, was founded by a group of local parents within an environmentally conscious residential development (also named Prairie Crossing) who sought to create a close-knit, alternative elementary school with an emphasis on caring for the natural environment. The three cornerstones of the school's charter are environmental stewardship, global citizenship, and parental participation. These objectives were not spelled out in any further detail within the charter, and implementation has been left to the faculty and staff. The school puts its global citizenship mission into practice by teaching children, in the words of the school's first principal, Kathleen Johnston, that a citizen is "a person who takes responsibility for what goes on in the world and is respectful toward all people."[11]

The most consistent way in which the Prairie Crossing curriculum has promoted global citizenship has been through teaching Spanish at every grade level. While a growing number of school districts in northern Illinois are introducing Spanish to middle school students in six-week modules, Prairie Crossing was the first elementary school in northern Illinois to be teaching Spanish to its entire student body—including kindergartners. True to the environmental concern of the school's founders, teachers at Prairie Crossing also have tried to demonstrate how the prairie landscape in their local community is embedded within the North American continent. As Victoria Ranney, a former school board member and codeveloper of the Prairie Crossing community, noted during an interview:

> Whereas many schools would be studying the rainforest, we're studying our own ecology and drawing conclusions that relate to the rainforest. You can understand flooding everywhere if you understand it here. The natural systems, if you understand them in your own backyard—with our prairies, our wetlands—they work similarly all over the globe. If local citizenship means being a steward of this environment, global citizenship is just a larger version of the same."[12]

In this regard, education for global citizenship at Prairie Crossing begins by helping youngsters understand their *local* environment in ways that can be applied to broader environmental concerns.[13]

Especially at the elementary-school level, one of the biggest challenges in education for global citizenship is to make the concept seem immediate and relevant to children who often might not even comprehend what it means to be a citizen of a town, let alone a country or the world. Asked if the school's kindergartners even have a sense of American citizenship, Linda Brazdil, who became the school's director in the summer of 2003, laughed and said: "They're pretty centered on themselves."[14] To help global citizenship become more salient, the school has tried to facilitate direct dialogue across cultures, between the pupils and people from other cultural backgrounds in the local community as well as from overseas. Close to home, the second and third graders met for a day with a Native American man and his young daughter to discuss their customs and traditions—an event that Brazdil said proved very revealing for the schoolchildren: "It's not that they don't think there were Native American children, but they think there *were* Native American children—and so to see a child their age, they were very impressed." In addition, youngsters in several classes at Prairie Crossing have corresponded (by e-mail and also through letters) with children at a school in Pakistan. Brazdil said the experience has been enriching for the children by shaking up their naive assumptions that everyone in the world goes to a school similar to their own. "When they hear things, for example, about how in many cultures girls don't go to school, or how they only go to school very young and then they stop, our girls go—'What? Why would they do that? I don't understand that.' For them to correspond with people in those cultures is so much better than my saying, 'Well, they believe this because. . . .' That has some value but certainly not nearly as much as hearing from people about what their experience is."

Promoting global citizenship through music education led to a tense episode at Prairie Crossing, illustrating how an agenda related to global citizenship can prompt unanticipated resistance. During the school's first holiday season, in late 1999, Kathleen Johnston thought that a useful way to bring home the idea of global citizenship would be to organize a musical performance featuring songs from numerous religious traditions, encompassing Christmas, Hanukkah, Kwanzaa, and Ramadan. The near-censorship in U.S. public schools of all references to religion was one reason Johnston had left her previous job in another school district, and at Prairie Crossing, she wanted to promote open dialogue about religion. Before long, however, Johnston began hearing rumblings of discontent from parents who objected to the idea of the multifaceted holiday program, fearing that "it was going to invade their Christmas celebration or what they perceived to be their Christmas celebration." This left Johnston in a quandary, because although global citizenship is one of the school's cornerstones, parental participation is another. She backed away and dropped the holiday sing-along, but Johnston and Brazdil managed to resurrect it in subsequent years. More recently, Brazdil said, some Protestant Christian parents have asked that their children be pulled from classrooms during lessons and celebrations related to the yearly Latin American festival El Día de los Muertos (Day of the Dead).

Both Johnston and Brazdil acknowledged that measuring the impact of the school's global citizenship initiatives remains a challenge. While some parents at Prairie Crossing have questioned whether or not activities related to global citizenship will help their children perform well on standardized tests[15] and help them gain admission to elite universities, other parents have argued that the school should launch more global citizenship activities.[16] Standardized-test scores in Spanish and geography serve as possible objective indicators of global citizenship, Johnston said, but the school is also trying to shape how young people view the world in ways that are not necessarily easy to measure: "What you really are trying to instill is a change in attitude, a change in values, feeling the value of global citizenship. That's much more difficult to measure, and you really can only do it, I think, over a period of time and very carefully, a lot by listening to what children say and by watching and reading what it is that they write." For example, during a lesson on the Olympics in September 2000, Johnston observed a group of second and third graders reflecting on the logic of the interlocking circles on the Olympic flag, and the students in a matter of seconds concluded, on their own, that the interlocking circles were to encourage friendship: "Nobody set them up; nobody gave them any prior knowledge of that. They got that from knowing that it was a big world event that brought a lot of athletes together, and then what interlocking circles might represent, and that's people getting along together. So that shows a change in attitude." Such shifts in attitude can be viewed as the earliest stages in a progression in which children begin to take on personal qualities related to global citizenship as awareness and cross-cultural empathy.

Eugene International High School, Eugene, Oregon

Perhaps the single most concerted effort to promote global education in secondary schools is the worldwide network of International Baccalaureate schools. Founded in Geneva in 1968, the International Baccalaureate Organization (IBO) created a secondary-school diploma based on a common, rigorous preuniversity curriculum and a standardized examination. Originally serving mainly the children of diplomats, foreign-service workers, and other internationally mobile families, the system has grown from a small cadre of founding secondary schools—located in Switzerland, Great Britain, Lebanon, Denmark, and Iran—to the current network of more than 1,700 schools in 122 countries.[17] The International Baccalaureate Organization has also created a curriculum used at hundreds of primary schools and middle schools around the world. Although the organization does not refer specifically to global citizenship in its mission statement, the diploma program from the outset has "sought to provide students with a truly international education—an education that encouraged an understanding and appreciation of other cultures, languages and points of view."[18]

One instructive case study within this model can be found in the development of Eugene International High School in Eugene, Oregon, which was founded in 1984 as an alternative secondary school and has set forth the mission of promoting global citizenship. In its humanities and social studies courses, Eugene International emphasizes an interdisciplinary approach in teaching world history and culture. Courses focus on literature from non-Western sources, comparative world values, comparative politics and economics, art, geography, and global public health issues. Although Eugene International is a separate public high school, the school does not occupy its own building but rather occupies wings of the city's four public high schools,[19] serving students who choose to attend the school and prepare for the International Baccalaureate exam. Its students take math, science, and language courses within the mainstream high schools (considered "host schools" by Eugene International) and take humanities and social sciences courses with Eugene International faculty. Enrollment is open to any student enrolled in the city's public schools, though only a minority of those who enroll choose to take the IB exam and pursue the IB qualification.[20]

The current Eugene International headmaster, Marilyn Curtis, said the school tries to instill in its students a capacity for lifelong learning and a willingness to become aware of "the complexity and diversity of the world." Eugene International promotes these qualities in its students not only through the interdisciplinary, globally oriented, and academically ambitious course content—with courses such as Comparative Values and Belief Systems and Theory of Knowledge—but also through international immersion experiences during the summer months. During the summer of 2004, for instance, students and teachers from Eugene International traveled together on study tours of India, Thailand, and Greece.

The term "global citizenship" entered the picture at Eugene International during the late 1980s, as the faculty struggled to resolve disagreement over exactly what should be included in a truly global education and what topics should be emphasized in the curriculum. The debate placed history and social studies teachers in tension with teachers who wanted a greater emphasis on literature, art, and music from around the world. "When I came here, for a while, I couldn't understand what the argument was," recalled Caron Cooper, a former head teacher at the school. "Why would it be one or the other?"[21] The social studies faction prevailed—approximately two-thirds of the school's course offerings fall within history, politics, economics, and geography—and the debate over the direction of the school produced the first mission statement, which was released in 1989 and stated: "Our mission at Eugene International High School is to challenge ourselves to value diversity, to recognize ambiguity, and to become empowered global citizens." This initial mission statement depicted global citizenship as a desired goal and not necessarily as something ever attained in full. Cooper said this statement served as a modest attempt to find some basic common ground among the faculty. Indeed, the emphasis on ambiguity reflected, in part, the tentative and often divisive period that the school underwent in its formative stages.

During the 1990s, Eugene International gained in popularity, its graduates went on to prosper in top universities, and teachers came and went. In 2000 the faculty revisited its mission and redefined its approach to global citizenship. The mission statement now reads: "As global citizens at Eugene International High School, we aspire to value diversity, ambiguity, and discovery and to act with responsibility, integrity, and compassion."[22] The new mission statement takes a much more activist approach: Global citizenship is presented as a background condition, and the ideals that follow are framed as personal qualities reflective of good global citizens. Rather than global citizenship being the ultimate goal, global citizenship is presented as a starting point from which to pursue other values.[23] The goals relating to embracing diversity and ambiguity remained in the second mission statement, and Cooper said that the emphasis on ambiguity remains especially important to the school's identity and approach: "We try to help students understand that there are multiple perspectives, that there are multiple theories, and that they weigh those thoughtfully—that we don't provide answers; we provide information, and we invite them to do research and explore and come to conclusions where discourse is really valued."

Britain's Curriculum Controversy

When the New Labour government in the United Kingdom began to revise the national school curriculum after Tony Blair became prime minister in 1997, the term "global citizenship" moved to the forefront of domestic public debate. The defining moment came in March 1998, when Michael Barber, head of the Standards Unit at the Department for Education and Employment (DfEE), spoke at a conference of secondary-school principals and called for schools to teach moral values under the rubric of citizenship education. Barber's speech, though not an official government statement, attracted considerable attention given his profile within the government and his claim that citizenship education could fill a moral vacuum left by what he considered the erosion of Christianity as a basis for moral education. As Barber noted in the speech, referring to global citizenship in a way that strongly signifies moral responsibility:

> Progressively over the last 200 years . . . the belief systems which sustained Western societies have crumbled away. Christianity, which established ethical codes for most of the last 2000 years, has become a minority interest, still hugely influential historically and culturally, but no longer able to claim unquestioning obedience. . . . There is a growing realisation that an amoral society of unfettered individuals competing in global markets on mobile telephones is inconsistent with ensuring a planet fit for future generations. Whatever else the school system in a country like ours achieves, the bottom line surely should be that it needs to strive to create a generation which is not only well-educated, in an academic sense, but also has a highly-developed sense of ethics and of global, as well as national, citizenship.[24]

True to the contested history of citizenship education in the United Kingdom,[25] Barber's remarks ignited controversy on three fronts. Some people worried that teaching global citizenship would undercut religious education. Others worried that promoting global citizenship would undermine loyalty to the United Kingdom. Across the board, critics worried that citizenship education would come at the expense of subjects such as history, geography, and English. The comments of one vocal critic, Nick Seaton of the Campaign for Real Education, serve to illustrate how citizenship education in Great Britain is a lightning rod for ideological conflict. In an interview, Seaton explained how he views global citizenship as a code word for pro-European Union and socialist political sentiments that he does not share: "It's one of these terms that the progressive left has claimed because it's appealing, and because it's difficult to argue against, but their intentions are to use it for something completely different from its normal meaning. . . . There's a shift away from any sort of national values or patriotism."[26]

Seaton's criticism of Barber's speech represented just one set of objections.[27] Even among those in favor of instilling in youngsters a sense of universal moral obligation, objections surfaced regarding the manner in which Barber seemed to frame global citizenship. In an interview for this study, Geoff Teece, director of the Westhill Religious Education Centre based at the University of Birmingham, said he still remembers "vividly" the moment he spotted an account of Barber's speech published in the *Guardian*. The newspaper headline declared: "Schools Adviser Urges Moral Code to Replace God."[28] Upon reading the details of the speech, Teece concluded that Barber had gone too far in marginalizing the Christian tradition in his plan for revising the curriculum:

> Reading his language was interesting because he used terms like "Christianity now is a minority interest," and you'd want to almost italicize the word "interest" . . . that because logical positivism has proved [that Christianity is] potentially nonsense, that it can't be proved, it's not proper knowledge; therefore it's a kind of hobby for people. It's something people do on Sundays or in their spare time and therefore has very little to contribute to public life in a modern society.

Teece immediately wrote a letter to the *Guardian* that was published in the next day's edition under the headline "All Hell Breaks Loose over God's (or god's) Role in the Curriculum." The letter stated:

> So Prof Barber believes pupils should learn the ethics of "global citizenship" to replace crumbling religious values? One wonders which religious values he is thinking of. Perhaps "You must love your neighbour as yourself," (Christian Gospels), "Show kindness to the neighbour who is related as well as the neighbour who is a stranger," (Qur'an Surah 4), "There can be no worship without performing good deeds," (Guru Granth Sahib 4). Such values are expressed in a variety of concepts—such as charity in Christianity, zakat (almsgiving) in Islam, tzedakah (justice) in Judaism and sewa (service for others) in Sikhism.[29]

Teece's letter argued that global citizenship, if cast as an ethical framework in education, need not be divorced from world religions but instead could be reconciled with religious teachings and even derive from them.[30] Indeed, many of the self-described global citizens whose thoughts and experiences were shared in the previous chapters of this book were inspired in part by their religious beliefs.

In an interview, Barber said that he did not intend for his speech to convey the impression that global citizenship education ought to crowd out religious education or any other subject. Furthermore, he agreed with Teece's point in the letter to the *Guardian*:

> There's no necessary conflict between global citizenship and religious values. On the contrary, I'd say some elements of some religions are the best examples of global citizenship I've come across. My argument in the speech was fifty years ago, you could, certainly in this country, be sure that nearly every child got the same set of religious values in the home, the school, and the church, and would be likely to attend church. That was no longer true. So you needed to find some other way to define the ethical basis, and that would be consis-

tent with religion, but you couldn't rely on religion to be providing it for every-body.[31]

The revised national curriculum, which took effect in September 2000, continues to require religious education, as well as a "predominantly Christian basis" to religious instruction within a syllabus agreed on by the local community, in order to account for specific religious traditions within the community. Therefore, urban communities with greater religious diversity often choose to develop a curriculum that explores a far wider range of religious traditions than communities in the countryside that are overwhelmingly Christian. Moreover, Barber added that news coverage of his twelve-page speech neglected one of his key points: that an essential component of citizenship education is helping students become "highly competent individuals who can think for themselves." In this regard, Barber's "global citizenship" agenda encompassed the concept of achievement—a concept that sparks little if any ideological discord—as well as the concepts of responsibility and cross-cultural empathy. Nevertheless, the episode served to illustrate how bringing the term "global citizenship" into an educational strategy can ignite conflict on divisive issues commonly simmering beneath the surface of domestic politics in many nation-states.[32]

Shared Futures: Beloit College and Rochester Institute of Technology

Perhaps the most concerted effort to date in the United States to put into practice education for global citizenship at the university level has been a program sponsored recently by the American Association of Colleges and Universities (AAC&U). Shared Futures: Liberal Education and Global Citizenship supported initiatives at eleven universities to give the specific idea of global citizenship a higher profile in university education. During the three years of the program, from 2001 to 2004, representatives from participating universities met annually and shared ideas at the AAC&U headquarters in Washington, D.C. Although the eleven selected institutions otherwise worked independently, the Shared Futures project represented the first instance in which a small collective of colleges and universities began to develop a network, albeit for a limited period of time, based on the institutions' interests in developing education for global citizenship.

The Shared Futures project grew out of several AAC&U initiatives dating back to the early 1990s aimed at promoting civic engagement and multicultural awareness on university campuses and beyond. Throughout this period, the organization expanded its global emphasis beyond more established approaches such as language learning and international exchange programs (especially with Japan) into an approach that would reflect the idea of the planet as a single unit. As Caryn McTighe Musil, the Shared Futures project director, recalled during an interview for this study:

> Global citizenship became, for us, a natural choice. It began to redefine for us the way in which "international" is sometimes interpreted—that is, there is the United States and it is the norm against which all other people or others are judged, and we are separate and distinct and each of us are autonomous nations. What we now know, because of all the "global" scholarship, is the way in which processes that link us, through flows of people, through economics, through culture, through language, through information, through military, through corporations—that that [approach centered on national autonomy] is a fiction—that we are already deeply connected in our very everyday processes with other countries. So we wanted to carry that idea forward.[33]

Beloit College and the Rochester Institute of Technology (RIT) provide an interesting contrast in how campus strategies related to global citizenship emerged in very different ways at colleges and universities participating in the project. While Beloit has championed international education for forty years and the AAC&U grant reinforced initiatives already supported by the central administration of the college, at RIT a group of junior faculty members worked to heighten the profile of international education and transform the nature of its liberal arts college within the larger university.

Since the early 1960s, Beloit has not only promoted study abroad among its 1,200 students; it also has brought scores of international students to its Wisconsin campus each year on exchange programs. By the late 1990s, approximately 45 percent of Beloit undergraduates were living abroad for a semester or more, and David Burrows, the dean of the college, said concern began to grow on campus that the 55 percent of the Beloit students not studying overseas were missing out on an international education. The AAC&U grant was used to develop activities and simulations for courses in several departments—especially political science, women's studies, religious studies, and chemistry. As Burrows noted: "What happened was not so much that we invented new ways of getting students involved as much as the consciousness of the faculty teaching courses in those areas was raised with respect to stressing the [civic] engagement piece."

The curriculum work was situated within a wider effort at Beloit to increase attention to international and global education on campus. In 2000, with the help of a hefty donation from an alumnus of the college, Beloit created a visiting chair in international studies, in which a diplomat, activist, or journalist—normally from outside the United States—takes up a two-week residency at Beloit to visit classes, hold seminar discussions with students and faculty, and give a keynote lecture. Beloit pays the visiting chair a stipend of $25,000 (plus travel and accommodation expenses), and Burrows said the college has found that the two-week residency brings in much more "bang for the buck" than paying distinguished speakers honoraria of several thousand dollars for single lectures that often turn out to be recycled talks. Burrows also said that the college initially wanted to bring in a visiting chair for one full semester at a time, but that such a long appointment would have prevented the college from bringing in presently active diplomats.[34]

At Beloit, the faculty use the term "world citizenship" rather than the term "global citizenship" to frame international education programs. Burrows said that faculty members were sharply divided over whether to use "international citizenship" or "global citizenship," with several political science professors arguing especially that "global" refers to processes that evoke planetary interdependence and interconnectedness while "international" refers to relationships among nation-states. "We've had hassles over what to call our international education office—which is still called the international education office, by the way," Burrows added, "so "world citizenship" is essentially my attempt at a compromise term."[35]

Burrows said that the faculty continues to discuss "in fits and starts" exactly what the college means by "world citizenship" and how this concept should figure into the university's academic offerings as well as campus life more generally. In a memo that Burrows circulated on campus in March 2004, Burrows proposed several possible qualities of world citizens, including "the ability to understand global forces that affect our lives . . . the ability to understand the diversity of human experience[36] . . . the ability to function effectively in a culture other than one's own . . . the development of a global identity . . . multidisciplinary perspective taking . . . the motivation for action to address global issues ethically and effectively." Burrows further emphasized in the memo that each academic discipline "has something important to contribute to the development of world citizenship" and argued that a "world-citizenship approach" should not warrant a restructuring of the college's graduation requirements but rather should amount to "integrating ideas about citizenship into our teaching." The memo continued: "I believe that world citizenship should be *infused* throughout the curriculum. We do not want to have courses dedicated to citizenship and designated with such terms as 'WC 101, Introduction to World Citizenship.' Rather, we should attempt to intentionally include connections to the theme of citizenship wherever appropriate."[37] During an interview, Burrows said that he would not argue that world citizenship courses per se are counterproductive, but that the culture at Beloit—which does not have a core curriculum and affords students a great deal of freedom in selecting courses—is not receptive to creating a required course dedicated to world citizenship. Although some members of the Beloit faculty have advocated a major in global studies, Burrows said that he does not expect it will emerge for some time.

While Beloit College represents an institution long dedicated to international education that is transitioning into education for global citizenship, Rochester Institute of Technology provides an example of an institution in a much earlier stage of developing a global education strategy. For RIT, the Shared Futures grant from the AAC&U was an opportunity to introduce a seminar on globalization and human rights into the liberal arts curriculum and increase the global awareness of a relatively parochial student body. Throughout the twentieth century, RIT functioned very much as a locally oriented feeder school for Rochester-based corporations such as Bausch & Lomb, Eastman Kodak, IBM, and Xerox. In recent years, these companies have cut tens of thousands of jobs in Rochester as manufacturing operations increasingly have been moved outside the United States.

With the leadership of Professor Robert D. Manning, a specialist in Latin American studies and international finance, the College of Liberal Arts at RIT created a senior-level course entitled Globalization, Human Rights and Citizenship that was offered alongside an ongoing lecture series on globalization featuring scholars including political philosopher Benjamin Barber and sociologist Saskia Sassen. Manning also assembled a group of six junior faculty members from several departments—anthropology, sociology, modern literature, philosophy, and political science—who created a series of courses focused on global issues in relation to their respective disciplines. The project's initial goal was for each participating faculty member to join forces with another colleague on the faculty and create an ever-expanding web of professors exchanging ideas and information on globally oriented courses. The expansion of the program is uncertain, however, partly because the academic administration within RIT's liberal arts college has not issued a sustained mandate for global citizenship education. As Manning noted:

> This was really a hard project to do, especially given the fact that the liberal arts college was not really well prepared to undertake such a broad, sweeping attempt to challenge the focus of the university and also to achieve this important sense of global citizenship as a theme that should be running throughout the college and influencing other people's courses. . . . One of the strengths

and weaknesses of the project was bringing in junior faculty. When the dean said this was important for their tenure process, then of course they put a lot of resources in it. And when the dean backed off and went to other issues, then their enthusiasm waned accordingly.[38]

Nevertheless, the courses created during the initiative have been incorporated into RIT's liberal arts offerings, and Manning said that the course on globalization, human rights, and citizenship seems to have reoriented the assumptions of many students with respect to the global economy. For the final project in the course, Manning required students to produce a "commodity chain" tracing the global roots of products such as computer chips, sneakers, duplicating paper, and McDonald's Happy Meals. The project went a long way in helping students comprehend some of the social costs of globalization that are often hidden to affluent Western consumers. "A lot of students did chocolate and were shocked to find out that what gives pleasure and joy in the United States is based on slave labor of young children in Africa. It was those kinds of topics that really enabled me to have the students connect to their disciplines." Similar to Beloit, a global studies minor is under consideration at RIT, though Manning does not expect this to emerge in the near future.

Chapman University

When the term "global citizenship" entered into the mission statement of Chapman University around 1994, the school in Orange, California, became perhaps the very first university in the United States to give global citizenship this sort of high profile. The statement reads: "The mission of Chapman University is to provide personalized education of distinction that leads to inquiring, ethical, and productive lives as global citizens."[39] And yet, even though the university's core seminar for first-year students for several years was entitled The Global Citizen, the faculty has never reached consensus on what it means to be a global citizen. Instead, a plurality of understandings can be found on campus. Don Will, a professor of political science and peace studies who coordinated the global citizenship seminar, approaches global citizenship as a metaphor encouraging political engagement and social responsibility.[40] In the anthropology department, professor Paul Apodaca looks skeptically at global citizenship as a potentially insidious form of Western ethnocentrism.[41] Economics faculty members, in contrast, think of the term primarily as a way of furthering free trade and international business in the world economy. Indeed, the school has awarded its Global Citizen Medal to some of the world's most notable conservatives, such as former U.S. presidents George H. W. Bush (2000) and Gerald Ford (2001), British prime minister Margaret Thatcher (2002) and former Spanish president José María Aznar (2004).

The integration of global citizenship into Chapman's offerings for first-year students emerged gradually. Previously, Will had taught an interdisciplinary seminar called War, Peace and Justice that emphasized world history, beginning with the Peloponnesian War. Around 1994, members of the faculty decided that the seminar should shift into contemporary issues and the natural sciences, especially topics such as the emerging global climate crisis:

> So for those kinds of reasons, we moved toward it, and somebody said, "Well, why don't we call it The Global Citizen? After all, it's in the mission statement." So what's happened now is a little bit of evolution in the thinking of a lot of the faculty that in some way, this is a cornerstone course in starting the general education core and fulfilling the mission statement. . . . I was not one of them who was that keen on changing it, partly because of the ambiguity of this term. We've never quite got this quite to the point of perfection after all these years.[42]

Content for the seminar varied from year to year, and Will said that some approaches provoked controversy. One year, Will and Apodaca collaborated on a module called Encounters that looked critically at the early settlement of North America and colonization around the world. The module examined Columbus's diaries, President Andrew Jackson's treatment of the Native Americans—particularly the forced relocation of the Cherokee Nation—and then moved on to a comparative unit on the settlement of South Africa and a study of human rights violations arising from the "encounters" of colonization. The approach turned out to be polarizing and sparked an intense backlash from many white male students.

> We tried not to make it too strident, but they complained, "Well, this is just making America look bad." But we tried to present it as a factual look at history. Let's not pretend that Columbus is all about the parade on Columbus Day. Read his diaries—this is a man with an avarice for gold . . . and you get the same kind of patronization from Andrew Jackson over the Cherokee. So student reaction was much more negative over that. Naturally, black students and Latino students didn't complain at all.

The faculty later dropped the Encounters section from the seminar, not so much because of the controversy that it caused but because of a decision to move the seminar further away from history and toward current affairs.

One objection that Will did *not* hear frequently from students was the view—often raised by political scientists skeptical of global citizenship—that citizenship is properly understood strictly within the boundaries of the nation-state. Instead, Will's students more commonly challenged the idea that global economic interdependence places moral responsibilities on their shoulders. When the course included an inquiry into sweatshop allegations against footwear and apparel companies, students often argued that despite their role as consumers, they were not personally responsible for the labor practices of Nike or Reebok in Southeast Asia. The perspective the seminar conveys on such issues depends on the outlook of whichever faculty member happens to be moderating the discussion:

> At our school, anyway, many of the economists have sort of a Chicago-school orientation, so they take the same attitude—there's a contract worked out between Nike and the Vietnamese government . . . and you don't have to buy Nike if you don't want to buy Nike. So you can opt out of being part of that, if it troubles you, and if it doesn't trouble you, you can be part of it. So they would say that there really isn't a moral obligation to control what Nike does over there.

As a result, although student attitudes influenced responses to the seminar, the perspectives presented by faculty members were remarkably divergent, as well.

Chapman's global citizenship agenda also has inspired efforts to promote mutual dialogue and respect across religious traditions on campus. Chapman was founded in 1861 by members of the Disciples of Christ, a tiny denomination that has long fostered ecumenical ties and social inclusion. Ever since opening, Chapman has admitted women as well as people from all racial backgrounds and religious traditions. However, the different religious groups on campus had been scattered. In an effort to bring these faith communities closer together, in 2004 the university opened the Wallace All Faiths Chapel as a home for religious services held by all denominations represented at the university. Located in the center of the campus, the new chapel displays no permanent symbolism, though it is designed to display, on a temporary basis, whatever symbols are appropriate for particular services.

Even before the chapel was ready to open, the dean of the chapel, Ronald Farmer, put into practice its ecumenical mission by coordinating interfaith services and leading discussions on campus about controversial issues, such as abortion: "We start with this metaphor," he said, "that our desire is to generate light, not heat." A professor of religious studies, Farmer added that from his vantage point, the virtue of toleration is not sufficient for global citizenship; in his mind, what matters is mutual respect across faith traditions and belief systems: "I know the word 'tolerance' has nice Latin etymological roots and all, but the way it's used today, it still sort of smacks of a hierarchy—a tolerator and a toleratee. So our goal is not to help people tolerate one another, because I personally don't want to be tolerated, I want to be appreciated."[43] The All Faiths Chapel, then, helps fulfill Chapman University's goal of educating "global citizens" who appreciate the interconnectedness of human life amid religious and cultural diversity.

Soka University of America

A similarly local approach to global citizenship and the enriching of public space can be found at a new, small, transnationally affiliated university that is also in Southern California. Soka University of America opened in September 2001 with the stated mission "to foster a steady stream of global citizens committed to living a contributive life."[44] Most of the five hundred students on campus are members of the university's parent organization, Soka Gakkai International (SGI), a lay Buddhist sect based in Japan.[45] The charter of SGI rests on three principles: "world citizenship, the spirit of tolerance and respect for human rights," and the organization's president, Daisaku Ikeda, frequently has referred to the idea of global citizenship in his writings and public lectures. In a speech given in June 1996 at Columbia University, Ikeda explained his own definition of the term, which corresponds with concepts of awareness, responsibility, and cross-cultural empathy:

> Certainly, global citizenship is not determined merely by the number of languages one speaks, or the number of countries to which one has traveled. I have many friends who could be considered quite ordinary citizens, but who possess an inner nobility; who have never traveled beyond their native place, yet who are genuinely concerned for the peace and prosperity of the world. I think I can state with confidence that the following are essential elements of global citizenship:
>
> - The wisdom to perceive the interconnectedness of all life and living.
> - The courage not to fear or deny difference; but to respect and strive to understand people of different cultures, and to grow from encounters with them.
> - The compassion to maintain an imaginative empathy that reaches beyond one's immediate surroundings and extends to those suffering in distant places.[46]

Note that this interpretation classifies individuals with these desired personal qualities as global citizens within local public space. In Ikeda's view, as stated in his speech, "to be meaningful, education for global citizenship should be undertaken as an integral part of daily life in our local communities."[47]

Asked to elaborate on the university's aim to foster global citizens, Eric Hauber, the dean of student recruitment, outlined two key imperatives: first, that students learn to value human diversity in all its forms—ethnic, cultural, spiritual, and so forth—and second, that students develop a broad perspective on international affairs:

> To be a global citizen, in our mind, a student needs to be able to not only not fear diversity, they need to be able to value it and to be able to see its ability to bring multiple views to the table and to see diversity as actually a highly desirable commodity if you are in a team environment. . . . So that hopefully when a student graduates, when they look at a world issue, they can look at it from a global perspective, not from a national self-interest perspective.

Similar to some of the other educational institutions profiled in this chapter, Soka University of America does not offer courses specifically related to global citizenship. Instead, a holistic approach prevails on the Aliso Viejo campus, and the mandatory core humanities courses engage philosophy, literature, and religious traditions from around the world. For instance, all first-year students are required to take a course called Pacific Basin, in which they explore how the Pacific Ocean—and the peoples and cultures living on both sides of the ocean—are connected in terms of history and migration, and how these dynamics have been viewed from the perspective of Asia and the Pacific islands. Students also are required to study two years of a language other than English and then travel to a country where the language is spoken. The study abroad experience, in the view of Michael Hays, the dean of faculty, is crucial to preventing students from being "more or less constrained within what are essentially Western paradigms of psychological or social thought."

All students at Soka University of America—even those who hail from outside the United States (nearly 60 percent of the student body)[48]—are required to go to a country in which they have never lived.[49] After considerable debate within the faculty about whether or not it would be fair to require international students and nonnative speakers of English to learn a third language, the faculty decided that this would be preferable to having a divided student body in which one group of students would study abroad in their junior year while the other group would remain on the Mediterranean-style campus for their entire university education. The intent of the interdisciplinary courses as well as the study abroad program is to place students repeatedly in situations in which they will feel uncomfortable—and indeed, this sense of discomfort seemed to emerge in Hays's thinking as an ad hoc indicator of whether or not students will grow into global citizens:

> The crucial thing, for me, is to be alienated—from self, from suppositions, and to have to struggle with that. For those students who came here and said, "We've already learned English. Why should we do another language?" I send them out, and not one of them has come back to complain. . . . One of the Japanese women who went to Spain e-mailed me and said, "I now understand why we need a United Nations of education," and she said, "I'm going to create one."

Dialogue across cultures on campus—in the classroom as well as less formal settings—often leads, in Hays's words, to "productive misunderstandings and objections, and that's good."[50] Hays encapsulated the university's approach to global citizenship thus: "Part of becoming a global citizen here, as we are dealing with it, is realizing that to understand and engage with other people, you must confront your own mental and discursive political and ideological structures. You must be aware of them. You must be aware that there will be conflict—that's crucial."

Global citizenship at Soka University of America also fits into the architecture and layout of the resortlike campus, which was contrived to suggest an egalitarian ethos and also promote collaboration and interaction among faculty and students. For instance, all the faculty and administrative offices are the same size, and the offices of the most senior administrators—such as the university president and the vice president for financial affairs—are located in the same buildings as classrooms. The campus also has no designated parking spaces. "These things are not directly connected with the question of global citizenship," Hays said, "but they are, I think, in their upshot." At Soka University of America, global citizenship involves creating a certain kind of atmosphere for inquiry and engagement within a very close-knit local community.

Tufts University: Institute for Global Leadership

Among some colleges and universities, education for global citizenship carries forth primarily within centers and institutes not formally affiliated with any particular academic department.[51] Especially active in this regard is the Institute for Global Leadership at Tufts University with its core program EPIIC— Education for Public Inquiry and International Citizenship, which is preoccupied especially with disentangling the most complicated issues in international relations. EPIIC was born in 1985 with a symposium on international terrorism and political violence following the hijacking of Trans World Airlines Flight 847. Under the leadership of founder and director Sherman Teichman, the symposium expanded into a larger, sustained program. Each year, EPIIC offers a yearlong interdisciplinary colloquium—an unusually rigorous undergraduate seminar focused on a global political theme. At the start of the academic year, participating students travel to the wilderness of northern New England to participate in an Outward Bound experience; it is a weekend that builds a sense of community among the new students and begins to motivate them to develop leadership and teamwork skills. The colloquium, in turn, amounts to an intellectual equivalent of an Outward Bound excursion.

Students who enroll face the challenges of completing an intense reading load and conversing with prominent guest lecturers, and they also serve on committees that plan and organize the annual public symposium on the year's chosen theme—an event that usually includes numerous panel discussions compressed into four or five days.[52] Typically the panelists are authors of the books studied in the seminar as well as leading diplomats, journalists, experts from public policy think tanks, and activists from nongovernmental organizations. The theme for 2006–2007 was "Global Crises: Governance and Intervention," while past programs have included themes such as "The Politics of Fear" (2006), "Oil and Water" (2005), and "Dilemmas of Empire and Nationbuilding" (2004). Unlike many panel discussions that run early in the evening and end after ninety minutes, the forums at EPIIC often last five or six hours and run well past midnight. Although the focus of the colloquium compares in academic rigor to a graduate seminar, EPIIC operates independently of any academic department at Tufts. Teichman has taught the EPIIC colloquium since its inception, but he and Heather Barry, EPIIC's associate director, are administrators, not faculty members. Thus during its twenty-year history, EPIIC has struggled repeatedly on campus for recognition and resources.[53]

In addition to providing students with what often amounts to the single most challenging intellectual experience of their university educations, EPIIC and its sister programs serve as a gateway for students to travel literally all over the world to participate in service opportunities, academic exchange programs,[54] advocacy work, and cross-cultural immersion. Each year, EPIIC selects one or more distinguished international figures to receive the Jean Mayer[55] Global Citizenship Award.[56] Asked why EPIIC chose "global citizenship" rather than another term, Sherman Teichman replied:

> For me, what citizenship means is an active role. What's happened in the U.S., at least, is we have become passive taxpayers, and we're not citizens. Citizenship

to me is a high calling of understanding the world in terms of either a public intellectual role, or—what I have asked our students to do in our program—is regardless of whether they're going into the military or the world of NGOs or into business, is to be a leader with integrity and accountability.[57]

Throughout two decades of programming, the themes and issues chosen for study by EPIIC consistently examine global problems—such as refugees and internally displaced persons; the future of democracy; the environmental dimensions of international security; global crime and corruption—that transcend international boundaries and defy conventional understandings of the sovereignty of nation-states. As Teichman put it: "For us, the idea of the sovereignty of the individual and the sovereignty of the nation are in conflict . . . and so we're interested in always challenging the idea of what citizenship means."

Conclusion

What it means, then, to be globally educated and to be a global citizen varies considerably depending on the perspective of the educational institution as well as the grade level in which particular global citizenship initiatives take shape. While global citizenship programs in elementary schools often focus especially on language learning and geography and begin to inspire children to think about global interdependence and cross-cultural empathy, programs in secondary schools typically emphasize world history and literature and often take the additional step of impressing on students the challenges they will face as professionals in the world economy. Colleges and universities, meanwhile, play a crucial role in global citizenship education. Not only do university initiatives offer students the opportunity to gain much more sophisticated understandings of policy dilemmas, urgent global problems, and the political, economic, and cultural dynamics that contribute to global interdependence in all its forms, but overseas immersion programs also help students to build bridges between thought and action and to begin to situate themselves, in tangible and meaningful ways, as members of an interdependent global community. Moreover, the diverse residential settings of colleges and universities provide students with unparalleled opportunities for sustained dialogue and deliberation.

The educational initiatives profiled in this chapter demonstrate that teaching skills and teaching values are far from mutually exclusive endeavors. Education for global citizenship works across objectives related to academic achievement, moral responsibility, and cross-cultural empathy. Similar to the ways in which global citizenship is now promoted by many international service and advocacy organizations, education for global citizenship also commonly emphasizes the development of competent, responsible, engaged, and culturally astute human beings rather than the development of global governing institutions. Moreover, true to understandings of global citizenship as an "attitude of mind"[58] rather than as any sort of formal membership or legal status, the term "global citizenship" in the educational arena tends to signify goals for students to attain through the gradual cultivation of personal qualities such as courage, empathy, and wisdom, as suggested by Daisaku Ikeda of Soka University of America.

Global citizenship within educational institutions often generates controversy. Initiatives that aim to deepen public space by including a religious dimension are prone to contention, especially within secular institutions that aim to promote an ecumenical spirit. When Kathleen Johnston attempted to organize a multicultural event to celebrate the holiday season at Prairie Crossing Charter School, she basically articulated the pluralistic ideal put forward across the Atlantic by Geoff Teece in his call for global citizenship education to engage the world's religions rather than ignore them. However, Johnston found herself at odds with parents who did not share the same objective, at least in the short term. At institutions such as Chapman University and Soka University of America—both of which are affiliated with religious or spiritual communities—efforts are under way to encourage students from many religious backgrounds to share common spaces and enter into mutual dialogue. Whether global citizenship is presented as secular morality or is embedded within religious pluralism, invoking the term within secular institutions invites ideological conflict. If ecumenical dialogue amounts to an unwelcome expansion or deepening of public space in the eyes of some detractors, global citizenship framed as secular morality can arouse fears of a contraction or a hollowing out of public space for dialogue. What is more, as illustrated by the dissent in the United Kingdom surrounding New Labour's revised school curriculum, efforts to use "global citizenship" as neutral terminology for promoting moral principles also are prone to objections, particularly from conservative critics, that citizenship education is "shot through with political correctness"[59] and wastefully redirects classroom time away from the more traditional subjects.

The schools, colleges, and universities discussed in this chapter represent just the tip of the iceberg of educational initiatives that now revolve around global citizenship. It might be premature to claim, at least within the United States, that education for global citizenship has moved into the political mainstream, but the idea has gained considerable ground. As far as education for global citizenship entails helping the next generation advance in political efficacy, community involvement, and moral responsibility at home and abroad, such initiatives instill in young people the same sorts of personal qualities that hearken back to ancient civic republican ideals. At the same time, education for global citizenship, as shown in this chapter, has expanded the portfolio of citizen education into areas such as international awareness; appreciation of art, music, and literature from around the world; and an ability to cultivate meaningful human relationship in communities in which one is an outsider, motivated to build bridges across languages, religions, and cultural traditions. Just as the idea of global citizenship has wide latitude within the educational arena—moving across old and new interpretations of what citizenship means—the same holds true, as we shall see in the next chapter, in public discourse about global citizenship in the context of multinational corporations.

CHAPTER SIX

Global Citizenship in the Marketplace

The idea of global citizenship has become dramatically more visible in the arena of international commerce. Just as many individuals now choose to think of themselves as global citizens in an interdependent world, some of the world's largest corporations also have employed the term "global citizenship" as a way to articulate goals of public accountability and responsible behavior in the global economy. Corporate global citizenship[1] now encompasses a range of practices, including philanthropic endeavors, voluntary codes of conduct and reporting procedures, monitoring of supply chains, and relationships with "stakeholders."[2] The idea of corporate citizenship, more generally, has also become a popular marketing tool, often framed within public relations campaigns and community outreach efforts. Such developments fit into a larger phenomenon in which corporations have formed networks and partnerships with independent organizations, some of them closer to the corporate arena than others. The ten principles of the United Nations Global Compact[3] regarding human rights, labor standards, environmental protection, and the curbing of political corruption; the SA8000 workplace standards advanced and monitored by the group Social Accountability International; and the Dow Jones Sustainability Index launched in 1999 are just a few of the initiatives and indicators that hundreds of corporations around the world now consider important benchmarks.

By emphasizing voluntary initiatives taken by corporations and widely eschewing calls for additional government regulation at any level,[4] adherents of corporate global citizenship often are consciously and unapologetically self-interested in linking global philanthropy and social accountability initiatives with prospects for expanded market opportunities and higher profits. An article published by the World Economic Forum notes:[5]

> Few if any of these actions are being driven by altruism. The rationale is clear. In the past decade, the rules of the game have started to change for business—driven by changing societal expectations and the impacts of globalization, technology and growing political openness. Issues once confined to "the philanthropy department"—and some that were not even on the radar screen of most companies—are becoming material business risks and opportunities.[6]

This line of argument—that corporations must now broaden their public roles to remain competitive—flies in the face of the conventional wisdom, as articulated in 1970 by economist Milton Friedman, that *the* singular social responsibility of business is simply to increase profits and that any movement beyond the immediate profit motive, narrowly defined, can only harm free societies.[7] And yet, if corporate global citizenship initiatives truly are consistent with profit maximization in a new global era, such strategies might be reconciled with Friedman's philosophy, after all. Indeed, many corporations now produce annual "citizenship reports" alongside their annual financial reports to shareholders,[8] and some corporations, such as Intel, Hewlett-Packard, and Abbott Laboratories, have gone so far as to appoint senior executives who hold the specific portfolio of "global citizenship."

The corporations examined in this chapter, as examples of organizations pursuing strategies related to the specific idea of global citizenship, represent just the tip of an enormous iceberg that will continue to expand as long as "citizenship" is increasingly regarded as a cornerstone of corporate governance. Moreover, as illustrated toward the end of this chapter, global citizenship is also a strategic idea in international commerce in the context of marketing products and services to an extremely wealthy and mobile bracket of consumers. This serves to illustrate, once again, how agendas related to global citizenship in the marketplace are sharply divided regarding articulations of collective responsibility, at least to a limited degree, and assertions of individual privilege.

Corporate Global Citizenship Strategies

Corporate global citizenship and its related term, corporate social responsibility, have moved in recent years from the periphery of international business to becoming key strategic principles. The phenomenon and the rhetoric of corporate global citizenship extend well beyond Western culture.

Consider this public statement by Sooho Cho, the chairman of Hanjin Shipping Co., Ltd., a cargo carrier based in South Korea that each year transports approximately fifty-seven million tons of goods worldwide: "We will remain a concerned global citizen who maintains our assets in a safe, environmentally responsible manner."[9] Examining how the idea of global citizenship has emerged in the corporate sector casts light on the sorts of public spaces in which the credibility of global free-market capitalism is now debated and defended. The ways in which multinational corporations have framed the term "global citizenship" also signal a decidedly capitalist strain within contemporary global citizenship discourse.

Corporate global citizenship carries forth in multiple public spaces for contestation and deliberation intersecting throughout business, government, and civil society. In many respects, the increasing deployment of the term "global citizenship" in the corporate sector reflects an attempt by business elites to gain the upper hand over critics and activists from civil society organizations in public debates about the efficacy and equity of economic globalization and the footloose nature of capital investment and business operations in the global economy. In some instances, corporate global citizenship initiatives have come in response to negative developments, such as the mammoth corporate governance scandals at corporations such as Enron, Tyco, and WorldCom, as well as growing public awareness of abusive and dangerous workplace practices at factories around the world that are often under contract to multinational corporations headquartered in the United States.

A more affirmative rationale for corporate global citizenship traces back to the position that the corporate sector can fill an important role alongside governing institutions in addressing formidable global problems, from the spread of AIDS and malaria to the lack of suitable educational resources and capital investment in many corners of the developing world. In an era where the annual cash flows of the world's major corporations exceed the gross domestic products of all but the world's largest nation-states, more and more corporations are professing a willingness to promote goals such as human rights, the rule of law, social justice, environmental sustainability, and public health and well-being. They can do so largely on their own terms, as no universally recognized or enforceable principles for corporate global citizenship exist in the same manner as they do in other realms of corporate governance, such as accounting and financial reporting. The following examples of Hewlett-Packard and Novartis illustrate how two corporations that have focused specifically on "global citizenship" for several years have situated this idea within their respective agendas.

Hewlett-Packard

The global citizenship strategy at Hewlett-Packard (HP), which today employs more than 140,000 people in more than 160 countries, has decidedly local roots dating back to the founding of the company in 1939. Even when HP was a relatively small business, operating out of one location in Palo Alto, California, founders William Hewlett and David Packard repeatedly stated that the company owed more to the community than supplying jobs, paying taxes, and not polluting the local environment. As David Packard stated in 1947: "The role of a corporation is not to make a profit. It is to make a difference." In 1957, when HP embarked on its first expansion, building a second facility in nearby Santa Clara, Hewlett and Packard worried that as they became less personally involved in daily business operations, their corporation would become less responsive to the local community. To address such concerns, Hewlett and Packard held a management retreat at which executives included citizenship in a list of seven strategic objectives. Throughout the 1960s, HP grew dramatically as the corporation opened branches in Europe and Japan and acquired other businesses based overseas. At this stage in its development, citizenship for HP still was interpreted primarily in a local context, especially in terms of community volunteer activities. Hewlett and Packard, in fact, were instrumental in setting up the local organization that evolved into the United Way of Santa Clara County, in the heart of Silicon Valley.

Citizenship horizons for HP began to expand during the 1990s, when HP launched an "e-inclusion" initiative that aimed to bring digital technology to economically and geographically isolated communities at the margins of the Internet boom. The program began in the United States with communities near Palo Alto, San Diego, and Baltimore and gradually has extended to nineteen countries on five continents. In 2004, HP opened "digital community centers," which focus on technology education and training programs, in relatively isolated cities in Jordan, Russia, and Ukraine. As these activities took off, many Hewlett-Packard executives believed that greater coordination was needed. In the words of Ken Larson, HP's former director of corporate social responsibility: "We had a philanthropy group that was doing good things; we had people working with educational institutions doing good things; we had people working in public affairs doing good things. But we didn't have any integrated strategy."[10] After Carly Fiorina became HP's chief executive officer in 1999, a strategy began to take shape. Senior executive Debra Dunn (who had served as chief of staff under the previous chief executive, Lew Platt) was given the title vice president of global citizenship and assigned a mandate to pull together the company's various civic and community initiatives into a coherent portfolio. Dunn assembled a new division called Corporate Affairs and Global Citizenship, which absorbed many staffers who worked as liaisons to various national governments and media outlets.[11]

Besides holding the aim of greater coordination of philanthropy and service projects, the globalization of HP's supply chain motivated the corporation to form a global citizenship strategy. Throughout the 1990s, HP manufactured fewer and fewer of its own components for computer hardware and printers. Manufacturing shifted largely to independent contractors, and HP changed its suppliers with increasing frequency during the late 1990s as profit gains from cost reductions became evident. Under continual pressure to increase profit margins, the company first opened a contract factory in Nashville, Tennessee, then moved operations to Guadalajara, Mexico, after eighteen months, and moved again one year later to the Guangdong province on the southern coast of China. HP managers who visited the independent contractors began returning from factories with warnings about poor living and working conditions, especially in China. Concerns ranged from the lack of safety guards on equipment to the substandard housing of the workers. As Larson noted: "At the time, we didn't have anything in our code or in our contract with [the supply contractors] about these kinds of issues. Whenever we were working with local contractors, there was really an assumption built in that we were going to work with companies that were like us and we could trust that they would operate in a way like HP. And that just fell apart when we moved farther and farther away."

This situation prompted HP to formulate its Supply Chain Code of Conduct, which was completed in 2002. Although the pressure to generate the code of conduct was primarily internal—from executives within the corporation— concerns about external pressure also were a driving force, as managers were aware that a number of advocacy groups were gearing up to target the electronics industry in the same way that campaigns in recent years have taken to task the garment industry, the shoe industry, and the toy industry for tolerating, and in some cases, spreading poor working conditions in the developing world. Although Larson candidly acknowledged during an interview for this study that HP would have done well to establish the code of conduct before setting up operations in China, HP nevertheless had one of the first codes in the electronics industry. In October 2004, HP and seven other companies (including IBM and Dell) signed a more sweeping code of conduct for supply contractors that includes general provisions on basic labor rights—such as freedom of association, mandatory overtime pay, and protection from discrimination—and workplace health and safety standards, as well as ethics provisions that ban bribery and extortion, and give rights to whistle-blowers.[12]

Like many codes of conduct, the document affirms a series of general principles and guidelines and leaves it up to individual corporations to choose exactly how to institute the guidelines. The minimum-wage provision, for example, states that corporations will pay workers according to "all applicable wage laws," which vary dramatically from country to country. Other guidelines are more specific: employers are told that workers should have at least one day off each week and should not work more than sixty hours a week, including overtime, and that any form of harsh or inhumane treatment, including sexual harassment, is absolutely forbidden. Despite the considerable flexibility and voluntary leanings of the supplier code of conduct, the document has triggered some resistance among supply contractors. As Richard Conrad, Hewlett Packard's senior vice president of global operations, told a conference of supply chain managers in 2004: "I would be less than candid if I said to you putting in place this policy was easy. It is not. Some of them [the supply contractors] took umbrage at being asked to sign the code; others wanted us to accept their citizenship reports as proof of their adherence; while some others flat-out refused and discussions continue."[13]

The process of developing codes of conduct for suppliers prompted HP executives to realize that their own corporation also needed clearer codes. As Larson recalled:

> We kind of reached this logical conundrum saying, OK, we're going to require all these things from our suppliers—no child labor, no forced overtime, no slave labor—and we kind of turned to ourselves and said, do we have commensurate policies for HP? And the reality was we didn't. In dealing with more and more NGOs and socially responsible investors, when they would ask us, "Well, what is your policy about child labor? What is your policy about slave labor?" And we didn't have one. All I could say was, "Trust us—we have good personnel policy and guidelines—and they'd say, "Yeah, right—thanks anyway." So we had a need to mirror what we were asking our suppliers to do and have our own policy.

Drafting a policy for HP brought about an internal struggle, as the legal department resisted the idea of the corporation's aligning itself with the United Nations Universal Declaration of Human Rights. Lawyers argued that making written commitments to good behavior could set HP up for criticism, at best—and lawsuits, at worst—if activists began making allegations that the corporation was not meeting its own standards. Dunn, Larson, and their colleagues gradually convinced the lawyers that greater transparency and commitments to accountability would prove more beneficial than burdensome for the corporation.

As stated in its frequent news releases and its annual global citizenship reports (which the corporation has published since 2003), Hewlett-Packard has included three key priorities in its global citizenship strategy: reducing electronic waste; raising social and environmental standards in supply chains; and increasing global access to information technology. With regard to environmental standards, in 2003 the corporation began to calculate greenhouse gas emissions from its operations and has tried to lower emissions from year to year. As of 2007, Hewlett-Packard has set the goal of reducing the combined energy consumption of its operations and products by 20 percent below 2005 levels by the year 2010.[14] In an effort to reduce the amount of computer hardware dumped in landfills around the world, Hewlett-Packard also has started a recycling program in thirty countries where it operates. In terms of philanthropy and investment, in January 2004 the corporation, along with partners from governments and voluntary organizations, launched a microfinance program in developing countries, providing very small loans—sometimes as low as $25—to independent businesses in need of financial help to get off the ground.[15]

In many respects, Hewlett-Packard has rebranded its philanthropy efforts—new initiatives as well as preexisting programs under its charitable foundation—under the umbrella of global citizenship. For instance, when HP awarded technology grants to twenty-six nonprofit community organizations in the United States and Puerto Rico in April 2003, the news release framed the grants as part of the corporation's global citizenship strategy.[16] Moreover, global citizenship initiatives at HP are often linked specifically to self-interested objectives to expand the corporation into emerging markets. When HP funded a group of entrepreneurial women setting up a photography business in Kuppan, a rural village in the Indian state of Andhra Pradesh, Debra Dunn acknowledged that the corporation's purpose was partly to explore new products and markets for itself: "We wanted to marry business development objectives and community development objectives. Companies such as HP are serving the top of the pyramid—probably only the top one billion people out of six billion. If we could figure how to serve another three billion, it would be a big market opportunity, even if they don't have a lot of money."[17]

Such initiatives from Hewlett-Packard, taking place in small and relatively isolated villages in developing countries, further demonstrate how global citizenship often unfolds within local public space. They also illustrate how businesses are taking affirmative steps to channel entrepreneurial energy into projects that aim to overcome global poverty and promote more sustainable economic development. In this instance, the philosophy comes in no small measure from HP's former chief executive, Carly Fiorina, who initiated the corporation's global citizenship strategy. Before leaving her post in early 2005, Fiorina echoed David Packard's words nearly fifty years earlier when she told participants at the World Economic Forum: "Business must play a role if only because we are so large and have such impact in the world. . . . We must do more than just make a profit. We must be a good global citizen[,] which is more than just doing no harm. Business must do well and do good."[18]

In 2006, Hewlett Packard was rocked by scandal when it was revealed that several company officials, including the chair, Patricia C. Dunn, had approved spying tactics known as "pretexting" when the officials sought to identify members of the corporation's board of directors who apparently had been leaking information to the news media. Revelations emerged that HP officials had enlisted, with Dunn's consent, private detectives who misrepresented themselves to telephone service providers in order to obtain personal phone records of HP board members and news reporters and identify connections between them. The case prompted hearings in the U.S. Congress on privacy issues, and criminal charges of felony identity theft and conspiracy were filed in California against Dunn and four other individuals. In December 2006, HP agreed to pay $14.5 million to the state of California to settle civil accusations of wrongdoing in the case, with $13.5 million of the settlement being used to create a fund that will help the state investigate and prosecute future privacy violations. Dunn resigned from the board in September 2006, and the charges against her were dropped in March 2007.[19] As of March 2007, the corporation's online global citizenship report included an apology for the scandal and a promise to reform its corporate governance.[20]

Novartis

Global citizenship became a key principle at Novartis, which employs more than 80,000 people in 140 countries, well before the idea's recent ascendancy within international business circles. Daniel Vasella, the chairman and chief executive of the pharmaceutical corporation, began to consider Novartis itself a global citizen during the 1996 merger between the corporation's predecessors, Ciba-Geigy and Sandoz.[21] At the time, the two Switzerland-based corporations estimated that the merger into Novartis would cause a net reduction of 12,000 jobs. During an interview for this study, Vasella said that global citizenship weighed heavily on his mind while he was thinking about how to lessen the merger's negative impact. In response to the job losses, Novartis created a fund worth approximately SF 100 million—about US$80 million—to assist any employees worldwide who wanted to start their own businesses. The fund eventually provided support to eighty offspring companies.

Since the merger, Vasella has continued to think of Novartis as a global citizen with the right to operate literally worldwide and the corresponding obligation, accepted voluntarily from within, to hold itself to the same workplace safety and environmental standards in relatively impoverished countries as in prosperous industrial countries. In fact, Vasella defined citizenship in fairly conventional terms of rights and duties, which he framed as both Western and universal:

> Citizenship, from my point of view, refers to a responsibility which an individual or an entity has towards the community. . . . It does have a moral or ethical aspect, but it also has a very rational one, which is a give and take, where basically, I think, you cannot live in a community without recognizing and respecting rules which allow us to live together in a civilized manner. I would say, too, here, that it's based on Western culture and an understanding of values, which is basically rooted in a Christian-Judaic basis of morality and what's good and bad. We look at human rights; we look at child labor—I'm aware that in some other cultures, not the same rules are applied and not the same things are seen as good or bad. Nevertheless, we have to ask, does the behavior fundamentally help a human being, or does it harm a human being?[22]

Postmerger, Vasella said, global citizenship has meant primarily two things for Novartis: avoiding doing harm to employees and local residents in the communities in which Novartis operates, and making contributions in support of economic and social development around the world.[23] This philanthropic aspect of global citizenship is pursued internationally mainly through a nonprofit arm of the corporation, the Novartis Foundation for Sustainable Development, which underwrites numerous programs in developing countries ranging from loans for small businesses to educational initiatives for children who have lost their parents to AIDS.

The Novartis Foundation helped spur the development of a malaria drug[24] that eventually became part of a landmark differential-pricing initiative. According to the foundation's director, Klaus Leisinger, in 1996 the pharmaceutical division (of Ciba-Geigy, a predecessor to Novartis) had declined to invest in developing the malaria drug after being approached by the government of China. The foundation was enlisted to provide assistance, and because malaria is one of the biggest killers of children, the foundation provided development funding though its "risk fund." One of the conditions was that if the drug were successful, Leisinger said, it would be sold in wealthier countries as one brand name and in poorer countries under a different brand name—and at a substantially lower price. In 1999, the drug was introduced in wealthy countries under the name Riamet, and in May 2001, Novartis and the World Health Organization negotiated an arrangement to sell the drug in developing countries under a different name, Co-Artem, at a cost of approximately US$2.30 per prescription pack.[25] This was dramatically below the drug's approximate cost, at the time, of US$50 in affluent countries such as Switzerland. Following the announcement, Vasella told a news reporter that the discounted price was equivalent to the cost of producing the drug.[26]

The foundation performs a dual function within Novartis: advocate for the developing world and strategic consultant and public relations vehicle for the corporation. Letters from nongovernmental organizations—some of them critical of the corporation—are routed to the foundation if they pertain to issues in developing countries. In this regard, the foundation fills several overlapping roles: manager of health and development programs worldwide, point of contact within Novartis for nongovernmental organizations and international organizations, and internal consulting unit for Novartis on corporate social responsibility: "And that also leads back to citizenship—the understanding that 'global citizen' Novartis also has a humanitarian or charity responsibility," Leisinger said. "This is a good understanding but if we—as part of a company—become active in a charitable way, we must do it on the highest possible professional level—the same quality as Novartis runs its business."[27] This emphasis on global citizenship as achieved through voluntary initiatives and codes of conduct, rather than as enforced by compulsory regulations from governments, projects the sense that Novartis has chosen to assume a public role within an emerging, albeit highly fragmented and incomplete, global public space.

Shareholder Activism and Global Citizenship

A corporation's characterization of itself as dedicated to global citizenship can provide activist groups with leverage to push for greater public accountability. Shareholder proposals at annual meetings have long served as a vehicle for critics and dissidents to raise their voices and focus attention on contentious issues—even if the proposals rarely gain much support—and the term "global citizenship" has given activists yet another hook. For example, the board of directors of Cisco Systems fended off a shareholder proposal at its annual meeting in November 2002 that would have required the computer networking company to disclose any equipment sold to governments or state-run businesses that could be used to intercept, record, or monitor traffic on the Internet. Although the proposed resolution did not mention any countries by name, the purpose of the proposal was to force Cisco to disclose equipment sold to the Communist government of the People's Republic of China. The proposal came from Ann Lau, the chair of the Visual Artists Guild in Los Angeles, who argued that Cisco should not tolerate its products being used to stifle free expression. In her presentation at the corporation's annual meeting in San Jose, Lau quoted several statements by Cisco's president and chief executive officer, John Chambers, including this one: "Cisco takes the responsibility as a global citizen seriously. It's the right thing to do and our success depends on it."[28] Lau then reminded shareholders that networking technology had enabled government authorities in China to step up the monitoring of China's citizens, and many dissidents had been imprisoned for criticizing the government in online communication. Among them was a twenty-two-year-old student at Beijing University, Liu Di, who had criticized the Chinese Communist Party online and written an essay published on the Internet stating: "My ideals are the ideals of an open society. . . . In my view, freedom does not just include external freedom, but freedom within our hearts and minds."[29] (Liu was held in prison in from November 2002 to November 2003.) Lau then reminded shareholders of Cisco's numerous contracts with the Chinese government and argued that Cisco should be as accountable on human rights as it is on financial reporting.

In its statement of opposition to the proposal, Cisco's board of directors maintained that the corporation is committed to freedom of speech and the use of the Internet to spread information around the world. However, the company argued that releasing the information, as requested, would "unnecessarily expend Cisco resources and could interfere with our customer relations," especially resellers and distributors that sell products directly to governments around the world.[30] Lau's proposal went down to overwhelming defeat, but her resolution succeeded in bringing into public debate concerns about electronic monitoring and the curtailment of freedom of speech. Yahoo, Microsoft, Google and Skype are among the other technology companies doing business in China that have been accused by human rights organizations of helping the Chinese government undermine freedom of speech and carry out censorship.[31] Similar issues have also been presented to Hewlett-Packard at its recent annual meetings. One recurring shareholder proposal called for HP to adopt eleven China Business Principles regarding human rights and labor standards, one of which included this sweeping promise: "We will not sell or provide products or technology in China that can be used to commit human rights violations or labor rights abuse." The proposal failed at three consecutive annual meetings, most recently in 2003, with HP's board of directors arguing that the proposal would "impair HP's ability to manage its operations in China and to control the scope and timing of the disclosure of sensitive business information. . . . We believe that the proposal is unnecessary, vague, costly and beyond HP's ability to implement."[32]

The ethical issue of how products are used after they are sold has been the main point of contention in another ongoing activist campaign targeting Caterpillar Inc. The manufacturer of construction equipment has come under intense critical scrutiny in recent years for selling more than one hundred bulldozers to the Israeli military. Numerous human rights monitors, most notably Human Rights Watch and Amnesty International, have reported that the Israeli military has used the bulldozers to destroy houses belonging to Palestinians in the occupied territories. According to Human Rights Watch, more than 2,500 houses have been demolished since 2000, and 16,000 people—many of them refugees—have lost their homes.[33] Several organizations holding shares of stock in Caterpillar—including Jewish Voice for Peace, the Catholic Sisters of Loretto, and the Mercy Investment Group, all have filed shareholder resolutions since the year 2003 calling for Caterpillar to review whether the sales of the D-9 bulldozers violate the corporation's code of conduct. Especially at issue was the following statement from Caterpillar's code of conduct:

> Caterpillar accepts the responsibilities of global citizenship. Wherever we conduct business or invest our resources around the world, we know that our commitment to financial success must also take into account social, economic, political, and environmental priorities. We believe that our success should also contribute to the quality of life and the prosperity of communities where we work and live.[34]

The emphasis placed on global citizenship in the code of conduct has become a lightning rod for critics. During the corporation's April 2004 annual meeting in Chicago, several dozen protesters gathered outside to demand that Caterpillar cease its sales of bulldozers to the government of Israel. Said one protester: "They say they are a global citizen [but] I don't think a global citizen sells the tools that people use to destroy the lives of other human beings."[35]

Activists who organized the campaign emphasized in interviews for this study that the corporation's promise that it accepts the responsibilities of global citizenship makes it all the more accountable to the public. As Liat Weingart of Jewish Voice for Peace put it: "We're using their branding against them."[36] The difficulty that the activists seem to have uncovered is that Caterpillar uses the term "global citizenship" in isolation, unaccompanied by specific measures or standards. The corporation has not explained to the public exactly what is meant by global citizenship—and since there is no clearly accepted definition or standard among corporations on what constitutes corporate global citizenship, Caterpillar's exact interpretation is left to speculation. Caterpillar's public relations department did not respond to requests for interviews for this study.

Asked during an interview what steps Caterpillar would need to take to live up to its declaration that the corporation accepts responsibility as a global citizen, Sarah Leah Whitson of Human Rights Watch said that at the very least, Caterpillar ought to investigate any allegations that their equipment, services, supplies, or products are being used in a manner that violates human rights: "And if that investigation shows you that, in fact, the equipment that you are selling is being used for the specific purpose of violating human rights of other people, you've got to stop. Otherwise, you're complicit in this."[37]

Whether or not Caterpillar ever launched such an investigation will be revealed, most likely, in the proceedings of two lawsuits filed in March 2005—in Haifa, Israel, and Seattle, Washington—by the parents of Rachel Corrie, a twenty-three-year-old activist from Olympia, Washington, who was crushed to death by a bulldozer as she tried to stop the demolition of a home in a refugee camp.[38] The lawsuit filed in Seattle accuses Caterpillar of being complicit in human rights violations and war crimes perpetrated by the Israeli military, while the lawsuit filed in Israel alleges that the Israeli military violated Corrie's human rights and right to life.[39] In response to the lawsuit as well as the shareholder resolutions, Caterpillar has repeatedly issued a written statement arguing that the corporation cannot be held responsible for how its products are used: "More than two million Caterpillar machines and engines are at work in virtually every region of the world each day. We have neither the legal right nor the means to police individual use of that equipment."[40]

Whitson said she realizes that corporations, generally speaking, might not be in a position to monitor exactly how each piece of equipment sold by the corporation is used, "but I think again, at minimum, what they should do is to get a representation in the contract, in the supply sale contract, that says, 'you represent, we represent, that we will not use your equipment in a manner that violates international humanitarian law or human rights law.'" Whitson further argued that parties to equipment sales contracts commonly agree to abide by domestic law, and that taking the next step to international humanitarian law makes sense for all concerned: "That way the company can say, 'We did our minimum due diligence; we obtained that we had no reason to believe that they were not in good faith going to comply with the law, and we had no knowledge of their actions and conduct in violation of law using our equipment.'"

Although both Whitson and Weingart shared ideas during their interviews about what would constitute good global citizenship for Caterpillar, neither Human Rights Watch nor Jewish Voice for Peace articulated a proposed standard for "global citizenship" during the course of the campaign. In fact, Weingart said that she is skeptical of the term and sees its value only as a lever to call for greater public accountability. Noting that her organization has never invoked or applied the term "global citizenship" in any other context—and did so in this case only in response to Caterpillar's code of conduct—Weingart argued: "There is zero accountability that is happening outside corporations, and the term 'global citizenship,' used within corporations to describe their own behavior, is meaningless—it has no teeth. It doesn't affect their bottom line. I find substance in the term only when there are outside mechanisms of accountability." Similar to the Cisco proposal from the Visual Artists Guild, shareholder proposals by human rights campaigners have been overwhelmingly defeated at Caterpillar's annual meetings, receiving less than 4 percent of votes cast. Nevertheless, such resolutions, protests and lawsuits have placed Cisco and Caterpillar as well as numerous other corporations that have faced similar proposals—under considerable public scrutiny and illustrated a gap in public space, with regard to ensuring corporate accountability, that advocacy groups such as Human Rights Watch, Jewish Voice for Peace, and the Visual Artists Guild are struggling to fill. The cases of Cisco Systems and Caterpillar also demonstrate the potential of corporate annual meetings as dynamic public spaces in ongoing public debates regarding the direction of global capitalism.

Marketing to "Global Citizens"

Alongside the burgeoning discourse of corporate global citizenship, many businesses have gravitated to the idea of global citizenship for an entirely different purpose: identifying and appealing to lucrative customer bases worldwide. While corporations seeking to portray themselves as dedicated to global citizenship seem to employ the term as they negotiate their roles within an emerging global public space, the marketing strain of global citizenship discourse seems to focus primarily on the development of *private* space for a small number of wealthy and privileged individuals. Some of the media references marketing products and services to "global citizens" appeal primarily to illusions of vanity, sophistication, and privilege. Consider this news release trumpeting a men's aftershave lotion released in ninety countries in September

2002: "Calvin Klein has introduced CRAVE Calvin Klein, its latest male fragrance for the man who is described as a global citizen, an influencer and an avid consumer of all media, music and technology."[41]

In the same vein, a fashion commentator in India, writing about the upscale Indigo Nation line of men's clothing, declared: "If clothes maketh a man then wearing Indigo Nation tells the world one is a 'global citizen, aggressive, spirited and supremely self-confident.'"[42]

In the investment arena, global citizens are often described as individuals who refuse to confine themselves to the stock markets of their home countries. In the words of Roger Ibbotson, a hedge fund manager and a professor at the Yale School of Management, "A true global citizen would have an equity allocation of nearly 50% to non-U.S. stocks. However, nobody I know invests this way. There's a home-country bias. People are more knowledgeable about their own market, so that's where they tend to invest."[43] The complexities faced by expatriates, as they move from country to country as their careers progress and accumulate wealth from all over the world, have opened up new business opportunities for global financial advisers and asset managers. As a journalist for the *Financial Times* noted:

> For many global citizens, family issues are the toughest nuts to crack. . . . In some cases, children may have been born overseas, and hold multiple citizenships. They may marry spouses from different countries, and make their lives scattered around the world. That means a global citizen who wants to bequeath a family business to his three children may need to consider three or four different sets of inheritance and gift tax laws—and their impact on the other children.[44]

Hence providers of private banking services around the world now aim to serve highfliers whom they have labeled global citizens. Many of the self-described global citizens profiled elsewhere in this book have put down roots within local communities, but the sorts of global citizens targeted by private banking services are characterized as seeking roots for their money, not for themselves. Consider this description from the head of the private client group of First Union National Bank, which has since been taken over by Wachovia:

> A very typical international client for us is an attorney in Costa Rica, whose son was schooled in the U.S. or Europe, his spouse is from Spain, and when he uses First Union bank, we're his broker. . . . We help with his U.S. activity; we'll be a dollar-based investor for him. Our international clients are very much global citizens who are very busy, very capable, holding businesses in several countries and looking for smart investments.[45]

The key modifiers to "global citizens" in this passage are revealing: The global citizens who depend on private client services are "busy, very capable, holding businesses in several countries" (not merely employed by a multinational corporation) and heavily invested. This would suggest that global citizens, at least from the bank's perspective, necessarily are members of a millionaires' club. Indeed, First Union's private client group worked only with investors with more than US$1 million in "investable assets," in the bank's words.

Across the Atlantic, Barclays Offshore Services, based on the island of Jersey, also markets its services to individuals the bank refers to as global citizens.[46] As the then managing director John Church noted in a 1999 article, "The growing number of global citizens living and working abroad and the increasingly international perspective of clients is driving demand for high quality international banking services."[47] This reference to "global citizens" was not a onetime accidental occurrence. The bank's multicurrency banking service, called Global Solutions, specifically targets individuals whom the bank's press releases have referred to as global citizens. Global Solutions offers Internet banking as well as services not traditionally associated with banks, such as property management, tax planning, and worldwide hotel discounts.

In an interview for this study, Martyn Scriven, managing director of Barclays Offshore Services, said that he considers the term "global citizen" more than a mere marketing phrase; rather, he sees it as "a real and accurate description of many people." He added that Global Solutions targets customers who own at least one residence outside the United Kingdom:

> We're not seeking for that particular Global Solutions package [for] the chap who lives in Reading and works in London. . . . That package is directed at the sort of person who might expatriate themselves, the sort of person who might live in a variety of jurisdictions. It's somebody who has gone from A to B and wants some hook, some reliable point that they can call back to. If you are becoming a global citizen, if you are moving about, you want security around your finances, and you want dependency. You want somewhere where you feel they are going to be here, now and the next day, and it's somewhere if you need money moving from A to B urgently, you'll know that organization has got the reach to do that.[48]

Law firms catering to the wealthy have also invoked the idea of global citizenship while jumping on the private-client bandwagon. In December 2001, the New York law firm Bergman, Horowitz & Reynolds merged with the London law firm Withers to create the world's first international law firm serving primarily, in the words of a news release announcing the merger, "high-net-worth individuals, their families and their advisers." Diana Parker, a senior partner of Withers, explained the rationale for the merger thus:

> A significant proportion of our clients are now global citizens with links all over the world. Indeed, many of our mutual private clients' personal wealth exceeds that of a number of companies listed on the London and New York Stock Exchanges and the NASDAQ. Such people want their affairs to be handled with the same commercialism that they encounter in other fields of business. They expect their advisers to be able to work across borders to tight deadlines.[49]

Consumer products and services marketed specifically to upscale global citizens also extend into areas such as air travel, television programming, deluxe mobile phone service, and health insurance plans. When United Airlines in 2002 launched a television advertising campaign aimed at elite travelers in Asia and the South Pacific, one of the airline's executives stated: "United's target in Asia is global citizens. They travel frequently and have a very international outlook . . . across cultures and language."[50] When the Discovery cable network launched a twenty-four-hour international lifestyle channel in India, its vice president promised to "offer an unparalleled selection of high quality, entertaining programmes on travel, cuisine, fitness and fashion that has been carefully chosen to appeal to an astute global citizen."[51] Iridium, a global telecommunications company that fell on hard times in early 2000, had intended to launch its World Roaming Service for "the global citizens who travel internationally and are heavy cellular users," explaining that "these global citizens need a communications solution that will provide continuity of communications across incompatible cellular standards as well as for those areas without any land-based communications."[52] Had Iridium succeeded, its customers would have been free to use their mobile phones practically anywhere on earth.

Meanwhile, some private health insurance companies based in the United States have marketed policies to individuals whom they call global citizens. In contrast with standard travel insurance plans, the policies typically claim that they can guarantee first-class medical care anywhere and include transportation costs to the United States in the event of a medical emergency. As California-based insurer Thomas Petersen explained, when asked during an interview why his company's marketing literature refers to "global citizens" rather than "global travelers" or "global migrants": "Global citizen, international traveler, multinational settings . . . I think when we use those terms, we do have to kind of give you the grain of salt in saying it is marketing when those words come out of our mouths."[53] Despite this figurative reference to global citizenship, Petersen's worldwide medical plan has clearly established objective criteria as to whether or not one can be classified as a global citizen. Citizens of the United States, in order to qualify for Petersen's worldwide health insurance, must reside outside the United States for at least five months of the year.

Conclusion

Global citizenship discourse within the corporate sector once again provides us with a striking contrast between articulations of collective responsibility, from corporations willing to hold themselves accountable at least to their own voluntary codes of conduct, and assertions of individual privilege. Images of wealthy and mobile global citizens, as portrayed by financial advisers, law firms, and insurance companies courting their business, contrast dramatically with the more public-spirited goals commonly articulated within corporate global citizenship initiatives. In some cases, they also depart from moral visions articulated by civil society organizations and educational institutions that emphasize the capabilities of individual persons to become motivated, responsible, and culturally perceptive global citizens. International-relations scholar Richard Falk, who has advocated for the idea of global citizenship in other contexts, has objected that when "the corporate or banking elite" describe themselves as world citizens, they are, in fact, referring to an international lifestyle rather than any meaningful understanding of citizenship: "The extreme thinness of such 'citizenship,' if it can even be so denominated, is exhibited by the lack of commitment to global public goods, by the absence of concern about the well-being of all persons on the planet, and by the lack of support for effective forms of global governance."[54]

While interview respondents whose stories are shared elsewhere in this book often indicated that global citizenship, for them, entails making decisions based on awareness of one's moral obligations in an interdependent world, many marketing specialists treat global citizenship as being based primarily on awareness of one's status. However, a rival marketing discourse of global citizenship is beginning to emerge among some providers of consumer goods that meet ethical standards with respect to issues such as workplace health and safety standards, fair trading practices, and environmental sustainability. When the Co-op supermarket chain in the United Kingdom launched a television advertising campaign in partnership with the Fairtrade Foundation, Co-op's vice president for branding noted: "Our customers want to play a more active part and be global citizens rather than just consumers."[55] Likewise, a Utah-based retailer of women's tops made with organic cotton fibers, free of synthetic pesticides and herbicides, can be found online at www.beaglobalcitizen.com. The Ireland branch of the United Nations Children's Fund (UNICEF) has changed the way it solicits donations from Irish businesses so as to appeal to corporations interested in promoting themselves as global citizens. In the words of UNICEF Ireland's executive director: "People want to know what is being achieved with their money. We had a company recently who wanted to give us money to be used very specifically on vaccines. We found a project to fit this and we are now reporting back to that donor with pictures of kids being vaccinated in Liberia—thanks to their donation."[56]

Plenty of debate continues regarding the extent to which corporations professing commitments to global citizenship truly behave as responsible actors in the world economy. At the very least, chief executives such as Daniel Vasella and Carly Fiorina have pushed their colleagues to consider more carefully the circumstances in which the actions of multinationals either help or harm human beings—and to minimize and mitigate the harm. The recent proliferation of global citizenship strategies has prompted corporations and, in many cases, their affiliated foundations to set higher standards for themselves and their subcontractors and also to launch social and economic development programs that otherwise might never have emerged. The onset of "corporate global citizenship" initiatives also has intensified public discussion about what kind of global capitalism should take hold in the twenty-first century. With corporate executives often competing with social and political activists for the moral high ground, vigorous public debate now thrives regarding the meaning of global citizenship; the appropriate roles, rights, and duties of multinational corporations; and the broader issue of how economic development should proceed in hopes of fostering human rights, social well-being, and environmental sustainability.

The bottom line, though, is that corporations trying to improve their images by turning to the idea of global citizenship are doing so largely out of calculated self-interest. The practices of corporate global citizenship are resolutely capitalist: corporations are implementing global citizenship strategies largely to make sure that access to markets around the world will not be curtailed. An article in *Business Week* summed up the rationale this way: "In an age of social activism and instant communication, when a Web log can energize a mass boycott overnight, some say it's essential to build a public narrative about your company as a good global citizen." Especially for multinational corporations based in the United States, global citizenship has taken a higher priority amid growing mistrust and, at times, violence overseas directed against American corporations. Sinking favorability ratings for the United States in international public opinion polling[57] have generated significant concern, as overseas markets account for about 40 percent of sales for American multinational corporations, and economic reliance on markets abroad is projected to increase in the coming years. A prolonged loss of luster for "brand America" would translate into lower profits and diminished prosperity for Americans. In the words of advertising executive Keith Reinhard, the founder and chairman of Business for Diplomatic Action,[58] "The world has changed. We are either going to be good global citizens, or we're going to be bad global citizens. But there's no longer a choice about whether we'll be citizens of the globe."[59]

CHAPTER SEVEN

Governing Institutions and Global Citizenship

The idea of global citizenship might appear, at first glance, to challenge the primacy of the nation-state as a global actor. After all, if one were to define citizenship narrowly—and in the familiar legalistic sense—as a permanent tie between an individual and a sovereign political community, then global citizenship would seem to require a world state. Of course, as we have seen in the preceding chapters, the sorts of persons and organizations around the world now adopting the term "global citizenship" allow for much more latitude in their understandings of citizenship. What is more, much of the contemporary public discourse surrounding global citizenship relates to the behavior of nation-states.

This chapter on governing institutions, then, begins by exploring how individual countries and their respective governments are often regarded and critiqued as global citizens in themselves. We will focus especially on how United States foreign policy has been depicted within global citizenship discourse, particularly in relation to the most controversial foreign policy decision of George W. Bush's presidency: the choice in March 2003 to invade and occupy Iraq. The chapter then examines how governing institutions at various levels in Japan, South Korea, and the United Kingdom, as well as the United Nations, have chosen to interpret and communicate the idea of global citizenship. These examples further illustrate how global citizenship often thrives within domestic public space and is framed by national governments as compatible with domestic and international policy objectives. As Gareth Evans noted when he proposed the idea of "good international citizenship" during his tenure as Australia's foreign minister in the 1980s, good citizenship on the part of nation-states is not "the foreign policy equivalent of Boy Scout good deeds. [It is] an exercise in enlightened self-interest: an expression of idealistic pragmatism."[1]

Nation-States as Global Citizens

As in the arenas examined in the previous chapters—civil society, education, and commerce—the meaning of global citizenship with regard to the behavior of nation-states remains in an ongoing process of clarification and contestation. The various ways in which individual countries are described as global citizens tend to reflect how the country, its people, and its political leaders regard themselves internally as well as how the country and its policies are perceived by politicians, journalists, and commentators from abroad. Of course, this means that judgments in media discourse about the merits of individual countries as global citizens depend on the respective positions and outlooks of each commentator. What follows, then, is not a comprehensive inventory of what counts—or ought to count—as good or poor global citizenship from nation-states, let alone a sweeping critique of any particular country's foreign policy. Rather, this discussion illustrates how the term "global citizenship" is often injected into contentious debates and how numerous competing perspectives can be found, at least within worldwide media discourse in the English language, as to whether the specific practices of any given national government can also be acclaimed as practices of global citizenship.

"Good International Citizenship"

In many cases, the term "global citizen" is applied to nation-states seeking to gain greater validation in the international arena. Russian president Vladimir Putin, for example, was labeled an aspiring global citizen in the aftermath of September 11, 2001, in light of his government's decision to increase oil production and help stabilize world oil prices amid international tension.[2] South Africa in the aftermath of apartheid has been framed as being in transition from "global pariah" to global citizen,[3] and speculation continues as to whether North Korea, with its secretive communist dictatorship, will ever become a global citizen.[4] China has been cast repeatedly in media discourse as an emerging global citizen in light of milestones such as Beijing's successful bid for the 2008 summer Olympics, the government's ratification of the Kyoto Protocol[5]— the international agreement to reduce greenhouse gas emissions relative to their 1990 levels by the year 2012—and China's successful entry into the World

Trade Organization, with the accompanying expectation that WTO member-ship would curb widespread counterfeiting practices and pirating industries.[6] Other, more critical media references to global citizenship have raised concerns about political oppression and China's control of Tibet. Following China's ele-vation in 1999 to most-favored-nation status in trade with the United States, a secondary-school student from Indiana advocated a consumer boycott of products from China: "When will the United States learn that China is not the type of global citizen that we want to be dealing with? Even at age 17, I realize that China is maliciously abusing its power and size."[7]

While the perceived global citizenship of authoritarian governments re-mains tenuous, at best, commentators and politicians in English-speaking constitutional democracies display more confidence in labeling their respec-tive countries as global citizens—while also subjecting their national govern-ments to critical scrutiny. In Australia, public discourse regarding global citi-zenship has become substantially more self-critical, especially among those who lamented the willingness of Prime Minister John Howard to join forces with the United States in Iraq.[8] Australia's military response to the East Timor crisis prompted one critic to suggest that despite Australia's "intentions to be-come a 'global citizen,'" in fact the national government has "little inclination to listen to foreign advice."[9] Australia's resistance to the Kyoto Protocol—in contrast with New Zealand's ratification of the agreement—also figures into Australians' self-perceived shortcomings of their country as a prospective global citizen.[10] "Environmental spoiler"[11] and "renegade state"[12] are some of the antonyms to "global citizen" that commentators have used to describe Australia when it comes to the issue of the emerging global climate crisis.

In Canada, global citizenship discourse often reflects ongoing public de-bates regarding the country's relationship with the United States. Does good global citizenship require Canada to distinguish itself from the United States—by ratifying the Kyoto Protocol, as it did in 2002, and staying out of Iraq? Or does global citizenship for Canada require the country to move closer to its neighbor to the south? Politicians and journalists have argued both sides of this question, especially in light of the government's decision to avoid sending troops to Iraq amid overwhelming public opposition to the March 2003 invasion.[13] When Canada's government ratified the Kyoto Pro-tocol in December 2002, its then prime minister, Jean Chrétien, said the act made Canada "a good global citizen"[14] despite concerns that the move would prove costly to the Canadian economy in the short term. On the other hand, as Paul Martin prepared to replace Chrétien as prime minister in December 2003, he argued that updating "our manual on global citizenship" required mending fences with the United States.[15]

Global citizenship discourse in Canada often portrays Canadians as global citizens in the context of the dramatic increase in immigration during the past two generations as well as the enthusiasm of younger Canadians to live and work overseas, especially as contributors to international organizations. In the words of essayist Pico Iyer:

> Canada has become the spiritual home, you could say, of the very notion of an extended, emancipating global citizenship. . . . Even as more and more of the world is in Canada, Canada is in more and more of the world. . . . Canadians— not burdened by the complicated obligations of the United States and not weighed down by centuries of history, as older cultures are—are taking their native senses of mobility and internationalism across the planet to help draw up what could be called the outlines of a global constitution.[16]

The United States of America garners mixed reviews as a global citizen. Perceptions of the United States as failing to live up to global citizenship have increased considerably during the presidency of George W. Bush, but the United States also received low marks for global citizenship during Bill Clinton's presidency. A newspaper commentary written in late 1999 described a widening gap between the flattering self-perceptions of Americans and the worries of the rest of the world about the behavior of the United States, especially as the U.S. government refused to ratify international agreements on the emerging global climate crisis, the prohibition of land mines, and the testing of nuclear weapons: "Americans may think of themselves as good global citizens who believe that the rule of law should guide international relations. But to much of the world, U.S. behavior frequently appears unilateral, capricious, and strategically incoherent."[17] Another commentator described international resentment of the United States, following air strikes on Iraq in December 1998, thus:

> Unable to challenge the United States directly, these states [China, Russia, France] and others are engaged in a poisonous whispering campaign against U.S. leadership. The U.S., they whisper, is unpredictable and trigger-happy. It's a poor global citizen: too unilateral, too violent, not a team player. Who says "no" to global efforts to control greenhouse gases? Who doesn't support, or rather, who opposes the International Criminal Court? Who doesn't pay its U.N. dues while trying to bully the Security Council?[18]

Alongside matters of war and peace, environmental issues consistently take a high profile in public discourse evaluating the credibility of the United States as a global citizen. The Kyoto Protocol is cited especially often in arguments that the United States is missing the mark.[19] First left in limbo by Bill Clinton's halfhearted support and then rejected outright by the Bush administration, the Kyoto Protocol came into force on 16 February 2005; as of December 2006, 166 countries have ratified or agreed to the pact. President George W. Bush announced in 2001 that the United States would withdraw from the Kyoto Protocol, stating: "We will not do anything that harms our economy, because first things first are the people who live in América."[20] According to Derek Heater, the most widely published historian of the idea of world citizenship, "Bush was acting to defend the economic freedom of U.S. citizens in preference to the environmental rights of world citizens."[21]

The lack of any comparable good-faith initiative coming from the U.S. government that would attempt to offset immediately the effects of the emerging global climate crisis and reduce carbon dioxide emissions has prompted many citizens to argue that the United States has awarded priority to its immediate, narrowly defined, and perhaps dangerously shortsighted preferences rather than work toward common goals for humanity and all life on the planet. One letter writer to a British newspaper argued, in the context of the Kyoto Protocol: "What happens when the freedom of American citizens affects the lives of other global citizens? The American reluctance to adhere to the Kyoto agreement so that Yanks have the freedom to drive their gas-guzzling cars when they want and where they want is a prime example."[22] This reference to global citizenship frames a bleak trade-off between the freedom of Americans to choose their preferred way of life, whatever the consequences, and the freedom of the rest of the world to protect the health of the earth itself and safeguard the planet's capability to sustain life.

Within the United States, as well, critics of the environmental policies of the Bush administration have marshaled the idea of global citizenship to make their points. In a June 2004 open letter to George W. Bush from several members of the U.S. Congress (both Democrats and Republicans), the authors argued that the Bush administration's planned weakening of emissions standards for coal-fired and oil-fired power plants would violate the Clean Air Act. The authors also urged for stronger measures to reduce mercury pollution both within the United States and around the world. The letter stated: "We believe that good global citizenship requires us to reduce and eliminate, wherever feasible, our domestic mercury and toxic air emissions for all sources and to cooperate with other countries to reduce this global health threat as soon as possible."[23] As this book moved into production in the spring of 2007, Bush proposed a new round of international negotiations to determine a new framework to replace the Kyoto Protocol when it expires in 2012.

At the same time, others have turned to the idea of global citizenship to convey their approval of actions taken by the U.S. government. One published reference from the Dow Jones financial news service gave credit to the U.S. Federal Reserve for being a good global citizen, in charting economic policy, for its refusal to "allow the world to plunge into recession"[24] during the 1997 Asian financial crisis. The U.S. military has also been credited at times with responsible global citizenship. One published reference in 1998 from the *Economist*, for instance, suggested that for the United Kingdom not to be a global citizen and participate in peacekeeping operations in Bosnia would be to "hitch a free ride from America."[25] When it comes to the question of global citizenship, such strikingly different perspectives on the United States illustrate how one commentator's rogue state can be another's model global citizen.

Global Citizenship and the Invasion of Iraq

Worldwide public debate regarding the United States as a global citizen reached a crescendo in the weeks leading up to the invasion of Iraq in March 2003 and the overthrow of Saddam Hussein's autocratic regime. The demise of the Iraqi dictatorship prompted barely any mourning. However, the single-handed determination on the part of George W. Bush to rush to war without the consent of key allies of the United States and without backing from the United Nations Security Council, the instability surrounding the occupation of Iraq that has prompted civil war and turned the country into a recruitment vehicle for terrorists, and the revelations of torture committed by U.S. soldiers at Saddam Hussein's former Abu Ghraib prison all have contributed to an erosion in public regard for the U.S. government—at home as well as abroad. In the aftermath of the invasion, some policy analysts framed a negative relationship between the Bush administration and global citizenship. As David Reiff of the Council of Foreign Relations wrote in July 2003:

> Here is the pessimists' case: Whatever else it may eventually accomplish, the war in Iraq seems to have put the final nail in the coffin of the dream of global citizenship that began more than half a century ago with the founding of the United Nations. Instead of a world order grounded, however imperfectly, in the idea of collective security, the war has made plain one of the central new realities of the post-9/11 world: The most powerful nation on earth, the United States of America, has decided to turn the international system on its head. . . . To say this is not to demand that people stop dreaming of a better world. Many of us may still aspire to the idea of global citizenship and long for the day when the words "international community" would not be cause for a bitter smile or a sardonic shrug. But it is important to understand how far we are from that day and to act accordingly.[26]

In this passage, Reiff chooses to define global citizenship as dependent on effective global governing institutions to keep the peace. The way the invasion of Iraq came to pass, therefore, left global citizenship all the more elusive. At the same time, though, other definitions of global citizenship with different areas of emphasis allowed for much more optimistic assessments regarding the feasibility of global citizenship in the face of U.S. militarism. Indeed, the protests that took place in approximately eight hundred cities in February 2003, with the most conservative estimates reporting six million participants in all, suggested that a growing symphony of global citizens was emerging as a countervoice, if not a counterweight, to the Bush administration. According to Kumi Naidoo, the leader of CIVICUS, a network of civil society organizations: "Never before has there been such widespread, sustained and truly global citizen mobilisation around an issue. The anti-war protests on 15 February 2003 were the largest issue-based global movement the world has ever seen."[27]

Around the world, critics of the Iraq war often argued that global citizens were on their side, and they tried to persuade their respective national governments to stay out of Iraq. At a protest march in Vancouver, Canada, one week before the invasion began, environmentalist David Suzuki declared: "We are here today as global citizens to show our firm opposition to the Bush administration's high-handed policies of ignoring the dissenting opinions in the U.N. [United Nations]. We urge our government to stay out of this war."[28] In Seoul, South Korea, activists boycotted Coca-Cola soft drinks and McDonald's fast food, while protesters marched in the streets as part of a "day of action of global citizens"[29] and filed petitions in court in an unsuccessful effort to stop the South Korean government from sending troops to join U.S. forces in Iraq. Many Australians critical of the war argued that the Australian government's collaboration with the United States made little sense and undermined Australia's standing as a global citizen. As one letter writer to the *Cairns Post* put it, using the term "global citizen" to describe himself but not his country: "Like a lot of global citizens, I still do not understand the logic of this current conflict. Wasn't Pol Pot a horrid dictator? Wasn't Idi Amin unrelentingly cruel to his people? Where was the United States when a peacekeeping corps was so badly needed in East Timor? It makes no sense to me at all."[30] In England, a critic of the planned invasion argued strongly for removing Saddam Hussein from power—but not through military force:

> The regime there really does need changing. It's evil. Saddam Hussein is a murderer. He kills his own people. As good global citizens we have a responsibility to get rid of him. . . . But not by raining death and destruction on millions of his victims, the people of Iraq. They need saving, not bombing."[31]

Within the United States, some opponents of the Iraq war argued that the United States would compromise its global citizenship if it invaded and occupied Iraq. Joyce Neu, the executive director of the Joan B. Kroc Institute for Peace at the University of San Diego, wrote just days before the invasion in March 2003:

> If we, as the world's strongest power, decide to short-circuit the United Nations and launch a pre-emptive strike on Iraq, we risk sacrificing core values that many of us hold dear. Are we prepared to say that peace is not worth every possible effort, that being a responsible and responsive global citizen is no longer essential, and that ignoring most of the world's populations is in our own national interest?[32]

As an illustration of how the term "global citizen" figured into public debate regarding the invasion of Iraq, we note that Neu's commentary in the *San Diego Tribune* prompted a rebuttal, published the following week, with an entirely different take on the United Nations, the United States, and prospects for global citizenship:

> The United Nations keeps talking and people keep dying and rogue nations keep building. Neu closes with a question about being a global citizen and the importance of giving peace a chance. I think I speak for the majority of the American people when I say that peace has had a chance in Iraq and peace has not been possible with Saddam Hussein at the helm any more than peace was possible with Adolf Hitler.[33]

Seen in this light—and, of course, resting on the assumption that Saddam Hussein was indeed preparing to launch some sort of attack—one could argue that George W. Bush led the way in global citizenship by forcibly removing Hussein from power.

Supporters of the Iraq war tended to follow this line of thinking by arguing that Saddam Hussein would never be a good global citizen and that the bravery of overturning his regime exemplified global citizenship. A Florida investment adviser, in a column sympathetic to Bush and skeptical of the United Nations weapons-inspection process that was cut short before the invasion, noted: "It is entirely possible that Saddam will have had an epiphany and released the true list of everything in his possession and resolved to be a good global citizen in the future, respecting the rights of women and minorities within his span of control. When elephants can fly."[34] A man from England essentially argued in a letter to his newspaper that supporters of the invasion could rightfully claim the upper hand on global citizenship: "Protesters are saying any country that is subject to poverty, slavery, torture or genocide by a dictatorial regime is not our problem, especially if by intervening we become threatened. Does this attitude make us good global citizens or does it make us soft, selfish and—dare I say—gutless?"[35] Likewise, an Australian supporter of the war rejoined critics of the invasion in especially strong terms, suggesting that the antiwar protesters would not defend the Iraqi people against an illegitimate government:

> The same left-wing activists and politicians who have for years begged governments to take a "moral" and "global citizenship" view when it comes to saving trees and fish, refuse to support the Government when it plans to intervene to save the lives of Iraqi people. Saddam has murdered and tortured and destroyed the lives of thousands of people, and unless stopped he will continue to do so, possibly on an even grander scale. I am proud that my country and my Prime Minister have the intestinal fortitude to stand up to dictators, and to stand up to evil. Only by saying "no" to what we know is wrong can the good people of the world hope to live in a peaceful, global community.[36]

Such associations of global citizenship with the moral courage to oust Saddam Hussein generally take for granted the view, much debated to this day, that invading Iraq to remove Saddam Hussein from power was absolutely and immediately necessary in March 2003 to safeguard world peace and global security. By invading and occupying Iraq, was the United States behaving admirably as a global citizen or despicably as an outlaw superpower? Did the invasion and occupation of Iraq represent a huge setback for global citizenship, if the goal of collective security was weakened, or did it illustrate how global citizenship is growing stronger than ever, if it triggered the unprecedented worldwide coordination of a citizen protest movement? On these sorts of questions, history will judge.

George W. Bush, the 2004 Election, and Global Citizenship

The polarizing attributes of George W. Bush and his administration have turned the U.S. presidency as never before into a point of contention concerning global citizenship. Perhaps the biggest change since 2000 in media discourse concerning the United States as a global citizen was an increase in published references that essentially described Bush as a personal barrier that separated the United States, at least temporarily, from good global citizenship. Critics of Bush and his deputies have minced no words in this regard. For example, a resident of Santa Rosa, California, wrote to his local newspaper, critiquing the Bush administration's resistance to the Kyoto Protocol and its chronic unwillingness to respond to concerns about the emerging global climate crisis: "The record of this administration shows the futility of looking there for sane environmental policy. Bush's eyes are wide shut on the need for our nation to behave as responsible global citizens."[37]

As would be expected, numerous media references to global citizenship focused specifically on George W. Bush in the months before the 2004 election. Although neither the Democratic National Party nor Bush's Democratic opponent, John Kerry, used the specific term "global citizenship" as a campaign catchphrase, Kerry's supporters occasionally did. A Green Party activist backing Kerry encouraged her classmates at the University of Minnesota one month before the election thus: "Raise hard questions, demand accountability and be a global citizen. It is not an overstatement to say that the future of our democracy and of our global relationships is at stake. . . . If Bush wins re-election, the world will see this as our endorsement of the Bush doctrine: Preemptive war, prisoner torture, disregard of international law and rejection of international treaties; an endorsement of arrogant, swaggering, cowboy justice."[38] The final sentence of this passage lists a series of practices—all attributed by the writer ultimately to Bush—that essentially are cast in the letter as a shameful repudiation of global citizenship.

Similarly, a resident of Illinois, in a letter to the *Daily Herald*, described Bush as the polar opposite of a good global citizen: "He promised to be a considerate, sensitive global citizen.[39] Instead, he squandered the goodwill of the world following the Sept. 11 terrorist attacks by launching a unilateral assault on another sovereign nation against the wishes of the majority of the world's major governments. He repeatedly has denigrated the world community while demanding their aid in resolving our problems."[40] Once again, practices that suggest the outright abandonment of global citizenship present themselves: "launching a unilateral assault . . . squandered the goodwill of the world . . . denigrated the world community while demanding their aid."

As the 2004 campaign proceeded, widening public recognition of the global impact of U.S. presidential elections worked its way into media references to global citizenship. One American voter—a former infantry solider in the U.S. Army—even linked the idea of a global citizenry with the principle of giving citizens around the world a voice in the election. Originally from Prescott, Arizona, and living in Malaysia in 2004, Eric Ossemig offered his vote to the people of Malaysia, the moderate Muslim country where he had lived for fourteen years. He invited Malaysians to cast their vote on a web page that he had set up, and he promised to cast his ballot, in turn, for the candidate who won. Ossemig told the Voice of America, the international news service run by the U.S. government, that non-Americans ought to be given a voice in deciding the leader of the world's superpower: "The global citizenry does not vote for its global leader. Americans vote for the next global leader, who happens to be the U.S. president."[41] Given the borderless nature of the Internet, it came as no surprise that as news of this gesture spread around the world, hackers at computers in South Carolina and in North Carolina added seven hundred votes for George W. Bush. In the end, Ossemig submitted his absentee ballot for John Kerry—the choice of 60 percent of the 7,876 votes recorded on the website.[42] Ossemig said he had wanted simply to make a symbolic contribution toward opening up U.S. foreign policy to stakeholders around the world:

> The U.S. president's responsibilities were once mostly limited to handling U.S. matters for U.S. citizens. Not anymore. . . . In an era where U.S. policy increasingly affects us all, why is it that only U.S. citizens can vote for a U.S. president who—reluctantly or not—is an increasingly global leader? Shouldn't we all have a say in who our global leader is to be?[43]

After George W. Bush proclaimed victory in November 2004 without a repeat of the Florida standoff that had occurred four years earlier, advocacy for worldwide participation in U.S. elections continued. One commentator from the Philippines wrote:

> Almost every country, every government and every citizen of the planet bet on either George W. Bush or John F. Kerry as though the world's fate depended on the choices to be made by American voters. . . . The global citizen simplified the U.S. elections to a personal security issue: A Kerry win will move the world away from the prevailing hawkish American foreign policy which wreaked havoc in every corner of the globe, while a Bush re-election will nudge the planet closer to World War III. In a shrinking world whose economies and body polities are intricately connected, the U.S. presidential election was not just a decision for American citizens to make. It was very well a collective decision for all non-Americans to make since we will all be affected by how America thinks and behaves.[44]

The prospect of giving citizens of other countries a say in U.S. presidential elections might strike many parochially minded Americans as absurd. Even many of the individuals profiled elsewhere in this book who think of themselves as both Americans and global citizens might not be comfortable with extending the franchise abroad. The hypothetical question was not posed to respondents during interviews—and not a single person interviewed for this study suggested on his or her own that extending voting rights to noncitizens in national elections might amount to a practice of global citizenship. Citizens of the twenty-seven countries belonging to the European Union now enjoy the right to live, work, vote, and run for public office in municipal elections and European Parliament elections in any other member state. However, even the institution of European Union citizenship—which some scholars consider a prototype for an international dimension of citizenship, although it is limited to citizens of the member states—does not confer the right to vote in the national elections of any member country.

In all likelihood, of course, presidents of the United States will continue to be chosen exclusively by United States citizens. Still, the growing public comprehension that American voters, whether they like it or not, are accountable to a global constituency speaks to profound transformations in how citizens around the world are thinking about political membership and obligation as they create new forms of public space for discussion and contestation. Even within the United States, many Americans unhappy with the outcome of the 2004 election seemed to be addressing a global constituency when they posted photos of themselves on a website (sorryeverybody.com) extending apologies to the rest of the world. Launched by a student at the University of Southern California, the website generated such tremendous interest—sixty million hits two weeks after the election—that a second website soon followed: apologiesaccepted.com was for people outside the United States to post photos and messages in response.[45] As long as the United States remains the world's only superpower, its presidential elections will continue to ripple around the planet like no other national election.

Governments and Global Citizenship Agendas

Governing institutions are not only cast in public discourse as global citizens and critiqued in relation to global citizenship. In some cases, governing institutions themselves claim to be proponents and facilitators of global citizenship. One of Japan's regional governments, for example, built a global citizenship complex that promotes international awareness as well as local civic engagement. In the United Kingdom, shortly after the 1997 election of the New Labour government, the Foreign & Commonwealth Office created the Global Citizenship Unit in an effort to promote voluntary codes of conduct for multinational corporations with headquarters in Great Britain. In South Korea, Nobel Peace Prize recipient and former president Kim Dae-Jung made a concerted effort to encourage Koreans to become linguistically and technologically skilled global citizens as the country competes for jobs in a global marketplace. Meanwhile, officials from the United Nations frequently advance the idea of global citizenship in speeches, especially with regard to developments in international law and the impact of transnational advocacy networks. These examples serve to illustrate, once again, how the practices of global citizenship emerge within the boundaries of nation-states—in domestic public space—as well as in the international arena.

Kanagawa Plaza for Global Citizenship

Nestled in a Japanese suburb between the massive modern seaport of Yokohama and the historic ancient capital of Kamakura sits a silver building that from the outside appears to be a hybrid of a traditional Western cathedral and a futuristic spaceship. This is the Kanagawa Plaza for Global Citizenship, a public hall and museum that opened in 1998.[46] The creators of the plaza within the Kanagawa regional government set out to promote international awareness among residents and visitors alike, and to strengthen the region's voice as an international player alongside Japan's national government. The plaza also reflects ideological differences within Japan, having been created by a regional government led by Social Democrats rather than the more conservative Liberal Democratic Party that has dominated Japanese national politics for the past half century. Finally, the creators of the plaza sought to strengthen the desire for world peace and to remind younger generations about the horrors of war experienced by their elders, many of whom remember the devastation of Yokohama during World War II.[47]

During the design stages, the proposed name for the complex was Kanagawa International Plaza for Children and for Peace. In 1992, the regional government changed the name to Kanagawa Plaza for Global Citizenship after a book on globalization, published by the Club of Rome, circulated among several leading Kanagawa officials.[48] The name change triggered some debate, as critics within the Kanagawa government objected that they had not heard of the term "global citizen" and did not understand what it meant. Shigeru Shiono, the coordinator of the project, said during an interview for this study that supporters defended the term by defining a global citizen as: (1) someone directly involved with international political and social causes, typically working with an international nongovernmental organization; and (2) anyone who directly or indirectly supports the activities of such organizations and takes the initiative to learn about global issues. It was mainly the second group of people that Shiono and other proponents of the Kanagawa plaza had in mind as global citizens. The plaza does not put forward any particular definition of a global citizen, and Shiono added that he does not consider it important for visitors to the complex to have a precise or clearly stated meaning of global citizenship drilled into their heads. Rather, Shiono believes that by becoming interested in international affairs, and through awareness and concern about one's personal roles in the world, each visitor can "just naturally grow into a global citizen."[49]

The plaza includes several lecture halls and meeting rooms for conferences and educational programs, along with an additional exhibit, which is geared toward younger children and provides a virtual voyage into other cultures around the world. Programs at the plaza have sought to encourage dialogue between native Japanese residents in Kanagawa Prefecture and the growing community of immigrants and international residents, who commonly hail from China, the Philippines, and Latin America. The plaza, in this respect, is part of a broader effort on the part of the Kanagawa government to bring home global citizenship by encouraging greater interaction among various segments of the local community. In effect, Kanagawa Prefecture is promoting global citizenship by expanding and deepening local public space. In recent years, international residents increasingly have become integrated within community education initiatives, thereby transforming civic life in the region. As Shiono put it: "Because [native] people are growing more aware of the foreign residents as they enter the daily life of our local communities, they will gradually end up becoming the kinds of global citizens that the plaza aims to create." A veteran official of the Kanagawa regional government, Shiono has come to believe that the regional level is increasingly fertile ground for people to become involved both as local citizens and as global citizens.

In renaming the public hall Kanagawa Plaza for Global Citizenship, the regional government broke new ground in Japan by introducing a term not widely used or clearly understood even in English, especially in 1992, the year of the plaza's name change.[50] Although Shiono and his colleagues spent much energy explaining their definition of global citizenship to skeptical Kanagawa assembly members and constituents, in many respects Shiono regards any specific definition of the term as relatively trivial:

> Global citizens and global society are image words for the future. We were taking the responsibility for the public to become aware of global issues by building an institution like this plaza. For the local people, I just want them to accept the term as a word for "coexistence" in the near future. There is no need for special explanations or a specific definition for the local people. This is because once people start sharing their knowledge, they will find the meaning of global citizenship for themselves.

Shiono added that he believes that individuals become global citizens primarily "through the experience of being in human relationships," not through any sort of legal status or notion of allegiance, and that communication at home about issues abroad is the most common way in which he envisions

Kanagawa residents becoming global citizens: "For example, to learn from people from developing countries, such as Malaysia, the important fact that there is the serious problem of deforestation. Even if someone doesn't go there in person, a mother who learns about such facts can pass on the knowledge to her children." In summary, the global citizenship agenda of the Kanagawa regional government aims to foster qualities related to awareness, participation, and cross-cultural empathy among local residents with respect to global issues as well as daily life in their own neighborhoods; to render the next generation of Japanese leaders in tune with responsible positions in addressing global problems; and to promote an active and constructive role in international society for Kanagawa as a region, much in the same way that certain regions within European Union member states have worked to carve out roles for themselves in the international arena.[51]

The United Kingdom Global Citizenship Unit

Following Tony Blair's May 1997 election as prime minister of the United Kingdom, the New Labour government launched two separate initiatives associated with global citizenship—one in foreign policy, the other with regard to launching a national school curriculum in England and Wales (see chapter 5). By all accounts, the two initiatives emerged in isolation from each other. In 1999, the then foreign secretary Robin Cook launched the Global Citizenship Unit as a component of his self-proclaimed ethical foreign policy, meant to encourage British multinational corporations to hold themselves on a voluntary basis to the same ethical standards abroad as they would maintain at home and thereby "ensure that responsible behaviour goes hand-in-hand with competitive advantage."[52]

In contrast with many civil society organizations and educational institutions discussed elsewhere in this book, the Foreign & Commonwealth Office did not craft a definition of global citizenship. Indeed, civil servants in the Foreign Office maintained that creating a precise definition of global citizenship would have added nothing to the unit's objective of encouraging corporations to hold themselves to high ethical standards when operating outside Britain. The head of the unit, Nick Coppin, noted in an interview for this study in December 2000: "I think people are quite happy to have a sort of woolly understanding of what exactly it [global citizenship] involves, because it means that you can bring more things in. If you start to set up definitional limits to what people are doing, then you may find yourself in a circumstance where what you're doing doesn't fall within the definition."

The Global Citizenship Unit did not last long; after Robin Cook left his post as foreign secretary following the 2001 election, it ceased to exist. The unit could claim one lasting accomplishment, though: the completion of a code of conduct for several multinational energy and mining corporations, which had headquarters in both the United Kingdom and the United States and had grappled with allegations of human rights violations involving private security forces in developing countries, especially in Africa. Collaborating with officials from the United States Department of State, the unit convened negotiations between representatives from the corporations and representatives from nongovernmental organizations. During several sessions that were held behind closed doors throughout 2000, mostly in London, the group worked to produce a statement of voluntary principles. The initiative required the rare collaboration of groups with clashing objectives and clashing visions of globally responsible policies, and the participating corporations viewed the process as a way to gain external validation for their internal policies. Nick Coppin said: "People like BP [British Petroleum] have already got fairly comprehensive systems for doing this [monitoring environmental and human rights standards], but they're internal systems; they don't have any sort of external stamp of approval, and they were interested in doing this and getting one."[53] By bringing to the table multinational corporations and international nongovernmental organizations from both sides of the Atlantic that normally might not have joined forces for any purpose, the negotiation of the code of conduct opened up transnational public space for deliberation.

The nonbinding agreement that resulted, a document entitled Voluntary Principles on Security and Human Rights, was unveiled in Washington, D.C., in December 2000. The document called for participating corporations to report any allegations of human rights abuses to the relevant government authorities; the corporations also agreed to monitor and support full investigations into allegations of human rights violations as well as allegations of any inappropriate uses of security equipment. Despite the peripheral role of the term "global citizenship" within the actual negotiations—and the absence of the term from the agreement itself—the Global Citizenship Unit nevertheless provides an example of a concerted effort by a national government to help fill a void in global governance: in the realm of influencing the behavior of multinational corporations, it facilitated a code of conduct mutually acceptable to numerous international actors holding competing agendas and interests.

Republic of Korea
The government of South Korea promoted the idea of global citizenship especially during the late 1990s in the public philosophy of Kim Dae-Jung, who served as president of the Republic of Korea from 1997 to 2003. Winner of

the Nobel Peace Prize in 2000, Kim spent much of his life as a political prisoner and survived relentless persecution from South Korean authoritarian regimes that he opposed. Kim's election as president in 1997 marked the first peaceful transfer of power from a ruling party to an opposition party since the end of World War II and Korea's liberation from thirty-five years of Japanese rule. The placement of the term "global citizenship" on the agenda of Kim's presidency can be traced back to a book entitled *DJnomics: A New Foundation for the Korean Economy*. Written in English and attributed to Kim, the book was published in February 1999 to commemorate the first anniversary of Kim's inauguration. The book includes the following passage:

> As rapid technological progress and globalization continue into the 21st century, the importance of national boundaries is diminishing. To prepare for the new global environment, the people of Korea must not only be required to have the necessary skills, but also become true global citizens by maintaining an open and inquisitive mind toward the world outside. Just as questionable collusion between the government and business is undesirable in today's world, so too are narrow-minded and backward-looking attitudes. We cannot simply resist liberalization and confine ourselves to the domestic market.[54]

This passage serves to link global citizenship not only to an international trade agenda but also to "an open and inquisitive" mind-set among Korean citizens. Moreover, the goal of developing international awareness is linked with economic development objectives. A government manifesto released in June 1999 focused on similar themes:

> The Government of People will utilize market liberalization to actively encourage Korean companies' participation in the international exchange of goods and services. It will also rework national institutions and practices to meet international standards in preparation for the global integration of capital markets. It will encourage the Korean people to become global citizens, helping them acquire an international outlook while retaining their cultural heritage.[55]

Kim continued to articulate this vision in speeches throughout his presidency, which ended in early 2003. In an announcement that schoolteachers with fifteen years of experience would be allowed to take sabbaticals, Kim reportedly urged educators "to foster children in such a way as to make them become global citizens, rather than mere 'frogs in the well.'"[56] Speaking before South Korean soldiers on the forty-ninth anniversary of the outbreak of the Korean War, Kim referred to the new millennium as "an age for global citizens" and urged the soldiers, for the sake of their futures at the end of their mandatory service, to study English and practice speaking what he called "the world language" during their off-duty hours. Across the board in these government statements, emphasis was placed on retaining Korean cultural heritage as well as furthering international awareness and economic competitiveness. In no way was the government of South Korea encouraging the abolition of state authority or national identity. Instead, the South Korean government's perception of diminishing national boundaries has led political leaders to advocate global citizenship, especially in terms of achievement and awareness, *within* the country's boundaries.

United Nations

One need only examine some of the key phrases in the preamble to the United Nations Charter, which was written in 1945, to see that the ideals of the United Nations evoke an aspiration of global citizenship: "dignity and worth of the human person," "better standards of life in larger freedom," "live together in peace with one another as good neighbours," "unite our strength," "combine our efforts."[57] Moreover, the 1948 Universal Declaration of Human Rights affirmed a broad array of rights to all human beings, including the right to citizenship within one's country of origin. And yet, the United Nations, with its constituent units of national governments, avoids any characterization of itself as an institution of global citizenship in any literal sense of the word. Instead, as articulated in numerous speeches from former secretary-general Kofi Annan, who completed his ten years in office in December 2006, the leadership of the United Nations instead has associated global citizenship mainly with voluntary endeavors of individuals, countries as international actors, and campaigns by transnational advocacy groups. A typical example can be found in the following reference to global citizenship in a speech given by Annan in November 1998:

> We are nearing the end of a tumultuous century that has witnessed both the best and worst of human endeavour. The challenges we face grow ever more complex. But, like it or not, modern communications mean that we are connected, inextricably and irrevocably. Those connections have helped give birth to a new phenomenon—an emerging sense of global citizenship and responsibility. We saw it at work in the movement that spurred governments to negotiate the treaty banning anti-personnel landmines last year, and the Statute of the International Criminal Court this year.[58]

Kofi Annan's speeches often have associated global citizenship with "people power" channeled through civil society organizations.[59] Such references to global citizenship often have tried to convey that the United Nations has become receptive to collaboration with nongovernmental organizations, which some transnational activists say was not the case in previous decades. In an interview for this study, one of the secretary-general's speechwriters, Richard Amdur, emphasized that the United Nations has no definition of global citizenship, although the term appears synonymous, at times, with global responsibility and global community:

> The term is very loose; there are many interchangeable expressions that sort of mean the same thing. It's just one of those terms/ideas whose time seems to have arrived, and therefore it's out there, floating, to be plucked when it seems right. I'm not sure any single person could lay claim to having introduced it.

Indeed, numerous speeches and statements released by top officials at the United Nations in recent years serve to illustrate how the United Nations has projected multiple meanings of global citizenship into public discourse. For example, a program officer for United Nations Volunteers, which sends adults to developing countries around the world, noted at a conference in Portugal in 1998 that "by shaping the world in which they [program participants] lived, they were also shaping their own character as global citizens."[60] Meanwhile, former UNESCO director-general Federico Mayor noted during a trip to Africa in 1999 that "we must share better all that we have in providing learning and the skills required by all citizens to cope with changing times. . . . The issue is how to provide each man and each woman the capacity to become a global citizen."[61] Furthermore, one of the more frequently quoted phrases from the 1999 *United Nations Human Development Report* appeared alongside a pie chart dramatically illustrating how Internet users are overwhelmingly concentrated in wealthy Western countries. Pointing out that the miracles of digital technology and mobile communications remain inaccessible to the vast majority of the global population, thus restricting the "global information society" to the relatively rich, the report noted with irony: "The market alone will make global citizens only of those who can afford it. Fulfilling the potential for global communications for development demands relentless effort in reaching out to extend and enhance the loop."[62]

These three references from the United Nations present contrasting images of global citizenship—volunteers who are caring and engaging, individuals born in impoverished surroundings who develop the capacity to escape poverty and thrive, and affluent individuals as well as multinational corporations that might claim rights and privileges related to global citizenship but do not necessarily take on corresponding responsibilities. All three of these images share one crucial common theme by portraying global citizenship as a quest for strengthening transnational public space largely within the associational arenas of civil society rather than the coercive ties of governing institutions. The United Nations has employed the idea of global citizenship to promote the first two of these images and to motivate international actors to improve living conditions and expand educational and economic opportunities for the world's least advantaged citizens. Contrary to frequent insinuations by skeptics of the United Nations, the use of the term "global citizenship" within the United Nations does not at all correspond with an agenda for world government. Richard Amdur noted: "What the U.N. works for is to have effective governments everywhere, not one single effective government from top down." Instead, the term "global citizenship," as invoked by the United Nations, aims to inspire national governments to reconcile their particular interests with consideration for common interests that reach across an interdependent world.

Conclusion

The examples of governing institutions presented in this chapter demonstrate how the primary and secondary concepts that speak to the practices of global citizenship are often employed in hopes of strengthening public space within nation-states as well as beyond them. In the United Nations, the term "global citizenship" is frequently placed into reports and speeches encouraging mobilization among nongovernmental organizations and national governments; in this regard, global citizenship as participation is paramount. In the United Kingdom Foreign & Commonwealth Office, the term operated in the background within an initiative promoting global corporate social responsibility on a voluntary basis. In South Korea, the term came to symbolize economic competitiveness in harmony with norms of democratic accountability and the rule of law; here global citizenship as achievement takes on a relatively high profile. Finally, in Kanagawa Prefecture, the term came to symbolize international awareness, cross-cultural empathy, and participation in community organizations.

The ways in which many nation-states are now depicted in the media as global citizens underscore how national governments are increasingly regarded as accountable to constituencies beyond their borders. This is not to say that the idea of global citizenship is an easy sell in the rough-and-tumble of national politics. Nowhere has any political party within any constitutional democracy ever run a national election campaign on a platform of global citizenship. The first presidential campaign with "A choice for global citizenship" as its slogan has yet to make history. Even political leaders who call for their national governments to be responsible global citizens tend to avoid the term on the campaign trail.

When Meg Lees served as party leader of the Australian Democrats, for example, she repeatedly appealed to the idea of global citizenship in public statements urging the government to ratify the Kyoto Protocol and reduce greenhouse gas emissions.[63] When asked during an interview for this study, however, if she would use "global citizen" during an election campaign or as any part of a strategy to build support among Australian voters, Lees responded with caution. She noted that "people do tend to look at their own backyards, particularly at election time," and that it would be all too easy for One Nation, a hard-line nationalist, anti-immigrant party in Australia, to seize on any mention of global citizenship by a competitor as evidence that the rival political party was neglecting Australian interests. Lees observed:

> It's a term that best would be described as selectively used, because it's so easy to misinterpret—not being Australian, or being more un-Australian or anti-Australian or whatever, rather than thinking globally. . . . It would be very easy during an election campaign to basically imply that by looking globally, you are not thinking nationally; you are not thinking about your own people; you're worrying too much about others; and it takes more than a thirty-second grab, frequently, to explain what you mean. . . . And so, during an election campaign, I think it would be something that would be deliberately misinterpreted by one's opponents.[64]

For any presidential hopefuls, party leaders or political consultants around the world who might consider the practices of global citizenship compelling enough to shout from the rooftops in a national campaign, these are sobering words.

Especially in the United States, there is a paradox: perhaps more so than anywhere else in the world, schools, colleges, universities, corporations, and voluntary organizations have gravitated to the idea of global citizenship. This should come as no surprise, as the U.S. Declaration of Independence in 1776 etched into the American creed much of the logic of global citizenship, if not the exact term, by championing the "unalienable rights" of "life, liberty and the pursuit of happiness" for all human beings, as well as the principle that each separate nation or people owes "a decent respect to the opinions of mankind."[65] In his 1961 presidential inaugural address outlining an imperative to "assure the survival and the success of liberty" around the globe, John F. Kennedy projected a vision of leadership and accountability to an emerging global public when he declared: "My fellow citizens of the world: ask not what America will do for you, but what together we can do for the freedom of man."[66] However, in the current American political climate, the idea of global citizenship is nearly invisible—and it is likely that any American presidential candidate or political party taking up the mantle of global citizenship would be vulnerable to blistering ideological attacks. One pundit in Washington, D.C., for instance, recently dismissed global citizenship as "liberal-speak for 'take more money from American taxpayers and ship it overseas in some planetary welfare program.'"[67]

The ease with which a term such as "global citizenship" can be caricatured and "deliberately misinterpreted" to smear a political contender is obvious. And yet, the ways in which nation-states are cast regularly as global citizens in contemporary public discourse do not discount the power of national governments but rather accentuate their impact as international actors. In this regard, the idea of global citizenship operates across competing schools of thought in the field of international relations. Global citizenship is by no means anchored to the idea of a universal, worldwide political community in which nation-states might find themselves submerged and subordinated. Rather, global citizenship can also be aligned with the "society-of-states" tradition of international relations envisaged by Hugo Grotius in the seventeenth century and reinvigorated in the late twentieth century in Hedley Bull's idea of the "anarchical society," with "neither complete conflict of interest between states nor complete identity of interest."[68]

Nation-states can be regarded as analogous to individual citizens operating in a partially formed, hazily defined, far from truly integrated international community. However, the kind of community that is emerging at the dawn of the twenty-first century, as illustrated in the preceding four chapters, is a more interconnected phenomenon than a society of states. No longer are national governments necessarily the dominant collective actors in a global public sphere. By taking on board the idea of global citizenship—and often launching initiatives around the world in association with this idea—multinational corporations, educational institutions, and voluntary organizations have projected themselves more deeply into world affairs alongside nation-states. We are now awakening to a global community in which actors in the arenas of government, business, education, and civil society will continue to build partnerships and strengthen networks of collaboration across borders. Global citizenship, then, now serves as a touchstone for growing numbers of individuals and organizations striving to enrich their immediate communities as well as the wider world.

Conclusion

The idea of global citizenship is rich, complex, and tangible. Throughout this book, we have seen how everyday people, at least within certain segments of the population, now find "global citizen" an appealing and meaningful way to frame their senses of membership, participation, and responsibility in political, social, cultural, and economic spheres. We also have seen how many organizations now use "global citizenship" deliberately, not haphazardly, as a principle to describe their activities and design programs and strategies. The legal institution of national citizenship might well remain in the hands of nation-states, and most of the world's population, including many self-described global citizens, might well continue to think of themselves as grounded mainly within their immediate political communities. Nevertheless, global citizenship continues to gain momentum. As this book has shown, global citizenship has become much more than an abstract and seemingly elusive ideal, espoused mainly by intellectuals and visionaries, and now takes on considerable significance in our world. The myriad practices of global citizenship demonstrate how the idea of citizenship itself is changing and evolving.

In the present day, global citizenship is an especially rich idea because it now signifies new ways of thinking about political action and belonging. Rather than simply transposing familiar models of domestic citizenship to the world as a whole, global citizenship often encompasses multiple meanings that vary depending on one's circumstances and view of the world and can shift throughout the course of one's life. The formative experiences of self-regarding global citizens are telling. For many individuals, as illustrated in chapter 1, global citizenship traces back to close family ties as well as the spirit of community and solidarity in one's immediate neighborhood. An American woman born in western Europe and cared for as a baby by a German-speaking nanny went on to run a language institute and develop a mission for the program to promote responsible global citizenship among young people.[1] A man from Brooklyn who formed close ties with his Irish relatives as a youngster went on to become a long-term benefactor for a village in Malawi.[2] A woman who read and dreamed as a child about kangaroos in the Australian outback went on to start an exchange program between nurses in the United States and Australia.[3] Other individuals who were interviewed for this study traced the roots of their global citizenship to the local immigrant subcultures in which they grew up: German Canadian, Chinese Filipino, Irish American, Hungarian English. Such childhood ties to family and neighborhood led several respondents toward international careers and outlooks as adults.

The meaning of global citizenship is found, for many individuals, not in international political campaigns or global governing institutions, but in face-to-face interaction among cultures in everyday life. Political activism in international causes is commonly preceded by community involvement in cities and towns, while many of the world's most internationally mobile citizens think about global citizenship mainly in terms of engagement within the local communities in which they reside overseas. Moreover, global citizenship often amounts to a state of mind, rather than any sort of reflection on the current realities of politics and government, and as a continual process of personal growth and awareness. The intertwined concepts of awareness, responsibility, and participation, as articulated in detail in chapter 2, together provide a vivid representation of the multiple personal qualities to which global citizens aspire, among them: being comfortable in the "universe" of one's own skin while navigating different settings; understanding how important issues are interconnected; erasing distinctions between "us" and "them," or insiders and outsiders; refusing to believe that one has a restricted, finite personal identity; thinking of oneself as a stakeholder, even a steward, in protecting the earth and its natural resources; thinking of proximity to others and to global problems as not defined or constrained by geographical boundaries.

To be sure, the abundant ways of interpreting and practicing global citizenship bring some dissonance, as well. As shown in chapters 3 and 6, some individuals and organizations, especially businesses marketing services to wealthy individuals, think about global citizenship not in terms of collective responsibility or communal solidarity that extends across humanity but rather in terms of individual privilege, even narcissism. Some associate the idea of global citizenship mainly with goals of accessing markets, consuming luxury products, or simply moving freely around the world—even if it means, at times, essentially "disowning" one's country of origin for the sake of maximizing one's financial assets. Even when looking beyond those who think about global citizenship mainly from the vantage points of the wealthiest segments of the world's population, a prominent strain of global citizenship discourse emphasizes success in the global marketplace. This is also the case among some civil society organizations and educational institutions, as shown in chapters 4 and 5. Some schools, universities, and service organizations link the idea of global citizenship to goals of promoting economic self-sufficiency within communities as well as furthering intellectual and professional accomplishments in the next generation.

Educational programs that seek to foster in youngsters the qualities of global citizens provide an especially vivid portrait of the many facets of global citizenship discourse. Global citizenship can be as basic and immediate as helping youngsters understand the earth around them, as in the case of Prairie Crossing Charter School (chapter 5). Some educational initiatives promoting global citizenship place emphasis primarily on academic achievement—especially with regard to developing analytical and communication skills—while other educational programs encourage cross-cultural dialogue and empathy, whether through finding pen pals abroad for elementary school children, organizing campus discussions on divisive issues, or facilitating overseas immersion experiences. As noted by some of the educators quoted in chapter 5, mutual respect and the appreciation of differences—not merely tolerance—serve as primary goals to be attained, along with viewing the idea of global citizenship as an "inner nobility" to be nurtured within hearts and minds. Confronting one's own beliefs and values and discovering—as articulated by the dean of Soka University of America—that one has become alienated from one's initial assumptions and preconceptions certainly illustrates how global citizenship is envisioned as a transformative principle in the lives of individuals, regardless of the extent to which political relationships and government institutions have evolved around the world.

Still other approaches to global citizenship have been introduced by corporations that have employed the term with respect to philanthropic community initiatives and, most of all, in framing voluntary codes of conduct that speak to a growing sense of public accountability. As discussed in chapter 6, corporate global citizenship is motivated ultimately by aims of opening markets, increasing profits (or at least maintaining them), and offsetting calls for greater government regulation of business in the global economy, thereby reiterating how some versions of global citizenship are highly pragmatic. Growing public recognition that it is desirable to attempt to mediate forces of national self-interest with aspirations for a global common good also has inspired some governing institutions—as well as many commentators—to invoke the idea of global citizenship in foreign policy discussions. Moreover, the term "global citizenship" in media discourse is occasionally employed now as a lever to evaluate the policies and behaviors of national governments, thereby holding nation-states accountable as ethical and collaborative actors within an international society, if not a community of humankind. As documented in chapter 7, some governing institutions also have taken on board the idea of global citizenship, often to articulate goals for their own citizens to pursue—such as being open and inquisitive toward the outside world, becoming proficient in language and technological skills that will help strengthen economic competitiveness, participating in nongovernmental organizations, and being ethical actors within the world economy.

With such a profusion of ideas under the umbrella of global citizenship, the complexities within this discourse come as no surprise. Indeed, in the minds of many individuals who contributed to this study by sharing their insights, to live as a global citizen is to recognize the growing complexity of the world. In some schools that have promoted global citizenship, the term itself is linked intentionally to ambiguity—as in the case of Eugene International High School, which emphasizes that gaining additional information about difficult moral dilemmas does not always ease the way to clear resolution, and that multiple and sometimes incompatible perspectives often sit together uneasily on contentious political issues. What is more, some self-described global citizens have gravitated to the label at least partly out of ambivalence toward their own personal identity in relation to their countries of origin. On the other hand, these individuals were a small minority of the interview respondents. For the most part, self-described global citizens seem to view the term as complementary to their national citizenship and not at all in conflict with their senses of national allegiance or patriotism, especially if this patriotism stems from principles as well as sentiment and solidarity. Just as one respondent noted how global citizenship for her meant "tradition, family, and landscape,"[4] many people who consider themselves global citizens are anchored deeply within their home countries and especially within their local communities. As Kwame Anthony Appiah once elaborated on the idea of rooted cosmopolitanism: "We cosmopolitans *can* be patriots, loving our homeland (not only the states where we were born but the states where we grew up and where we live). Our loyalty to humankind—so vast, so abstract, a unity—does not deprive us of the capacity to care for people closer by; the notion of global citizenship can have a real and practical meaning."[5]

The practices of global citizenship often thrive within the most immediate of public spaces, especially if global citizenship for many individuals means self-awareness, principled decision making, and engagement across cultures. In addition, some activists choose to think of global citizenship as a verb, rather than a noun—as an everlasting quest for goals such as world peace, social justice, poverty eradication, and environmental sustainability. While in some respects global citizenship thrives within multiple, cross-cutting public spaces, in other respects global citizenship amounts to an ongoing quest to build public spaces on an international scale for contestation, deliberation, and problem solving. Indeed, the end goal of global citizenship varies considerably from person to person, depending on which concerns and issues are most important to each self-described global citizen. Sometimes the term "global citizenship" is tied very closely to ideals of civic engagement and moral obligation to humanity, sometimes not. Some individuals associate global citizenship with advocacy for stronger channels of international collaboration, while other individuals equate global citizenship with defending small and distinctive villages, cities, and nations against forces of centralization and uniformity. The competing perspectives presented throughout this book invite further debate as to which understandings of global citizenship might be more valid than others.

The richness and complexity of global citizenship discourse make one thing clear: Global citizenship has become a practical, tangible idea. No longer is global citizenship consigned largely to the ivory towers of academia; on the contrary, global citizenship gives meaningful expression to the daily lives of countless individuals around the world. The vast majority of today's self-described global citizens do not think of citizenship mainly as a sorting mechanism separating members of a nation-state from outsiders. With a few exceptions, the self-described global citizens are not starry-eyed dreamers of a singular overarching world government—not even those who are fighting for more effectiveness or greater democratic accountability within international institutions. Nor do these individuals generally believe that sustained democratic participation is necessarily limited to a small political community. Instead, for many of the interview respondents quoted in this study, embracing global citizenship depends at least in part on thinking about citizenship as far more malleable in nature, and contingent on the lives and decisions of individuals as well as the agendas of organizations, than more conventional definitions of citizenship that are firmly anchored in statehood or nationality would seem to allow. Global citizenship in nonacademic discourse, then, amounts to a fundamentally different phenomenon than simply projecting the more familiar model of national citizenship into the international arena.

Global citizenship, in the minds of the vast majority of the interview respondents, did not trace back to understandings of national citizenship that revolve primarily around formal membership rights and compulsory duties, though many self-described global citizens were strong advocates of universal human rights. Nor did the concept generally amount to a worldwide extrapolation of national allegiances, though in many cases self-described global citizens and advocates of global citizenship did articulate senses of moral responsibility and common loyalty toward all humanity. Even among the set of those self-identifying global citizens who were active in transnational advocacy groups concerned with global problems—such as the management of international trade, the eradication of world hunger and disease, the protection of the environment, the reduction or elimination of nuclear weapons, and so forth—none claimed to be global citizens in the same sorts of ways in which citizens normally are required to contribute to their respective countries, such as voting, paying taxes, serving on juries, or joining the military.

The thoughts and activities of numerous interview respondents do converge, however, with ancient and enduring civic ideals that champion active and responsible participation in a political community. Many individuals now seem to regard themselves as members of a formative global community as well as of their local, regional, and national communities; many have joined political or social movements or formed professional and personal relationships that leave them feeling as if they belong to the world as a whole. However, they tend to think that global citizenship can be cultivated gradually through education and life's experiences and need not be conferred by any government or legal authority. Whatever pathways they might follow in their lives or whatever agendas their respective organizations might pursue, they believe that they are free to adopt global citizenship for themselves, simply by virtue of inhabiting this earth, and build on this citizenship throughout the courses of their lives. What we see in today's manifold understandings of global citizenship, then, provides new articulations and practices of the more general idea of citizenship in ways that reflect the realities of our interdependent and interconnected world.

Notes

Introduction

1. Charles Jones has defined cosmopolitanism thus: "The fundamental idea is that each person affected by an institutional arrangement should be given equal consideration. Individuals are the basic units of moral concern, and the interests of individuals should be taken into account by the adoption of an impartial standpoint for evaluation." See Charles Jones, *Global Justice: Defending Cosmopolitanism* (Oxford: Oxford University Press, 1999), 15. Kwame Anthony Appiah has helpfully articulated that "the one thought that cosmopolitans share is that no local loyalty can ever justify forgetting that each human being has responsibilities to every other." See Kwame Anthony Appiah, *Cosmopolitanism: Ethics in a World of Strangers* (New York: W. W. Norton, 2006), xvi. Joshua Cohen has provided another helpful definition, noting that according to cosmopolitanism, "our highest allegiance must be to the community of humankind, and the first principles of our practical thought must respect the equal worth of all members of that community." See Joshua Cohen, "Editor's Preface," in *For Love of Country: Debating the Limits of Patriotism*, ed. Cohen (Boston: Beacon Press, 1996), vii. Although the essays in it now date back more than a decade, *For Love of Country: Debating the Limits of Patriotism* remains the most accessible volume containing a variety of perspectives on global citizenship by North American scholars. Centering on an essay by moral philosopher Martha Nussbaum arguing that one's strongest allegiances should be directed toward humanity at large—an essay followed by numerous brief critiques and rejoinders—the book treats the terms "world citizenship" and "global citizenship" and the idea of cosmopolitanism as interchangeable, even though this is not always the case in the contemporary literature. For a recent contribution that differentiates between an idealistic

form of "world citizenship" and a more pragmatic and practical version of "global citizenship" in an interdependent world, see Darren J. O'Byrne, *The Dimensions of Global Citizenship: Political Identity beyond the Nation-State* (London: Frank Cass, 2003).

2. Brian Barry, for one, has stressed that although "a cosmopolitan is, by definition, a citizen of the world," cosmopolitanism, in his view, is "a moral outlook, not an institutional prescription." See Brian Barry, "Statism and Nationalism: A Cosmopolitan Critique," in *Global Justice* (Nomos XLI), ed. Ian Shapiro and Lea Brilmayer (New York: New York University Press, 1999), 35. Similarly, Charles Beitz has insisted that cosmopolitan liberalism "is not a view about the best institutional structure for international politics," nor, in his view, is cosmopolitanism about "how persons should understand their individual identities and loyalties." Rather, Beitz has framed cosmopolitan liberalism as a moral doctrine that aims to identify principles for existing governing institutions, at all levels, that account for all human persons rather than all members of a particular country or society. See Charles R. Beitz, "Social and Cosmopolitan Liberalism," *International Affairs* 75, no. 3 (1999): 519.

3. In recent years, a competing, pluralistic strain of cosmopolitan thinking has downgraded ethical universalism, especially as articulated by Immanuel Kant, to "a contestable act of faith" and instead emphasizes "rooted cosmopolitanism," which, as Mitchell Cohen has coined the term, "accepts a multiplicity of roots and branches and which rests on the legitimacy of plural loyalties, of standing in many circles, but with common ground." See Mitchell Cohen, "Rooted Cosmopolitanism," *Dissent* (Autumn 1992): 478–83. Even a longtime advocate of world citizenship such as Derek Heater recently has taken a turn toward endorsing a comparatively "rooted" approach to cosmopolitanism, arguing that ideals of universal human rights and moral obligation need to be translated into "terms relevant to the present and future world's peoples, who are of diverse religions, or none, and who, for the most part, are limited in their mental horizons to their local and national cultures, sanctified by long generations of loyalty." See Derek Heater, "Does Cosmopolitan Thinking Have a Future?" *Review of International Studies* 26 (2000): 186. On the other hand, James Clifford worries that such translation efforts will prove "unmanageable" and yield nothing more than confusion: "The term cosmopolitan, separated from its European universalist moorings, quickly becomes a traveling signifier, a term always in danger of breaking up into partial equivalences: exile, immigration, migrancy, diaspora, border crossing, pilgrimage, tourism." See James Clifford, "Mixed Feelings," in *Cosmopolitics: Thinking and Feeling beyond the Nation*, ed. Pheng Cheah and Bruce Robbins, (Minneapolis: University of Minnesota Press, 1998), 63.

4. For good accounts of cosmopolitan ideas throughout history, see Derek Heater, *World Citizenship and Government: Cosmopolitan Ideas in the History of Western Political Thought* (New York: St. Martin's Press, 1996) as well as April Carter, *The Political Theory of Global Citizenship* (London: Routledge, 2001).

5. For the sake of brevity, this book frequently uses "national citizenship" as shorthand for citizenship as full legal standing or membership within a state or a nation-state, as well as citizenship as allegiance and loyalty to a domestic political community held together in part by national ties, whether largely civic, cultural, or ethnic in nature. The usage of these terms is not at all intended to conflate the various conceptions of statehood and nationality. As Christian Joppke has outlined the conceptual terrain, the nation-state is a dual concept, with the modern state going back to the Peace of Westphalia, and nationalism tracing back to Protestantism, the Enlightenment, and "the rise of vernaculars," with both concepts of nation and state fused in the French Revolution: "*Qua* states, nation-states are territorial organizations characterized by the monopolization of legitimate violence; *qua* nations, nation-states are membership associations with a collective identity and a democratic pretension to rule." See Christian Joppke, "Immigration Challenges the Nation-State," in *Challenge to the Nation-State: Immigration in Western Europe and the United States*, ed. Christian Joppke (Oxford: Oxford University Press, 1998), 8.

6. See David Miller, "Bounded Citizenship," in *Cosmopolitan Citizenship*, ed. Kimberly Hutchings and Roland Dannreuther (London: Macmillan, 1999), 60–80; Will Kymlicka, *Politics in the Vernacular: Nationalism, Multiculturalism and Citizenship* (Oxford: Oxford University Press, 2001), 317–26. For a good case in favor of global citizenship, see David Held, "The Transformation of Political Community: Rethinking Democracy in the Context of Globalization," in *Democracy's Edges*, ed. Ian Shapiro and Casiano Hacker-Cordón (Cambridge: Cambridge University Press), 84–111. For a good reply to Miller, see Daniel Weinstock, "Prospects for Transnational Citizenship and Democracy," *Ethics and International Affairs* 15, no. 2 (2001) 53–66.

7. Aleš Debeljak, *The Hidden Handshake: National Identity and Europe in the Post-Communist World* (Lanham, MD: Rowman & Littlefield, 2004), ix.

8. Some of the people interviewed for this study expressed misgivings about this phrase. In the words of an information technology consultant from California who has worked to expand Internet access in developing countries: "I think people misinterpret it to just think locally, act locally, and I think that thinking globally and acting locally doesn't really work either. . . . I think it creates an opportunity for people to not get themselves out of their box." (Janine Firpo, interview with the author, San Francisco, 16 November 2000.)

9. One helpfully concise definition comes from Robert Keohane, who frames globalization as the increasing volume and speed of flows of capital and goods, information and ideas, and people and forces that connect actors between countries. See Robert O. Keohane, *Power and Governance in a Partially Globalized World* (London: Routledge, 2002) 194. David Held and his colleagues have offered a sweeping definition of globalization as "a process (or set of processes) which embodies a transformation in the spatial organization of social relations and transactions—assessed in terms of their extensity, intensity, velocity and impact—generating transcontinental or interregional flows and networks of activity, interaction, and the exercise of power." See David

Held, Anthony McGrew, David Goldblatt, and Jonathan Perraton, *Global Transformations: Politics, Economics and Culture* (Cambridge: Polity Press, 1999), 16. Further definitions of "global" and "globalization" are noted in chapter 2 of this book.

10. In many respects, the individuals whose insights are shared in this book resemble what Bhikhu Parekh has labeled "globally oriented" citizens, whom Parekh differentiates from citizens of a world polity: "A globally oriented citizen has a valued home of his own, from which he reaches out to and forms different kinds of alliances with others having homes of their own. Globally oriented citizenship recognises both the reality and the value of political communities, not necessarily in their current form but at least in some suitably revised form." See Bhikhu Parekh, "Cosmopolitanism and Global Citizenship," *Review of International Studies* 29, no. 1 (2003): 12.

11. Pippa Norris has provided a helpful analysis, in this regard, of data in the World Values Survey, which repeatedly has asked people in seventy countries the following survey question: "Which of these geographical groups would you say you belong to first of all?" Respondents were given five answer choices: their city or town, their state or region, their country, their continent, or the world as a whole; they also were given the option to specify a second choice. The overwhelming majority of respondents identified mainly with domestic political communities. The proportion of respondents identifying primarily with their continent or with the world came to 15 percent. Just 2 percent of all respondents identified themselves exclusively with their continent or the world, with no secondary territory in mind. See Pippa Norris, "Global Governance and Cosmopolitan Citizens," in *Governance in a Globalizing World*, ed. Joseph S. Nye Jr. and John D. Donahue (Washington, DC: Brookings Institution Press, 2000), 161–62.

12. As Judith Shklar famously observed: "There is no notion more central in politics than citizenship, and none more variable in history, or contested in theory." See Judith Shklar, *American Citizenship: The Quest for Inclusion* (Cambridge, MA: Harvard University Press, 1991), 1. Among the fault lines in competing theoretical interpretations of citizenship are: passive legal status versus active practices and habits; formal membership versus voluntary participation; and the rights of the individual versus the good of the community.

13. My original database, which I first assembled in the year 2000 by searching electronic archives of news sources, included more than five hundred documents published from late 1997 until the end of 1999. In the year 2000, I obtained documents using *Westlaw All News Plus*; more recently, to update the database, I have used *Factiva*. The database now contains more than four thousand documents awaiting further study.

14. To appreciate how the idea of global citizenship has gained momentum, consider that the usage of "global citizenship" and its cognates in media references from 1991 to 2000 increased by 335 percent relative to the corresponding increase in the usage of "citizenship." In contrast, other keywords evocative of an international dimension of citizenship—world citizenship, international citizenship, earth citizenship, and planetary citizenship—barely increased in usage relative to "citizenship" during the 1990s.

15. Most of the 157 interviews were conducted by telephone from March 2000 to August 2001, a period that followed the massive protests in Seattle outside the World Trade Organization meeting in November 1999 and preceded the terrorist attacks of September 11, 2001. To update my findings as I prepared this book, I contacted the respondents again during 2004 and 2005 and completed thirty additional interviews with new respondents. Of course, many of the respondents have moved, graduated, retired, or changed positions since their interviews. I have tried to note these changes whenever this information is relevant.

16. Nevertheless, the phenomenon of reactivity—how values and objectives of the researcher influence the procedures and conclusions of any qualitative study— was inescapable. As Joseph Maxwell has written: "What the informant says is always a function of the interviewer and the interview situation. Although there are some things you can do to prevent the undesirable consequences of this, such as avoiding leading questions, trying to minimize your effect is not a meaningful goal for qualitative research . . . what is important is to understand how you are influencing what the informant says, and how this affects the validity of the inferences you can draw from the interview." See Joseph A. Maxwell, *Qualitative Research Design: An Interactive Approach* (London: Sage, 1996), 91.

17. The interviews were transcribed word for word and compiled into a second database in which computer software was used to classify and arrange countless small passages of text into thematically and conceptually relevant categories. For a good explanation of the origins of the software and its rationale, see Lyn Richards and Tom Richards, "From Filing Cabinet to Computer," in *Analyzing Qualitative Data*, ed. Alan Bryman and Robert G. Burgess (London: Routledge, 1994).

Chapter 1

1. Indeed, discussion about "world citizenship" in the period following World War II basically revolved around the world federalist movement and advocacy of world government institutions, and this discussion waned after the onset of the Cold War weakened the United Nations almost immediately after the organization's founding.

2. Don Will, interview with author, Orange, CA, 15 September 2000. Another university educator and advocate of global citizenship also credited a communal housing environment—housing for married graduate students and their families—for turning his children into "the most color-blind kids I know." Eric Hauber, interview with author, Aliso Viejo, CA, 6 April 2000.

3. Nelly Ukpokodu, interview with author, Kansas City, MO, 14 September 2000.

4. Janet Sipple, interview with author, Bethlehem, PA, 14 April 2000.

5. Rosie Brown, interview with author, Tulsa, OK, 21 June 2000.

6. Christian Eckart, interview with author, New York, 9 May 2001.

7. Washington SyCip, interview with author, 21 September 2000.

8. Michael Szabo, interview with author, Cambridge, UK, 23 November 2000.

9. Robert Harper, interview with author, Mattituck, NY, 26 September 2000.

10. Hazel Henderson, interview with author, St. Augustine, FL, 8 July 2000.

11. Maude Barlow, interview with author, Ottawa, 19 April 2000.

12. Pat Montandon, interview with author, San Francisco, 3 October 2000.

13. Brown, interview.

14. Jean-Jacques Rousseau, *Émile*, trans. Allan Bloom (New York: Basic Books, 1979), 38.

15. For instance, Janet Sipple (profiled earlier in this chapter) recalled that her boisterous personality as a youngster prompted an elementary school teacher to grade her citizenship as unsatisfactory! Little did Sipple know that fifty years later, she would be honored with a "global citizen" award by the Pennsylvania State Nurses Association.

16. This state of affairs is beginning to change with the next generation. As illustrated in chapter 5, educational programs related to global citizenship have become increasingly common at schools, colleges, and universities.

17. Sarah Willcox, interview with author, Dallas, 14 September 2000.

18. Laura Seay, interview with author, New Haven, CT, 27 September 2000.

19. Blake Burleson, quoted in "African Studies Prove Valuable for Baylor U. Students," *U-Wire*, 19 January 1999.

20. Nava Swersky Sofer, interview with author, Tel Aviv, Israel, 10 October 2000.

21. Imogen Mkhize, interview with author, Johannesburg, 6 August 2000.

22. Al Dizon, e-mail correspondence with author, Singapore, 11 October 2000.

23. Francis Woong-il Lee, commencement speech delivered at Roanoke College, Salem, VA, 2 May 1998.

24. Robin Madell, "Pharma Stars—Women in the Industry," *Pharmaceutical Executive*, 1 June 1999.

25. Cynthia Hogan, interview with author, East Hanover, NJ, 2 October 2000.

26. Miles Colebrook, interview with author, London, 26 July 2000.

27. Benjamin R. Barber, "Constitutional Faith," in *For Love of Country: Debating the Limits of Patriotism*, ed. Joshua Cohen (Boston: Beacon Press, 1996), 34.

28. Elsewhere, I have explored how two overarching discourses, a civic republican discourse and a libertarian discourse, are especially prominent within the idea of global citizenship. See Hans Schattle, "Communicating Global Citizenship: Multiple Discourses beyond the Academy," *Citizenship Studies* 9, no. 2 (2005): 119–33.

29. "CivWorld Citizens Campaign for Democracy," at www.civworld.org/about.htm (accessed 15 December 2005). Elsewhere, Barber has written that the goal of democratic reformers should be "global civic cooperation" rather than any sort of world government: "Citizenship has always been attached to activities and attitudes associated with the neighborhood: this means that imagining what global citizenship entails actually is a daunting task. Still, it is absolutely necessary, because while participation is local, power is global: unless local citizens can be globally engaged, the true levers of power will remain beyond their grasp." See Benjamin R. Barber, *Fear's Empire: War, Terrorism and Democracy* (New York: W. W. Norton, 2003), 223.

Chapter 2

1. Juliette Beck, interview with author, San Francisco, 11 July 2001.

2. This person elaborated: "Something as simple as taking a shower and letting the water run . . . I know there are people in Ethiopia and the Sudan and other places that desperately need water. And that's not to suggest they're going to get my shower water, but yet that's how strongly my veins are connected with my resource use." Claudine Cmarada, interview with author, Boulder, CO, 22 November 2000.

3. Pat Montandon, interview with author, San Francisco, 3 October 2000.

4. Kenneth R. Garren, interview with author, Roanoke, VA, 29 November 2000.

5. Daniel Vasella, interview with author, Basel, Switzerland, 11 January 2001.

6. Benjamin R. Barber, *Strong Democracy: Participatory Politics for a New Age* (Berkeley: University of California Press, 1984), 223.

7. Note that Held does *not* require that "cosmopolitan citizens" reason from an abstract, neutral position (as some strains of liberalism would require) but from other particular points of view. See David Held, "Regulating Globalization?" in *The Global Transformations Reader*, ed. David Held and Anthony McGrew (Cambridge: Polity Press, 2000), 425.

8. T. H. Marshall, *Class, Citizenship and Social Class* (Cambridge: Cambridge University Press, 1963), 26.

9. Roland Robertson and Habib Haque Khondker, "Discourses of Globalization: Preliminary Considerations," *International Sociology* 13, no. 1 (March 1998): 29.

10. Martin Shaw, *Theory of the Global State: Globality as Unfinished Revolution* (Cambridge: Cambridge University Press, 2000), 11 (Shaw's italics). Similarly, Malcolm Waters has defined globalization as "a social process in which the constraints of geography on economic, political, social, and cultural arrangements recede, in which people become increasingly aware that they are receding and in which people act accordingly." See Malcolm Waters, *Globalization*, 2nd ed. (London: Routledge, 2001), 5.

11. James Rosenau, *Distant Proximities: Dynamics beyond Globalization* (Princeton, NJ: Princeton University Press, 2003).

12. Oscar Arias, interview with author, San Jose, Costa Rica, 13 February 2001.

13. Roger Scruton, who believes that citizenship ultimately stems from the bonds of nationhood, puts forward shared language, shared associations, shared history, and common culture as essential ingredients in the formation of national consciousness. Lest there be any doubt, Scruton does not believe the potential for shared consciousness exists beyond the nation. See Roger Scruton, *The Philosopher on Dover Beach* (New York: St. Martin's Press, 1990), 314–15. Even a cosmopolitan sympathizer such as Pheng Cheah also regards national consciousness as highly resilient: "It is precipitous to consider nationalism as an outmoded form of consciousness. An existing global condition ought not to be mistaken for an existing mass-based feeling of belonging to a world community (cosmopolitanism) because the globality of the everyday does not necessarily engender an existing popular global political consciousness." See Pheng

Cheah, "The Cosmopolitical Today," in *Cosmopolitics: Thinking and Feeling beyond the Nation*, ed. Pheng Cheah and Bruce Robbins (Minneapolis: University of Minnesota Press, 1998), 31.

14. Denise Chávez, interview with author, Las Cruces, NM, 20 April 2000.

15. Sherry Dean, interview with author, Dallas, 19 April 2000.

16. Jasmine Kim, interview with author, Sunnyvale, CA, 7 May 2001.

17. Christian Eckart, interview with author, New York, 9 May 2001.

18. This deploys, with a different interpretation, Benedict Anderson's language of the nation as an imagined political community that is also imagined as "both inherently limited and sovereign." See Benedict Anderson, *Imagined Communities: Reflections on the Origin and Spread of Nationalism*, 2nd ed. (New York: Verso, 1991), 6.

19. Kikujiro Namba, interview with author, Tokyo, Japan, 7 December 2000.

20. Courtney Vallade, interview with author, Oxford, OH, 26 May 2001.

21. Cathy Guthrie, interview with author, Toronto, 15 November 2000.

22. Kevin Danaher, interview with author, San Francisco, 31 August 2001. However, such universal moral visions are regarded elsewhere with extreme skepticism; as two theorists of identity formation have noted, "we-they" perceptions, for better or for worse, have been "central to politics since time immemorial." See Yale H. Ferguson and Richard W. Mansbach, "History's Revenge and Future Shock," in *Approaches to Global Governance Theory*, ed. Martin Hewson and Timothy J. Sinclair (Albany: State University of New York Press, 1999), 205.

23. Wendy Kvalheim, interview with author, New York, 8 May 2001.

24. Nelly Ukpokodu, interview with author, Kansas City, MO, 14 September 2000.

25. Linda Braun, interview with author, Invercargill, New Zealand, 25 September 2001.

26. Randall Wiesenmayer, interview with author, Morgantown, WV, 28 August 2000.

27. Kristin Cox, interview with author, Oregon City, OR, 18 April 2000.

28. Rosie Brown, interview with author, Tulsa, OK, 21 June 2000.

29. Kwame Anthony Appiah, *Cosmopolitanism: Ethics in a World of Strangers* (New York: W. W. Norton, 2006), xvi.

30. The voluntary nature of cosmopolitan citizenship is not lost on proponents such as Andrew Linklater, who has acknowledged that this can be a lightning rod for critics who emphasize the absence of a structured global institutional framework. Note how in the following passage Linklater refers to "world citizenship" as an ethic rather than as an institution: "One objection to the ethic of world citizenship is that it has few of the qualities and demands traditionally associated with national citizenship. Indeterminate and voluntary duties to the rest of humanity characterise the ethic of global responsibility, and the absence of political community rules out the possibility of institutionalising the Aristotelian ideal of civic participation." See Andrew Linklater, "Cosmopolitan Citizenship," in *Cosmopolitan Citizenship*, ed. Kimberly Hutchings and Roland Dannreuther (London: Macmillan, 1999), 40.

31. The United Nations Global Compact is a partnership between the United Nations, nongovernmental organizations, and multinational corporations that have agreed to follow a voluntary code of conduct.

32. Georg Kell, interview with author, New York, 3 July 2001.

33. Paul Shay, interview with author, New York, 6 November 2000.

34. Geoff Strong, interview with author, Melbourne, Australia, 4 December 2000.

35. Louise Arbour, interview with author, Ottawa, 10 January 2001. From 1996 to 1999, Arbour served as chief prosecutor for the International Criminal Tribunals for war crimes in Rwanda and in the former Yugoslavia. In May 1999, Arbour indicted Slobodan Milošević, at the time the president of Yugoslavia, for alleged war crimes and crimes against humanity in Kosovo.

36. Andrew Mitchell, interview with author, Oxford, UK, 30 November 2001.

37. Carol North, interview with author, St. Paul, MN, 4 May 2000.

38. Note the connection this respondent made between awareness, principled decision making, and her own behavior. Janine Firpo, interview with author, San Francisco, 16 November 2000.

39. Lester Brown, interview with author, Kingston, RI, 12 September 2001.

40. Kristin Cox, "U.S. Makes Heavy Impact on Globe," *Oregonian*, 19 October 1999. This critique resembles David Korten's metaphorical argument that modern industrial societies, particularly the United States, "are practicing a cowboy economics" in what has become a "spaceship world." See David C. Korten, *When Corporations Rule the World* (San Francisco: Berrett-Koehler, 1995), 26–27.

41. Kristin Cox, interview. Cox's rationale here closely parallels recent arguments by political economists concerned with promoting such "global public goods" as a cleaner environment and ample food for the world's population; the arguments state that national governments are accountable to international constituencies as well as to domestic ones and therefore "must assume full responsibility for the cross-border effects their citizens generate." See Inge Kaul, Isabelle Grunberg, and Marc A. Stern, eds., *Global Public Goods: International Cooperation in the 21st Century* (Oxford: Oxford University Press, 1999), xxvii.

42. The notion of countries as ethical actors within an international society of states can be linked with Immanuel Kant's vision of a "pacific federation" of free and independent states. See Immanuel Kant, "Perpetual Peace: A Philosophical Sketch," trans. H. B. Nisbet, in *Kant: Political Writings*, ed. Hans Reiss (Cambridge: Cambridge University Press, 1991), 93–130. In the contemporary literature, Keith Faulks has argued that in light of a world order structured around states, not individual persons, "an important step towards a more global citizenship must therefore be a greater willingness for states to exercise global obligations and build stronger links with other countries." See Keith Faulks, *Citizenship* (London: Routledge, 2000), 154. Hence the term "global citizenship," when deployed in the context of countries rather than individuals, fits more closely with the state-centered rather than the cosmopolitan school of thought in international relations.

43. Michael Szabo, interview with author, Cambridge, UK, 23 November 2000.

44. Brian Dill, interview with author, Cambridge, MA, 20 April 2000.

45. Kim, interview.

46. In the French understanding of *solidarité*, notions of fellowship or cohesion take a backseat to conditions of joint liability, joint responsibility, or interdependence. In fact, the noun *solidarité* derives from the much older French adjective, *solidaire*, which traces back to 1462 and means jointly liable or jointly responsible. As historian J. E. S. Hayward documents, early ideas of *solidarité*, as extracted from eighteenth-century French legal documents, appear to have focused on obligations to repay debts and uphold contracts, especially with regard to property transactions. See J. E. S. Hayward, "Solidarity: The Social History of an Idea in 19th Century France," *International Review of Social History* 4 (1959): 270–71.

47. The Oxford English Dictionary (www.oed.com) defines "solidarity" as "community or perfect coincidence of or between interests" and "the fact or quality, on the part of communities, etc., of being perfectly united or at one in some respect, especially in interests, sympathies or aspirations."

48. The phrase "preferential option for the poor" emerged in twentieth-century Roman Catholic social teaching. Michael Murphy, interview with author, Saskatoon, SK, 11 April 2000.

49. This person did qualify her statement, noting that she also takes her responsibility as a citizen of France seriously, particularly with respect to French global policy: "France has always taken the wrong side in the last 100 years, unfortunately. In that sense I feel a bit more responsible . . . and a bit more ashamed for what is happening in Rwanda and in ex-Yugoslavia, because of the role of the French authorities. But otherwise, in general terms, I don't feel any closer to any problem in Europe or anybody in Europe than I would to anybody anywhere else in the world." Anne-Christine Habbard, interview with author, Paris, 26 June 2001.

50. Martha C. Nussbaum, "Patriotism and Cosmopolitanism," in *For Love of Country: Debating the Limits of Patriotism*, ed. Joshua Cohen (Boston: Beacon Press, 1996), 3–17, and *Cultivating Humanity: A Classical Defense of Reform in Liberal Education* (Cambridge, MA: Harvard University Press, 1997).

51. Barber, *Strong Democracy*, 223.

52. Bruce Kent, interview with author, London, 22 November 2000.

53. Danaher, interview.

54. Catherine Harper, interview with author, Mattituck, NY, 26 September 2000.

55. Aristotle, *The Politics*, trans. Carnes Lord (Chicago: University of Chicago Press, 1984), 1277b.

56. This was all the more the case since the interviewing process began in the aftermath of the 1999 demonstrations outside the World Trade Organization meeting in Seattle.

57. Cynthia Hogan, interview with author, East Hanover, NJ, 2 October 2000.

58. This respondent noted that he places "no boundaries" on his understanding of community. Francis Woong-il Lee, interview with author, Seoul, 29 September 2000.

59. Ruth Wardwell, interview with author, Orange, CA, 10 April 2000.

60. Murray Campbell, interview with author, Auckland, New Zealand, 15 May 2001.

61. David Shenk, interview with author, New York, 6 April 2000.

62. David Fuller, interview with author, Wollongong, Australia, 29 November 2000.

63. Sharon Cobban, interview with author, Toronto, 7 April 2000.

64. Vasella, interview.

65. Murphy, interview.

66. Habbard, interview. The objective of strengthening transnational democratic control is cast as an uphill battle from the perspective of democratic theory, which as noted by Robert Dahl, emphasizes that smaller political systems "at least hold out the theoretical potential for greater citizen effectiveness than larger systems, even if in practice that potentiality is not always realized." See Robert A. Dahl, "A Democratic Dilemma: System Effectiveness versus Citizen Participation," *Political Science Quarterly* 109, no. 1 (1994): 28.

67. Peter Rosset, interview with author, Chiapas, Mexico, 15 February 2001.

68. David Hallman, interview with author, Toronto, 5 June 2001.

69. Danaher, interview.

70. When asked to clarify whether "global" applied to the movement or the citizens, this person replied "both." Maude Barlow, interview with author, Ottowa, 19 April 2000.

71. Barlow said that she would "start over" the IMF and World Bank and maintain the WTO but remove its jurisdiction in areas such as health, education, food, and water.

72. This is consistent with theoretical arguments that human rights regimes cannot be upheld worldwide, and that instead, "human rights protections need firm anchoring in the local political regime in order to be effective." See Herman van Gunsteren, "Four Conceptions of Citizenship," in *The Condition of Citizenship*, ed. Bart van Steenbergen (London: Sage, 1994), 7.

73. Rosset, interview.

74. Danaher, interview.

75. Gwen Noyes, interview with author, Cambridge, MA, 18 June 2000.

76. Strong, interview.

77. James Ensor, interview with author, Melbourne, Australia, 9 October 2000.

78. Mitchell, interview.

79. Noyes, interview.

80. Susan Vallade, interview with author, Oxford, OH, 26 May 2001.

81. Shigeru Shiono, interview with author, Hyama, Japan, 18 April 2001.

Chapter 3

1. Denise Chávez, interview with author, Las Cruces, NM, 20 April 2000.

2. As alleged by Anthony Smith, who has argued that the idea of "global culture" is an impossibility, lacking any sort of shared global identity: "Where the nation can be constructed so as to draw upon and revive latent popular experiences and needs,

a 'global culture' answers to no living needs, no identity-in-the-making. . . . There are no 'world memories' that can be used to *unite* humanity; the most global experiences to date—colonialism and the World Wars—can only serve to remind us of our historic cleavages." See Anthony D. Smith, "Towards a Global Culture?" in *Global Culture*, ed. Michael Featherstone (London: Sage Publications, 1990), 179–80. This is a far more monolithic conception of global culture than the conception articulated by Denise Chávez in the text.

3. Gloria Anzaldúa, *Borderlands/La Frontera: The New Mestiza* (San Francisco: Aunt Lute, 1987), 79.

4. The term "outsider" is employed in this discussion rather than "foreigner," as "foreigner" more decisively signifies a person from a different country, whereas many individuals who display the qualities of global citizenship as cross-cultural empathy do so within their local communities. Even such terms as "outsider" and "other" are imperfect, as many individuals who might perceive themselves as outsiders—or individuals who might be perceived as outsiders—are in fact on their way to becoming insiders, such as immigrants in the process of becoming citizens. Furthermore, in multicultural nation-states, many so-called outsiders, at least within the sphere of a particular cultural milieu, already are full citizens as far as legal or political membership is concerned.

5. Geoff Strong, interview with author, Melbourne, Australia, 4 December 2000. Contrast this culturally embracing outlook with the xenophobia of Filip Dewinter, the leader of Vlaams Belang (previously Vlaams Blok), the Flemish nationalist party in Belgium that recently held 40 percent of the city council seats in Antwerp: "I don't believe in all these cultures living together. . . . We should not try to organise some kind of multicultural society. . . . I sometimes go into the Moroccan communities. These Moroccan restaurants, they have Arabic writing on the walls. And the music they play. The women dress in hijabs. It's not our culture, and *I feel threatened*. What is wrong with these people adopting our way of life? They should assimilate into our way of life or leave." Quoted in Burhan Wazir, "Race Fears Fuel Rise of Antwerp's Own Haider," *Observer*, 15 October 2000 (italics added).

6. Note that this person's view of global citizenship, although discussed in the context of cross-cultural engagement, was derived heavily from awareness. In fact, the respondent noted that global citizenship for her is 100 percent "a state of mind; it's perspective-taking." Ruth Wardwell, interview with author, Orange, CA, 10 April 2000.

7. Francis Woong-il Lee, commencement speech delivered at Roanoke College, Salem, VA, 2 May 1998.

8. This attribute of a global citizen also relates back to the concepts of awareness and responsibility, as discussed in chapter 2, in terms of recognition of universalities of the human experience and respect for humanity.

9. Emily Drabble, interview with author, London, 28 September 2000.

10. David Fuller, interview with author, Wollongong, Australia, 29 November 2000.

11. Stephen Frosh, "Psychoanalysis, Identity and Citizenship," in *Culture and Citizenship*, ed. Nick Stevenson (London: Sage Publications, 2001), 62.

12. Robert Harper, interview with author, Mattituck, NY, 26 September 2000.

13. Imogen Mkhize, interview with author, Johannesburg, 6 August 2000.

14. Louise Arbour, interview with author, Ottawa, 10 January 2001.

15. "White House Statement on Medal of Freedom," *U.S. Newswire*, 15 January 1998.

16. Brian O'Sullivan, interview with author, Woodbridge, ON, 28 September 2000.

17. Linda Braun, quoted in "Principal Urges International Outlook," *Southland Times* (Invercargill), 28 July 1999.

18. As Murray Bookchin has written, with respect to ancient Greece: "The polis was not only a treasured end in itself; it was the 'school' in which the citizen's highest virtues were formed and found expression. Politics, in turn, was not only concerned with administering the affairs of the polis but also with educating the citizen as a public being who developed the competence to act in the public interest." See Murray Bookchin, *From Urbanization to Cities: Towards a New Politics of Citizenship* (New York: Cassell, 1995), 59.

19. See the work of Lawrence Mead, who has defended work requirements in welfare programs as a means of promoting "social competence" and securing equal citizenship. For example, Lawrence Mead, *Beyond Entitlement* (New York: Free Press 1986), 250–56. For a rejoinder that lambastes the New Right welfare reform agenda as "a mean and truncated conception of social obligation and citizenship," see Michael Katz, *The Price of Citizenship: Redefining the American Welfare State* (New York: Metropolitan Books, 2001), 358–59.

20. Herman van Gunsteren, *A Theory of Citizenship* (Boulder, CO: Westview Press, 1998) 24–25, 27.

21. Bryan Turner reiterates that these sorts of cosmopolitan citizens make up an elite segment of the population with lives "characterised by contingency, risk and mobility. The postmodern citizen is only moving on." Turner contrasts these so-called reflexive citizens with "the 'ethnic patriots' of the nation-state," namely the relatively immobile working classes and underclasses, who maintain "hot loyalties and thick patterns of solidarity." See Bryan Turner, "Liberal Citizenship and Cosmopolitan Virtue," in *Citizenship and Democracy in a Global Era*, ed. Andrew Vandenberg (New York: St. Martin's Press, 2000), 28.

22. Aihwa Ong, "Flexible Citizenship among Chinese Cosmopolitans," in *Cosmopolitics: Thinking and Feeling beyond the Nation*, ed. Pheng Cheah and Bruce Robbins (Minneapolis: University of Minnesota Press, 1998), 142.

23. Robert B. Reich, *The Work of Nations: Preparing Ourselves for 21st-Century Capitalism* (New York: Knopf, 1991), 177–80.

24. Reich, *Work of Nations*, 309.

25. Rick Ellis, interview with author, Auckland, New Zealand, 12 October 2000.

26. Miles Colebrook, interview with author, London, 26 July 2000.

27. Barbara Moses, interview with author, Toronto, 20 September 2000.

28. Ironically, this strain of cosmopolitanism presumes the existence of autonomous, stable, and liberal nation-states in which internationally mobile individuals are free to live in comfort and peace. As Michael Ignatieff has observed: "Globalism in a post-imperialist age permits a post-nationalist consciousness only for those cosmopolitans who are lucky enough to live in the wealthy West. . . . In this sense, therefore, cosmopolitans like myself are not beyond the nation; and a cosmopolitan, post-nationalist spirit will always depend, in the end, on the capacity of nation-states to provide security and civility for their citizens." See Michael Ignatieff, *Blood and Belonging: Journeys into the New Nationalism* (New York: Farrar, Straus and Giroux, 1993), 13.

29. Linda Braun, interview with author, Invercargill, New Zealand, 25 September 2000.

30. Francis Woong-il Lee, interview with author, Seoul, 29 September 2000.

31. Murray Massey, "Retirement Gets New Meaning for Japanese," *Business Review Weekly*, 27 October 1997.

32. Cynthia Hogan, interview with author, East Hanover, NJ, 2 October 2000.

33. Mkhize, interview.

34. Rosie Brown, interview with author, Tulsa, OK, 21 June 2000.

35. Chávez, interview.

36. Joseph H. Carens, "Aliens and Citizens: The Case for Open Borders," in *Theorizing Citizenship*, ed. Ronald Beiner (Albany: State University of New York Press, 1995), 230.

37. As this person noted, Ukrainian Canadians were in the forefront of helping the revived Ukraine form its constitution and democratic institutions following the collapse of the Soviet Union. Haroon Siddiqui, interview with author, Toronto, 10 April 2000.

38. Jonathan Chevreau, "Guide to Offshore Investment Funds: Expat Makes No Bones about Appeal for Canadians," *National Post*, 14 August 1999.

39. Jonathan Chevreau, interview with author, Toronto, 6 April 2000.

40. As Davidson and Rees-Mogg advise their readers: "Citizenship is obsolete. To optimize your lifetime earnings and become a Sovereign Individual, you will need to become a customer of a government or protection service rather than a citizen. Instead of paying whatever tax burden is imposed upon you by grasping politicians, you must place yourself in a position to negotiate a private tax treaty that obliges you to pay no more for services of government than they are actually worth to you." See James Dale Davidson and William Rees-Mogg, *The Sovereign Individual: How to Survive and Thrive during the Collapse of the Welfare State* (New York: Simon & Schuster, 1997), 373.

41. As of April 2000, when Chevreau was interviewed, the Canadian taxation rate on retirement savings plans was 25 percent for early withdrawal, compared with 50 percent upon retirement, making it, in Chevreau's words, a "relative bargain" to take the money and run.

42. Clearly Chevreau's take on global citizenship is symptomatic of a backlash against the welfare state, and the so-called privatization of citizenship has attracted attention in academic debate. As Margaret Somers has lamented, "We are seeing citizenship morph from that of public participation into that of obligatory customership in the ever-expanding world of consumer and financial markets." See Margaret Somers, "Romancing the Market, Reviling the State: Historicizing Liberalism, Privatization, and the Competing Claims to Civil Society," in *Citizenship, Markets and the State*, ed. Colin Crouch, Klaus Eder, and Damian Tambini (Oxford: Oxford University Press, 2001), 25.

43. Christopher Lasch, *The Revolt of the Elites and the Betrayal of Democracy* (New York: W. W. Norton, 1995), 6.

44. I am grateful to Renée Legatt for suggesting that these terms might work to frame this divide.

45. Falk and Urry have proposed numerous categories of prospective global citizens, such as "global activists," "global reformers," "global managers," and "global capitalists." See Richard Falk, "The Making of Global Citizenship," in *The Condition of Citizenship*, ed. Bart van Steenbergen (London: Sage Publications, 1994), 127–39; and John Urry, *Sociology beyond Societies* (London: Routledge, 2000). Falk has since cast a more skeptical view of global citizenship, which he sees as "essentially a Western experience" that is subordinated to the dynamics of economic globalization; see Richard Falk, "The Decline of Citizenship in an Era of Globalization," *Citizenship Studies* 4, no. 1 (2000): 3–17.

Chapter 4

1. Michael Walzer, "The Civil Society Argument," in *The Citizenship Debates*, ed. Gershon Shafir (Minneapolis: University of Minnesota Press, 1998), 291–92.

2. Richard Falk, "The Making of Global Citizenship," in *The Condition of Citizenship*, ed. Bart van Steenbergen (London: Sage Publications, 1994), 127–39; and John Urry, *Sociology beyond Societies* (London: Routledge, 2000).

3. Margaret E. Keck and Kathryn Sikkink, *Activists beyond Borders: Advocacy Networks in International Politics* (Ithaca, NY: Cornell University Press, 1988). Likewise, in his depiction of how domestic and transnational actors in civil society successfully mount pressure, from above and below, on repressive states, Thomas Risse avoids likening these actors to "global citizens" or any similar term. See Thomas Risse, "The Power of Norms versus the Norms of Power: Transnational Civil Society and Human Rights," in *The Third Force: The Rise of Transnational Civil Society* (Tokyo and Washington, DC: Japan Center for International Exchange and Carnegie Endowment for International Peace, 2000), 177–210.

4. John Gaventa, "Global Citizen Action: Lessons and Challenges," in *Global Citizen Action*, ed. Michael Edwards and John Gaventa (Boulder, CO: Lynne Rienner, 2001), 278. See also Michael Muetzelfeldt and Gary Smith, "Civil Society and Global Governance: The Possibilities for Global Citizenship," *Citizenship Studies* 6, no. 1 (2002).

5. Anne-Christine Habbard, quoted in Roger Cohen, "Growing Up and Getting Practical since Seattle," *New York Times*, 24 September 2000.

6. John Cavanagh, Jerry Mander, and others, ed., *Alternatives to Economic Globalization: A Better World Is Possible*, 2nd ed. (New York: Berrett-Koehler, 2004), 344.

7. Notes from Nowhere, ed. *We Are Everywhere* (London: Verso, 2003).

8. The purpose of the interviews was *not* to provide a platform for activists in reiterating objections to the WTO, the IMF, or any other institution. Certainly the respondents conveyed their critical perspectives as well as their hopes for change, such as democratic reforms in decision making, elimination of debt in developing countries, or, in some cases, outright abolition of the WTO, IMF, and their ilk. However, the main objective of the interviews was to trace the roots of each respondent's activism and to examine how and to what extent, if at all, these individuals had reflected on the meaning of citizenship.

9. The lyrics from "God Bless the USA," by Lee Greenwood, the song crafted for Ronald Reagan's 1984 campaign for reelection as president of the United States.

10. Chelsa Mozen, interview with author, Prague, 28 November 2000.

11. Jeffrey Ferguson, interview with author, Annandale-on-Hudson, NY, 25 January 2001.

12. Arthur Foelsche, interview with author, Plainfield, VT, 17 November 2000.

13. In Murray Bookchin's view, modern urbanization and the rise of the nation-state fell far short of the caliber of citizenship in the ancient polis, in which people strengthened their character through participation in public affairs: "Later ideals of citizenship, even insofar as they were modeled on the Athenian, seem more unfinished and immature than the original." See Murray Bookchin, *From Urbanization to Cities: Towards a New Politics of Citizenship* (New York: Cassell, 1995), 83.

14. With fourteen affiliate members in ten countries in central and eastern Europe and in the Commonwealth of Independent States, Bankwatch monitors projects sponsored by international financial institutions and often proposes alternative projects, particularly addressing such issues as energy and transportation.

15. Tomasz Terlecki, interview with author, Kraków, 13 November 2000.

16. Terlecki does not use any Polish equivalent of "citizen of the world" or "global citizen." Indeed, Terlecki noted that many English-language terms, such as "sustainable development" and "facilitation," lack suitable counterparts in Polish.

17. In correspondence with the author in March 2005, nearly five years after his interview for this study, Evan Henshaw-Plath said that his sense of cultural continuity with the United States had eroded: "It's true that I'm increasingly frustrated with the political climate in the U.S., but it's the culture which makes me want to leave— its alienated consumerism, suburbia, disrespect for family ties, culture of perpetual work, nonexistent social safety net, and environmentally destructive polices. . . . For me citizenship has become a thing of which passport can I get the right to carry and where do I have a right to live and work." Evan Henshaw-Plath, e-mail correspondence with author, 21 March 2005.

18. Evan Henshaw-Plath, interview with author, Arcata, CA, 17 November 2000.

19. No relation to the sociologist Martin Shaw.

20. Richard Pendlebury, "My Son the Anarchist," *Daily Mail*, 30 September 2000.

21. Martin Shaw, interview with author, Oxford, UK, 5 December 2000.

22. As with the other interview respondents within this group, Martin Shaw made the first reference to the idea of a world citizen.

23. David Miller, "Bounded Citizenship," in *Cosmopolitan Citizenship*, ed. Kimberly Hutchings and Roland Dannreuther (London: Macmillan, 1999), 78.

24. "Canada World Youth—Mission," at www.cwy-jcm.org/en/aboutus/mission (accessed 14 November 2005).

25. "Global Visionaries," at www.global-visionaries.org (accessed 25 March 2005).

26. "About the Global Citizen Corps," at www.netaid.org/global_citizen_corps/About.html (accessed 4 January 2006).

27. Bettina Mok, interview with author, Oakland, CA, 15 June 2005.

28. Yvette Gillespie, quoted in Margaret Wenham, "Cultural Exchange," *Courier-Mail* (Queensland), 6 March 2004.

29. Ben Romeril, quoted in "Raise Funds for Tanzania," *Knox Leader*, 20 April 2004.

30. "World Vision Australia—Major Poverty Reports," at www.worldvision.com.au/aboutus/povertyreports/ (accessed 5 January 2006).

31. Tim Costello, quoted in "Understanding Big Issues," *Illawarra Mercury*, 3 August 2004.

32. "Global Gang," at www.globalgang.org.uk/ (accessed 28 June 2005).

33. More than 60,000 volunteers have joined Earthwatch field research projects, and approximately 120 scientists sponsored by Earthwatch travel each year with volunteers to more than forty countries on projects that normally last for one or two weeks.

34. Andrew Mitchell, interview with author, Oxford, UK, 30 November 2001.

35. This global think tank was formed in 1968 and is best known for its much-debated report, *The Limits to Growth*, published in 1972, which argued that continued economic growth would be impossible given the planet's limited natural resources. See Donella H. Meadows et al., *The Limits to Growth: A Report for the Club of Rome's Project on the Predicament of Mankind* (London: Earth Island, 1972). Donella Meadows went on to write a syndicated newspaper column, which she called "The Global Citizen," until her death in February 2001.

36. As Kikujiro Namba, during a separate interview, recalled his contribution: "Global citizenship means Earthwatch members are always looking for the future of our planet, so they are considered as having global consciousness and attacking the global problems." Kikujiro Namba, interview with author, Tokyo, 7 December 2000.

37. Tally Forbes, internal Earthwatch memorandum provided to author by Andrew Mitchell, 6 May 1997.

38. Even the term "citizenship," standing alone, has suffered from a historically low profile among British subjects. As Ivor Crewe argued in a lecture delivered around the same time as Earthwatch was grappling with the global citizenship question, "The

vocabulary of citizenship is foreign to the British; it does not speak to them." See Ivor Crewe, "Citizenship: The Revival of an Idea," in *Citizenship and Civic Education* (London: Citizenship Foundation, 1997), 4.

39. Carol North, interview with author, St. Paul, MN, 4 May 2000.

40. When North was asked during her interview what "citizen" meant to her on its own, removing any modifiers such as "global" or "national," her immediate reply was: "Well, it is hard to think of it without the global, because it was kind of a package deal."

41. *The Purple Dawn*, newsletter of the Global Citizens Association, July 2000.

42. David Held's version of cosmopolitan democracy, for example, proposes an elected worldwide assembly, an international judiciary, military force and economic policy institutions, as well as transnational referenda and public scrutiny of international nongovernmental organizations. See David Held, *Democracy and the Global Order* (Cambridge: Polity Press, 1995), 270–83, as well as Richard A. Falk and Andrew Strauss, "Toward Global Parliament," *Foreign Affairs* 80, no. 1 (2001): 212–20.

43. Duncan Graham, interview with author, Vancouver, BC, 13 October 2000.

44. Jürgen Habermas conceives of the public sphere thus: "The public sphere can best be described as a network for communicating information and points of view (i.e., opinions expressing affirmative or negative attitudes); the streams of communication are, in the process, filtered and synthesized in such a way that they coalesce into bundles of topically specified *public* opinions." See Jürgen Habermas, *Between Facts and Norms: Contributions to a Discourse Theory of Law and Democracy*, trans. William Rehg (Cambridge, MA: MIT Press, 1996), 360 (Habermas's italics).

45. James Bohman, "The Public Spheres of the World Citizen," in *Perpetual Peace: Essays on Kant's Cosmopolitan Ideal*, ed. James Bohman and Matthias Lutz-Backmann (Cambridge, MA: MIT, 1997), 196. Likewise, Seyla Benhabib has argued that public space should not be defined as an arena reserved for political elites but instead framed as "the creation of procedures whereby those affected by general social norms and collective political decisions can have a say in their formulation, stipulation and adoption." See Seyla Benhabib, "Models of Public Space," in *Habermas and the Public Sphere*, ed. Craig Calhoun (Cambridge, MA: MIT Press, 1992), 87.

Chapter 5

1. For two recent books that have explored citizenship education from an international perspective, see Nel Noddings, ed., *Education for Global Awareness* (New York: Teachers College Press, 2005); and Robert Jackson, ed., *International Perspectives on Citizenship, Education and Religious Diversity* (London: Routledge, 2003). For an argument that schools need to go much further in realigning their purposes toward "a universal commitment to global values," thereby preparing students to become "competent citizens in an age of globalization," see Fernando Reimers, "Citizenship, Identity and Education: Examining the Public Purposes of Schools in an Age of Globalization," *Prospects* 36, no. 3 (2006): 275–94.

2. Carole L. Hahn, "Promise and Paradox: Challenges to Global Citizenship," *Social Education* 48, no. 4 (April 1984): 297.

3. For an argument that students need to develop the capacity to reflect and deliberate on global issues as ethical "multidimensional citizens," see Walter C. Parker, Akira Ninomiya, and John Cogan, "Educating World Citizens: Toward Multinational Curriculum Development," *American Educational Research Journal* 36, no. 2 (Summer 1999): 117–45.

4. Robert Muller, "A World Core Curriculum," in *Holistic Education: Principles, Perspectives and Practices*, ed. Carol Flake (Brandon, VT: Holistic Education Press, 1993).

5. Christine Drake, "Education for Responsible Global Citizenship," *Journal of Geography* 86, no. 6 (November–December 1987): 300–306.

6. Lynne M. O'Brien and William E. Pulliam, "Media and the Global Citizen," *Social Education* 42, no. 7 (November–December 1978): 624–29.

7. Martha C. Nussbaum, *Cultivating Humanity: A Classical Defense of Reform in Liberal Education* (Cambridge, MA: Harvard University Press, 1997), 60–61.

8. I am indebted to Carole Hahn for bringing this to my attention.

9. For example, a recent report sponsored by the Carnegie Corporation of New York—to which nearly sixty leading scholars and educators contributed and which aimed to reinvigorate citizenship education within grade schools—steered clear of discussing the relationship between citizenship education and global education; likewise, the report set forth goals for citizenship education exclusively within the context of domestic politics. See *The Civic Mission of Schools*, Carnegie Corporation of New York and The Center for Information and Research on Civic Learning and Engagement (CIRCLE), 13 February 2003.

10. For an argument that citizenship education of any kind undercuts the goals of educating youngsters in pursuit of universal moral principles such as social justice and democratic accountability, see Amy Gutmann, "Democratic Citizenship," in *For Love of Country? Debating the Limits of Patriotism*, ed. Joshua Cohen (Boston: Beacon Press, 1996), 66–71.

11. Kathleen Johnston, interview with author, Grayslake, IL, 15 September 2000.

12. Victoria Ranney, interview with author, Grayslake, IL, 20 July 2004.

13. Ranney added that in teaching the global interconnectedness of the local environment, the school quite literally puts forward a rooted approach to global citizenship: "The kids learn that the prairie plants, some of them have roots that are fifteen feet deep, and that's why they're useful in holding the soil and taking water down to the lowest area and bringing water up. Roots are important, and locality is important, and I think for kids, you've got to have that sense of being comfortable with your own place before you can go on to think about global citizenship. Otherwise it's just a bunch of words."

14. Linda Brazdil, interview with author, Grayslake, IL, 7 July 2004.

15. According to Brazdil, students at Prairie Crossing generally have scored within the 70–90 percentile range on standardized tests.

16. In 2003, when Prairie Crossing's charter came up for its first renewal, the school board briefly considered removing "global" as a modifier from the goal of promoting "responsible citizenship," but advocates on the board argued that global citizenship served as an essential reminder of the need to educate students in relation to other societies. As Linda Brazdil noted: "Between environmental stewardship and global citizenship, we saw huge links of care for the earth and care for other people—that you really couldn't have one without the other."

17. About 1,350 of these schools are secondary schools that grant the International Baccalaureate diploma. See "Number and Location of IB Schools," at www.ibo .org/programmes/slidef.cfm (accessed 21 January 2006).

18. "History of the International Baccalaureate Organization," at www.ibo.org/ ibo/index.cfm?page=/ibo/about/ibo_history&language=EN (accessed 12 August 2004).

19. Eugene International grew rapidly in its first decade: during the 1980s, the school enrolled just fifty students and operated in two host schools; today, the school enrolls approximately 1,500 students.

20. The International Baccalaureate qualification also requires a community service commitment and participation in athletics and arts activities.

21. Caron Cooper, interview with author, Eugene, OR, 7 July 2004.

22. Eugene International High School, at schools.4j.lane.edu/ihs/ (accessed 12 August 2004).

23. The term "global citizenship" triggered greater debate in the year 2000 than in 1989, when the school's original mission statement was written, mainly because one teacher questioned whether the term carried some baggage from socialism and communism. Other teachers, in response, defended not only the usage of "global citizenship" but also the right of the school to define "global citizenship" affirmatively in its own terms. Faculty members also debated using "world" and "international"— rather than "global"—as modifiers for citizenship, and teachers decided that the first two modifiers carried too much baggage in terms of national sovereignty, imperial conquest, and colonization, while "global" was seen as more neutral and inclusive. In addition, some faculty saw the term "empowered," which was in the 1989 mission statement, as having an unintended imperial connotation, rather than as reflective of the school's goal simply to empower students with knowledge of the world's cultures, languages, histories, traditions, and value systems. Hence the term "empowered" also was dropped from the 2000 mission statement. Cooper, interview.

24. Michael Barber, speech delivered to a conference of the UK Secondary Heads Association, Birmingham, 22 March 1998.

25. For good summaries of this history, see Ian Lister, "Citizenship and Citizenship Education in Britain," in Citizenship and Citizenship Education in a Changing World, ed. Orit Ichilov (London: Woburn Press, 1998), and Bernard Crick, Essays on Citizenship (London: Continuum, 2000).

26. Nick Seaton, interview with author, York, UK, 18 July 2000.

27. This was a familiar set of objections, as educators within the United Kingdom who began to promote global citizenship during the 1980s as "global consciousness,"

in an interdependent world, and local action" were rebuffed by educational traditionalists and other conservative groups. Lister, 1998.

28. John Carvel, "Schools Adviser Urges Moral Code to Replace God," *Guardian*, 23 March 1998.

29. Geoff Teece, "All Hell Breaks Loose over God's (or god's) Role in the Curriculum," *Guardian*, 24 March 1998.

30. For a compelling argument that churches can fill an important role in shaping a "global common good," see David Hollenbach, *The Common Good and Christian Ethics* (Cambridge: Cambridge University Press, 2002).

31. Michael Barber, interview with author, London, 1 August 2000.

32. With the revised school curriculum now in place across the entire United Kingdom, various British educational institutions and advocacy groups have launched networks of information sharing and collaboration among teachers. Three relevant websites are sponsored by the UK Development Education Association: www.globaldimension .org.uk/, the Faculty of Education of the University of Glasgow and the International Development Education Association of Scotland (IDEAS) (www.global–citizenship .org/), and Oxfam UK (www.oxfam.org.uk/coolplanet/teachers/globciti/).

33. Caryn McTighe Musil, interview with author, Washington, DC, 13 August 2004.

34. Holders of the Weissberg Chair have included Palestinian diplomat Hanan Ashrawi; Alain Destexhe, the executive director of Médecins Sans Frontières; and Cuban diplomat Carlos Alzugaray.

35. David Burrows, interview with author, Beloit, WI, 16 August 2004.

36. This point on recognizing the diversity of human experience offers an interesting contrast to the view from several people interviewed for this study, as noted in chapter 2, that global citizenship involves recognition of the universalities of human experience.

37. David Burrows, "World Citizenship" (internal Beloit College memorandum, 11 March 2004).

38. Robert D. Manning, interview with author, Rochester, NY, 20 August 2004.

39. "Chapman University—About Chapman—Chapman Facts—Mission," at www.chapman.edu/about/mission.asp (accessed 13 January 2006).

40. In the custom-edited text for the seminar, Will defined a global citizen as "a person who develops an awareness of world affairs, who has acquired the critical thinking skills to analyze such events, and who can evaluate the ethical dimensions of complex issues—possibly leading to actions to make the world a better place." See Don Will, ed., *The Global Citizen*, 2nd ed. (New York: Pearson Custom Publishing, 1999), 8.

41. Paul Apodaca, "Regarding Global Citizenship," in *The Global Citizen*, 21.

42. Don Will, interview with author, Orange, CA, 15 September 2000.

43. Ronald Farmer, interview with author, Orange, CA, 23 August 2000.

44. The Japanese word *soka* means "value creation," which Daisaku Ikeda has described as "the capacity to find meaning, to enhance one's own existence and contribute to the well-being of others, under any circumstance."

45. SGI was founded in 1939, the same year that Nazi Germany invaded Poland and Japan itself was headed into World War II. In the postwar years, the organization prospered; SGI now has chapters in 128 countries and runs several educational institutions in Japan and in the United States. Soka University of Japan, located just to the west of Tokyo, enrolls nearly nine thousand students. In addition, a political party created by the organization in 1964, the Komeito, often takes part in governing coalitions in Japan.

46. Daisaku Ikeda, "Thoughts on Education for Global Citizenship" (speech, Columbia University Teachers College, New York, 13 June 1996), 3–4.

47. Ikeda, "Education for Global Citizenship," 6.

48. Approximately 40 percent of the student body at Soka University of America comes from East Asia, namely, China, Japan, and South Korea. Another 40 percent comes from the United States, with an additional 15 percent from Latin America and the remaining 5 percent from Africa, Europe, and Central Asia.

49. In practice, this means that students from East Asia go either to Japan, Spain, or Latin America, while students from Latin America and the United States generally go to Japan, as Japanese tends to be the most accessible East Asian language for the students to learn.

50. Michael Hays said that when the university first opened in 2001, fostering positive interaction among the students of different ethnic backgrounds and from multiple continents was not always easy: "A big shock for the American students was to meet students from abroad who had utterly different notions about behavior, about dress, about food, about manners, and there were some sharp exchanges. . . . The American students thought the international students were holding them up because their English language proficiency wasn't sufficient. The Latin American students thought that the Japanese students, for example, and the Asian students and Americans were all too uptight. The East Asian students thought that some of the behavior patterns and aggressiveness of both the Latins and the Americans was a little inappropriate. And so they would come, one or the other, to various members of the faculty and complain, and this was a wonderful opportunity for us to tell them, 'Well, work it out, think about it . . . and that's part of the education process here—confronting one's own assumptions."

51. Other global citizenship centers include the Center for Peace and Global Citizenship at Haverford College, a clearinghouse for service opportunities and student research support at home and abroad; the Ford Motor Company Center for Global Citizenship at Northwestern University's Kellogg School of Management, a hub for research on the political and social impacts of multinational corporations; and the Mark Lindenberg Center for Humanitarian Action, International Development and Global Citizenship at the University of Washington, which promotes education on issues related to global poverty and public health.

52. Many students also participate in Inquiry, an initiative that creates simulation programs to educate secondary-school students on global issues. In the 2003–2004 academic year, EPIIC students worked with four hundred secondary-school students in thirty high schools in seven states.

53. An evaluation, completed by the U.S. Department of Education, noted that despite the overwhelmingly positive educational impact of EPIIC, some former students in the colloquium reported resistance from their professors. As one student reported: "There was a lot of tension between my international relations advisor and EPIIC. He didn't really approve of my decision to do EPIIC, and all of that, it was hard. It was hard to work out." See Nancy S. Haydu, *Creating a Blueprint for Leadership and Citizenship Development: The EPIIC Educational Process*, Fund for Innovation in Post-Secondary Schools, U.S. Department of Education, June 2003.

54. Another offshoot of the Tufts University Institute for Global Leadership is TILIP, or Tufts Institute for Leadership and International Perspective. Students participating in TILIP travel to Hong Kong for a summer internship in which they are paired with a student from a Chinese university.

55. Jean Mayer, a renowned nutritionist and activist, served as president and chancellor of Tufts University from 1976 until 1992.

56. Past recipients have included Nobel Prize–winning economist Amartya Sen; Archbishop Desmond Tutu; authors David Halberstam and Conor Cruise O'Brien; Mary Robinson, the former president of Ireland and the former United Nations High Commissioner of Refugees; and Romeo Dallaire, the retired Canadian general who commanded the United Nations Assistance Mission in Rwanda and forcefully argued for intervention to stop the early stages of genocide there in 1994. In addition to honoring Mayer and the recipients, the award also helps EPIIC attract top-notch speakers.

57. Sherman Teichman, interview with author, Medford, MA, 26 April 2000.

58. Rick Ellis, interview with author, Auckland, New Zealand, 12 October 2000.

59. Chris Woodhead, "Empty Lessons for Citizen Ignorant," *Sunday Times*, 21 April 2002.

Chapter 6

1. For literature exploring possible definitions of corporate global citizenship, see James E. Post, "Global Corporate Citizenship: Principles to Live and Work By," *Business Ethics Quarterly* 12, no. 2 (2002): 143–53; Sandra Waddock and Neil Smith, "Relationships: The Real Challenge of Corporate Global Citizenship," *Business and Society Review* 105, no. 1 (2000): 47–62; and Noel M. Tichy, Andrew R. McGill, and Lynda St. Clair, eds., *Corporate Global Citizenship: Doing Business in the Public Eye* (San Francisco: New Lexington Press, 1997).

2. This is a widely applied and often vaguely interpreted term, encompassing everyone from employees to residents of local communities where multinationals do business.

3. For a good overview of the UN Global Compact, authored by its director, see Georg Kell, "The Global Compact: Origins, Operations, Progress, Challenges," *Journal of Corporate Citizenship* 11 (2003): 35–50, and John Gerard Ruggie, "The Theory and Practice of Learning Networks: Corporate Social Responsibility and the Global Compact," *Journal of Corporate Citizenship* 5 (2003): 27–36.

4. For a good overview of the development of international standards for industry "self-regulation," see Thomas A. Hemphill, "Monitoring Global Corporate Citizenship: Industry Self-Regulation at a Crossroads," *Journal of Corporate Citizenship* 14 (2004): 81–96. For a critique arguing that voluntary codes of conduct have stalled the development of more binding forms of international regulation in the world economy, see James K. Rowe, "Corporate Social Responsibility as a Global Business Strategy," in *Globalization, Governmentality and Global Politics: Regulation for the Rest of Us?* ed. Ronnie Lipschutz (London: Routledge, 2005). Notably, economist and Nobel laureate Joseph E. Stiglitz has called for multinational corporations that profess high ethical standards to align themselves with stronger government regulations at home and abroad. In his words: "Corporations are becoming adept at image manipulation and have learned to speak in favor of social responsibility even while they continue to evade it. Those who are really serious about higher standards should welcome regulations that support the codes of conduct they publicly endorse, for such regulations would protect them from unfair competition from those who do not adhere to the same standards." See Joseph E. Stiglitz, *Making Globalization Work* (New York: W. W. Norton, 2006), 199.

5. During 2003 and 2004, the World Economic Forum, with its annual international summit of elites in business, government, and academia, declared on its website its commitment to "improving the state of the world by engaging particularly its corporate members in global citizenship." While this statement still appears on World Economic Forum news releases, the reference to global citizenship was replaced in 2005 with the phrase "improving the state of the world by engaging leaders in partnerships to shape global, regional and industry agendas." See "World Economic Forum—Homepage," at www.weforum.org (accessed 12 January 2006).

6. Jane Nelson, "Turning Ethical Values into Business Value," *Global Agenda* (Davos and London: World Economic Forum and World Link Publications, 2003). Similarly, as James Muldoon has argued: "Survival in today's business environment has as much to do with successfully managing complex interactions with governments, multilateral institutions, and global social movements as with efficiency and competitiveness." See James P. Muldoon Jr., "The Diplomacy of Business," *Diplomacy and Statecraft* 16, no. 2 (2005): 355.

7. Milton Friedman, "The Social Responsibility of Business Is to Increase Its Profits," *New York Times Magazine*, 13 September 1970. Similar to some contemporary critics of "corporate citizenship" and "corporate social responsibility" initiatives, Friedman argued that discussions of the social responsibilities of business suffered from "analytical looseness and lack of rigor."

8. The extent to which corporate global citizenship reports are taken seriously varies. As a trade journal for human resources professionals notes: "The value that social reports offer in building corporate reputation is clouded by questions about their completeness, accuracy, and credibility. Social reports generally tend to generate more critique than appreciation." See Philip Radhika, "Corporate Social Reporting," *Human Resources Planning*, January 2003.

9. "Hanjin Shipping Co., Ltd.—Company View," *Datamonitor Company Profiles*, 19 June 2004.

10. Ken Larson, interview with author, Roseville, CA, 11 May 2005.

11. In early 2005, the division included 120 staffers around the world.

12. "Electronic Industry Code of Conduct," at www.hp.com/hpinfo/globalcitizenship/environment/pdf/supcode.pdf (accessed 20 January 2006).

13. Dick Conrad, "ISM Launches Social Responsibility Activity for Supply Managers," *Supplier Selection & Management Report*, June 2004.

14. "HP Global Citizenship Report: Energy Efficiency," at hp.com/hpinfo/globalcitizenship/gcreport/energy.html (accessed 20 August 2007).

15. Typically such loans are used by people starting up small businesses who need to buy basic equipment and merchandise in order to open.

16. "HP Provides $1.3 Million in Technology Grants to Non-Profit Organizations Nationwide," *BusinessWire*, 18 April 2003.

17. Debra Dunn, quoted in Alison Maitland, "Business Also Benefits from Helping the Poor," *Financial Times*, 29 September 2003.

18. Carly Fiorina, quoted in Diane Francis, "From Isolation to Integration," *National Post*, 24 January 2004.

19. Benjamin Pimentel, "Court Dismisses Charges against Former HP Chair," *San Francisco Chronicle*, 15 March 2007, and Matt Richtel, "Charges Dismissed in Hewlett-Packard Spying Case," *New York Times*, 15 March 2007.

20. "HP Global Citizenship Report—Governance and Ethics Complicance" at www.hp.com/hpinfo/globalcitizenship/gcreport/ethics.html (accessed 16 March 2007).

21. Daniel Vasella, interview with author, Basel, Switzerland, 11 January 2001.

22. Vasella added that he uses the term "global citizenship" on purpose, not by accident or by chance, and that he has used it repeatedly but not regularly: "First, it works best in English—it doesn't work in all languages; and secondly, it doesn't work with all people that don't know what it means, not what I believe it means." Vasella said that in his view, the French term *citoyen du monde* and the German term *Weltbürger* both lack notions of moral responsibility and "humanistic values" that are implicit, in his mind, within the term "global citizen."

23. When Novartis sponsored a "peace summit" for youngsters from the Middle East, Vasella noted that "as a global citizen, Novartis wants to promote peace and security, a fundamental condition to human well-being and economic development." See Daniel Vasella, quoted in "First Middle East Youth Summit Held during Israeli/Palestinian Negotiations," *PR Newswire*, 28 April 1998.

24. According to World Health Organization (WHO) estimates, malaria infects more than three hundred million people each year and kills one million people annually. Only tuberculosis claims more lives.

25. Alexander G. Higgins, "Malaria Drug Costs to Be Cut," Associated Press, 24 May 2001. News of this differential pricing came as the pharmaceutical industry was under considerable pressure from nongovernmental organizations, most notably

Médecins Sans Frontières, to improve the accessibility of medicines deemed essential. Also in May 2001, a group of large pharmaceutical companies, including Novartis, dropped an internationally denounced lawsuit against South Africa that would have prevented the South African government from importing inexpensive versions of patented drugs, especially drugs related to AIDS.

26. Daniel Vasella, quoted in Melody Peterson, "Novartis Agrees to Lower Price of a Medicine Used in Africa," *New York Times*, 3 May 2001.

27. Klaus Leisinger, interview with author, Basel, Switzerland, 22 January 2001.

28. "Corporate Citizenship," at www.cisco.com/en/US/about/ac227/about_cisco_corporate_citizenship_home.html (accessed 21 January 2006). Cisco's public relations department declined to provide an interview with John Chambers for this study or to explain the context of the quotation.

29. Lui Di, quoted in Ann Lau, "Presentation of Proposal to Annual Meeting of Cisco Stockholders," at www.visual-artists-guild.org/VAG/Pages/_start.html (accessed 12 June 2005).

30. "Notice of [2002] Annual Meeting of Shareholders," at www.cisco.com/en/US/about/ac49/ac20/ac19/ar2003/proxy/ (accessed 11 June 2005).

31. "Race to the Bottom: Corporate Complicity in Chinese Internet Censorship," at www.hrw.org/reports/2006/china0806/index.htm (accessed 29 June 2007).

32. "Notice of [2003] Annual Meeting and Proxy Statement," at www.hp.com/hpinfo/investor/financials/annual/2002/03proxy.pdf (accessed 11 June 2005).

33. "Razing Rafah: Mass Home Demolitions in the Gaza Strip," at hrw.org/campaigns/gaza/ (accessed 11 June 2005).

34. "Code of Worldwide Business Conduct," at www.cat.com/cda/layout?m= 39260&x=7 (accessed 6 June 2005). As of March 2007, Caterpillar's code of conduct linked to this web page contains a reference to "global citizenship" in language different from before: "We are global citizens and responsible members of our communities who are dedicated to safety, care for the environment, and manage our business ethically."

35. Cheryl Brodersen, quoted in "Caterpillar's Sale of Bulldozers to Israel to Destroy Palestinian Homes Protested,"Associated Press, 14 April 2004.

36. Liat Weingart, interview with author, Oakland, CA, 7 June 2005.

37. Sarah Leah Whitson, interview with author, New York, 6 June 2005.

38. The Israeli military has maintained that the driver of the bulldozer did not see Rachel Corrie. Her colleagues who witnessed the incident have disputed that account. See Greg Myre, "Israeli Army Bulldozer Kills American Protesting in Gaza," *New York Times*, 17 March 2003.

39. As of March 2007, the lawsuits were still pending in both jurisdictions. The case attracted much interest in international law circles as it marked the first time when two lawsuits regarding the same incident were filed concurrently in more than one country. See Henry Weinstein and Laura King, "Activist's Parents Sue Caterpillar Inc.," *Los Angeles Times*, 20 March 2005.

40. "Notice of [2004] Annual Meeting of Stockholders," at www.cat.com (accessed 6 June 2005).

41. "Calvin Klein Craves a Global Citizen," *Cosmetics International Cosmetic Products Report*, July 2002.

42. Sravanthi Challapalli, "How Indigo Nation Engineered a Kumble Makeover," *Hindu*, 31 July 2002.

43. Roger Ibbotson, quoted in Donald Jay Korn, "Overseas, Underpriced," *Financial Planning*, November 2002.

44. Suzanne McGee, "Caution for Continent-Hoppers," *Financial Times*, 2 November 2004.

45. F. Daniel Prickett, quoted in Jennifer Zajac, "Active Management," *Private Banker International*, 11 October 1999.

46. Barclays has operated on the island of Jersey since 1925 and also has branches in offshore jurisdictions such as Cyprus, Gibraltar, and various Caribbean islands.

47. John Church, "The Changing Face of Offshore Banking," *International Money Marketing*, 19 February 1999.

48. Martyn Scriven, interview with author, Helier, Jersey, UK, 19 June 2001.

49. Diana Parker, quoted in "Transatlantic Merger Leads to World's First International Law Firm," *Business Wire*, 4 December 2001.

50. Jim Brennan, quoted by Normandy Madden, "Campaigns: United Connects with Flyers," *Ad Age Global*, July 2002.

51. Pankaj Sazena, quoted in Vidyashree Amaresh, "For High Living," *Hindu*, 12 November 2004.

52. "Iridium North America Announces New Pricing Structure," *Business Wire*, 24 June 1999.

53. Thomas R. Petersen, interview with author, Valencia, CA, 10 April 2000.

54. Falk also casts a skeptical eye upon corporate global citizenship initiatives. In his words: "The corporate embrace of globalism should perhaps not even be associated with citizenship as it posits and acknowledges no accompanying global community, and hence contains no bonds of solidarity with those who are weak and disadvantaged, or with people generally." See Richard Falk, *The Declining World Order: America's Imperial Geopolitics* (London: Routledge, 2004), 181.

55. David Croft, quoted in Rachel Barnes, "Fairtrade Enters the Mainstream," *Marketing*, 4 March 2004.

56. Maura Quinn, quoted in "Eur9 Saves a Life, Does Business Care?" *Business & Finance*, 4 December 2003.

57. An international public opinion survey, released by the Pew Research Center for the People and the Press just before the invasion of Iraq in March 2003, found sharp drops in public regard for the United States even in countries with governments that had supported the invasion. In the United Kingdom, 48 percent of the public had a favorable view of the United States in early 2003, compared with 83 percent three years earlier. In France, the favorability rating dropped from 62 percent to 31 percent;

Germany, 78 percent to 25 percent; Italy, 76 percent to 34 percent; Poland, 86 percent to 50 percent; Russia, 37 percent to 28 percent; Spain, 50 percent to 14 percent; and Turkey, 52 percent to 12 percent. See "America's Image Further Erodes, Europeans Want Weaker Ties," at people-press.org/reports/display.php3?ReportID=175 (accessed 14 June 2005). Favorability ratings for the United States recovered slightly in Pew's 2004 survey but remained well below levels prior to 2003.

58. Formed in the aftermath of September 11, 2001, Business for Diplomatic Action is an association of executives and professionals with the aim of rebuilding the global image of American business.

59. "Businesses Decide to Tackle Problems of Being American," *Gannett News Service*, 23 February 2004.

Chapter 7

1. Gareth Evans, "Making Australian Foreign Policy," *Australian Fabian Society Pamphlet 50* (Canberra, 1989), 42. For Evans, good international citizenship meant that Australia would rise to the occasion on challenges such as international peacekeeping, arms control, environmental protection, curbing drug trafficking, and opening the country to refugees.

2. Simon Marks, "Oil Futures Price Rises during Price War Conflict," transcript of *Marketplace*, Minnesota Public Radio, 27 November 2001.

3. Simon Mills, "Five Stars for 2002," *Guardian*, 29 December 2001.

4. "Rush of S-N Contacts May Help Doves in Bush Administration," *Korea Times*, 15 August 2002, and "An Odd Time to Pick a Fight," *Buffalo (NY) News*, 5 December 2001.

5. Paul Cleary, "China, India Now Likely to Ratify," *Australian Financial Review*, 30 August 2002.

6. "China Is Hoping Accession to the World Trade Organization Will Jolt Its Economy into Faster Growth," *Banker*, May 2002.

7. Gregory Bair, "Stopping the Chinese Abuse of Power," *Indianapolis Star*, 8 April 1999.

8. Carmen Lawrence, "It's Time to Face the Real Reasons for Defeat," *Australian Financial Review*, 30 November 2001, and Jurgen Gregersen, "Every Child Counts," *Gold Coast Bulletin*, 17 June 2002.

9. Walter Tonetto, "The Death of Symbolism in Australia," *Jakarta Post*, 16 December 1999.

10. Noel Ryan, "Australia—Future Pollution Haven," *Illawarra Mercury*, 5 November 2002, and Robert Messenger, "Charcoal Plant to Cost $1b—Adviser," *Canberra Times*, 29 May 2002.

11. "Australia Seen as Laggard State," *Tasmanian Country*, 23 August 2002.

12. Melissa Fyfe, "Track Record Earns Australia Environmental 'Renegade' Status," *Age*, 19 August 2002.

13. Canadian soldiers remained alongside United States troops in Afghanistan.

14. Jean Chrétien, quoted in Richard Gwyn, "Good Global Citizenship Matters to Canadians," *Toronto Star*, 4 January 2003.

15. Paul Martin, "It's Time to Revisit Nuclear Fuel Storage," *Saskatchewan Business*, November 2003.

16. Pico Iyer, "Canada: Global Citizen," *Canadian Geographic*, 1 November 2004.

17. Robert A. Manning, "Saving U.S. Foreign Policy From Its Worst Instincts," *Boston Globe*, 27 December 1999.

18. Walter Russell Mead, "A Fading Coalition on Iraq," *Los Angeles Times*, 20 December 1998.

19. Tim Rochford, "Leadership Required," *Dominion*, 13 December 2001, and David Crane, "America's Failure on Climate Change," *Toronto Star*, 29 June 2002.

20. George W. Bush, quoted in Derrick Z. Jackson, "Who's to Blame on Global Issues," *Boston Globe*, 6 April 2001.

21. Derek Heater, *World Citizenship: Cosmopolitan Thinking and Its Opponents* (London: Continuum, 2002), 125.

22. Unsigned letter to the editor, *Express*, 2 March 2003.

23. "Sen. Snowe Urges EPA to Strengthen Domestic Regulation of Mercury Levels," *U.S. Fed News*, 29 June 2004.

24. "Global Disarray," Dow Jones News Service, 14 August 1998.

25. "George Robertson Punches above His Weight," *Economist*, 11 July 1998.

26. David Rieff, "Goodbye, New World Order," *Mother Jones*, 1 July 2003.

27. Kumi Naidoo, "Civil Society at a Time of Global Uncertainty," *OECD Observer*, May 2003.

28. David Suzuki, quoted in "200,000 Anti-War Protesters March through Montreal," *Kitchener-Waterloo Record*, 17 March 2003.

29. "Civic Groups Challenge Constitutionality of Troop Dispatch," *Organisation of Asia-Pacific News Agencies*, 3 April 2005.

30. Barb Johns, "Your Letters," *Cairns Post*, 5 April 2003.

31. Tony Troughear, letter to the editor, *Newcastle Herald*, 15 February 2003.

32. Joyce Neu, "A Slow, Frustrating—and Valuable—U.N.," *San Diego Tribune*, 16 March 2003.

33. Byron Litsey, "Regarding 'A Slow, Frustrating—and Valuable—U.N.'," *San Diego Tribune*, 22 March 2003.

34. Brian Presley, "Brian Presley Column," *Port Charlotte Sun*, 8 December 2002.

35. Graham Egan, letter to the editor, *Sunday Mail*, 30 March 2003.

36. Dave Kitchen, letter to the editor, *Age*, 11 March 2003.

37. Bob Tunks, "Sustainable Course," *Santa Rosa Press-Democrat*, 21 October 2003.

38. Amy Lange, "Students Must Take Advantage of Their Power on Nov. 2," *Minnesota Daily*, 7 October 2004.

39. It does not appear that George W. Bush has ever made a specific public reference to global citizenship. The writer, in this instance, might be referring to an often-cited statement from Bush, made during a debate with Al Gore on 11 October

2000 at Wake Forest University, regarding how the United States is regarded around the world: "If we're an arrogant nation, they'll resent us. If we're a humble nation, they'll respect us." "The Second Gore-Bush Presidential Debate," at debates.org/pages/trans2000b.html (accessed 12 December 2005).

40. David Shroder, "Only Fools Believe Bush Promises Now," *Daily Herald (IL)*, 6 October 2004.

41. "American Offers His Presidential Election Vote to Malaysian Public," *Voice of America Press Releases and Documents*, 22 September 2004.

42. "Final Analysis: John Kerry Gets One 'Malaysian' Vote," at www.malaysiakini .com/letters/30839 (accessed 19 December 2005).

43. Eric Ossemig, quoted in Steven Gan, "American Offers His Vote to Malaysiakini Readers," at www.malaysiakini.com/news/30170 (accessed 19 December 2005).

44. Argee Guevarra, "Fast Forward; Rock the Vote," *BusinessWorld*, 8 November 2004.

45. Michelle Young, "Bush's Election Spurs Student-Created Site," at media.www .dailytrojan.com/media/storage/paper679/news/2004/11/19/News/Bushs.Election .Spurs.Student.Created.Site-811477.shtml (accessed 16 March 2007).

46. In Japanese, "global citizen" is pronounced as *chi-ku shi-min*.

47. In recent years, the left-leaning Kanagawa government has campaigned for the closure of several U.S. military bases located in the prefecture.

48. Alexander King and Bertrand Schneider, *The First Global Revolution: A Report by the Council of the Club of Rome* (New York: Pantheon Books, 1991).

49. Shigeru Shiono, interview with author, Hyama, Japan, 18 April 2001.

50. And yet, the Kanagawa government was not the first entity in Japan to use the term "global citizenship." In the early 1980s, a grassroots organization based in Kyushu went by the name Global Citizens Association.

51. For a good overview of regional development policy in the European Union, see Liesbet Hooghe, ed., *Cohesion Policy and European Integration: Building Multi-Level Governance* (Oxford: Oxford University Press, 1996).

52. Despite the widespread usage of "ethical foreign policy" during his tenure as foreign secretary, Cook distanced himself from the phrase, calling it "too easily capable of being misunderstood as grandstanding." See Robin Cook, "Beyond Good Intentions—Government, Business and the Environment," speech, Business and the Environment Dinner, St. James Palace, London, 17 November 1998.

53. Nick Coppin, interview with author, London, 11 December 2000.

54. "Pres. Kim Calls on Koreans to Become Global Citizens," *Korea Times*, 25 February 1999.

55. "Koreans Urged to Become Global Citizens," *Korea Times*, 5 March 1999.

56. "Sabbatical Leave Introduced for Teachers," *Korea Times*, 11 June 1999.

57. "Preamble to the Charter of the United Nations," at www.un.org/aboutun/charter/preamble.htm (accessed 17 June 2005).

58. Kofi Annan, "Television's Power Must Be Harnessed to Best of Human Endeavour, Says Secretary-General," *M2 Presswire*, 20 November 1998.

59. Kofi Annan, "Secretary-General Says 'Global People-Power' Best Thing for United Nations in Long Time," *M2 Presswire*, 9 December 1999.

60. Kofi Annan, "Hope Expressed that Declaration to Be Adopted at Lisbon Conference Will Be Reference for Future Action," *M2 Presswire*, 13 August 1998.

61. Felix Njoku, "Africa's Future Lies in Education—Mayor," Africa News Service, 21 April 1998.

62. Richard Jolly et al., *Globalization with a Human Face*, United Nations Human Development Programme (Oxford: Oxford University Press, 1999), 63.

63. In a statement calling for Australia's Conservative government to pledge to reduce greenhouse gas emissions to 10 percent below 1990 levels without imposing a carbon tax, Lees stated: "The Government now has before it dozens, if not hundreds, of ideas on how to address the greenhouse problem as a responsible global citizen. . . . The Democrats challenge them to take action now and to save face at Kyoto." See Meg Lees, quoted in "Greenhouse Solution—A Carbon Tax–Free Model," *Australian Environment Review*, November 1997. More than three years later, in another party statement urging Australia's Conservative government to avoid following the United States in its abandonment of the Kyoto accord, Lees stated that the American withdrawal was "hugely disappointing; we should be working with Britain and Europe and being responsible global citizens." See Lees, quoted in "Democrats Say Would Be Wrong to Dump Kyoto," AAP Newsfeed, 2 April 2001.

64. Meg Lees, interview with author, 6 November 2000.

65. Thomas Jefferson et al., "The Declaration of Independence," at www.ushistory.org/declaration/ (accessed 15 March 2007).

66. John F. Kennedy, "Inaugural Address," 20 January 1961 at www.yale.edu/lawweb/avalon/presiden/inaug/kennedy.htm (accessed 16 March 2007).

67. Robert E. Heiler, "Snake Oil Pundit," *Washington Times*, 20 January 2002.

68. Hedley Bull, *The Anarchical Society*, 2nd ed. (New York: Columbia University Press, 1995), 25.

Conclusion

1. Christine Schuzle, interview with author, Moorhead, MN, 13 April 2000.

2. Robert Harper, interview with author, Mattituck, NY, 26 September 2000.

3. Janet Sipple, interview with author, Bethlehem, PA, 14 April 2000.

4. Denise Chávez, interview with author, Las Cruces, NM, 20 April 2000.

5. Kwame Anthony Appiah, "Cosmopolitan Patriots," in *For Love of Country? Debating the Limits of Patriotism*, ed. Joshua Cohen (Boston: Beacon Press, 1996), 26–27.

Recommended Readings

Ackerman, Bruce. "Rooted Cosmopolitanism." *Ethics* 104 (1994): 516–35.

Aleinkoff, T. Alexander, and Douglas Klusmeyer, eds. *From Migrants to Citizens: Membership in a Changing World.* Washington, DC: Carnegie Endowment for International Peace, 2000.

Anderson, Benedict. *Imagined Communities: Reflections on the Origin and Spread of Nationalism.* 2nd ed. New York: Verso, 1991.

Anzaldúa, Gloria. *Borderlands/La Frontera: The New Mestiza.* San Francisco: Aunt Lute, 1987.

Appiah, Kwame Anthony. "Cosmopolitan Patriots." In Cohen, *For Love of Country: Debating the Limits of Patriotism.*

———. *Cosmopolitanism: Ethics in a World of Strangers.* New York: W. W. Norton, 2006.

———. *The Ethics of Identity.* Princeton, NJ: Princeton University Press, 2004.

Archibugi, Daniele, David Held, and Martin Köhler, eds. *Re-imagining Political Community: Studies in Cosmopolitan Democracy.* Cambridge: Polity Press, 1998.

Barber, Benjamin R. "Constitutional Faith." In Cohen, *For Love of Country: Debating the Limits of Patriotism.*

———. *Fear's Empire: War, Terrorism and Democracy.* New York: W. W. Norton, 2003.

———. *Jihad vs. McWorld: How Globalism and Tribalism Are Reshaping the World.* New York: Ballantine, 1995.

———. *Strong Democracy: Participatory Politics for a New Age.* Berkeley: University of California Press, 1984.

Barry, Brian. *Culture and Equality: An Egalitarian Critique of Multiculturalism.* Cambridge, MA: Harvard University Press, 2001.

————. "Statism and Nationalism: A Cosmopolitan Critique." In Shapiro and Brilmayer, *Global Justice*, Nomos XLI.

Bauböck, Rainer. "Expansive Citizenship—Voting beyond Territory and Membership." *PS: Political Science & Politics* 38, no. 4 (2005): 683–87.

————. *Migration and Citizenship: Legal Status, Rights and Political Participation*. Amsterdam: Amsterdam University Press, 2006.

————. *Transnational Citizenship: Membership and Rights in International Migration*. Aldershot, UK: Edward Elgar, 1994.

Beck, Ulrich. "The Cosmopolitan Perspective: Sociology of the Second Age of Modernity." *British Journal of Sociology* 51, no. 1 (2000): 79–105.

————. "Democracy beyond the Nation-State" *Dissent*, no. 46.1 (1999).

————. *What Is Globalization?* Cambridge: Polity Press, 1999.

Beiner, Ronald, ed. *Theorizing Citizenship*. Albany: State University of New York Press, 1995.

Beitz, Charles R. "Cosmopolitanism and Sovereignty." In Brown, *Political Restructuring in Europe: Ethical Perspectives*.

————. *Political Theory and International Relations*. 2nd ed. Princeton, NJ: Princeton University Press, 1999.

————. "Social and Cosmopolitan Liberalism." *International Affairs* 75, no. 3 (1999): 515–29.

Benhabib, Seyla. *Another Cosmopolitanism: Hospitality, Sovereignty, and Democratic Iterations*. Oxford: Oxford University Press, 2006.

————. "Borders, Boundaries, and Citizenship." *PS: Political Science & Politics* 38, no. 4 (2005): 673–77.

————. *The Claims of Culture: Equality and Diversity in the Global Era*. Princeton, NJ: Princeton University Press, 2002.

————. "Models of Public Space." In *Habermas and the Public Sphere*, edited by Craig Calhoun. Cambridge, MA: MIT Press, 1992.

————. *The Rights of Others: Aliens, Residents, and Citizens*. Cambridge: Cambridge University Press, 2004.

Bohman, James. "The Public Spheres of the World Citizen." In *Perpetual Peace: Essays on Kant's Cosmopolitan Ideal*, edited by James Bohman and Matthias Lutz-Backmann. Cambridge, MA: MIT Press, 1997.

Bohman, James, and Matthias Lutz-Backmann, eds. *Perpetual Peace: Essays on Kant's Cosmopolitan Ideal*. Cambridge, MA: MIT Press, 1997.

Boli, John, and George M. Thomas, eds. *Constructing World Culture: International Non-Governmental Organizations since 1875*. Stanford, CA: Stanford University Press, 1999.

————. "World Culture in the World Polity: A Century of International Non-Governmental Organization." *American Sociological Review* 62, no. 2 (1997): 171–90.

Bookchin, Murray. *From Urbanization to Cities: Towards a New Politics of Citizenship*. New York: Cassell, 1995.

Bosniak, Linda. *The Citizen and the Alien: Dilemmas of Contemporary Membership.* Princeton, NJ: Princeton University Press, 2006.

———. "Denationalizing Citizenship." In *Citizenship Today*, edited by T. Alexander Aleinkoff and Douglas Klusmeyer. Washington, DC: Carnegie Endowment for International Peace, 2000.

Boulding, Elise. *Building a Global Civic Culture.* New York: Teachers College Press, 1988.

Brown, Chris. *Political Restructuring in Europe: Ethical Perspectives.* London: Routledge, 1994.

Bull, Hedley. *The Anarchical Society.* 2nd ed. New York: Columbia University Press, 1995.

Carens, Joseph H. "Aliens and Citizens: The Case for Open Borders." In Beiner, *Theorizing Citizenship.*

Carter, April. *The Political Theory of Global Citizenship.* London: Routledge, 2001.

Castles, Stephen, and Alastair Davidson. *Citizenship and Migration: Globalization and the Politics of Belonging.* Basingstoke, UK: Macmillan, 2000.

Cavanagh, John, Jerry Mander, and others, eds. *Alternatives to Economic Globalization: A Better World Is Possible.* 2nd ed. New York: Berrett-Koehler, 2004.

Cheah, Pheng. "The Cosmopolitical Today." In Cheah and Robbins, *Cosmopolitics: Thinking and Feeling beyond the Nation.*

Cheah, Pheng, and Bruce Robbins, eds. *Cosmopolitics: Thinking and Feeling beyond the Nation.* Minneapolis: University of Minnesota Press, 1998.

Cohen, Mitchell. "Rooted Cosmopolitanism." *Dissent* 39, no. 4 (1992): 478–83.

Cohen, Joshua, ed. *For Love of Country: Debating the Limits of Patriotism.* Boston: Beacon Press, 1996.

Commission on Global Governance. *Our Global Neighbourhood: The Report of the Commission on Global Governance.* Oxford: Oxford University Press, 1995.

Crewe, Ivor. "Citizenship: The Revival of an Idea." In *Citizenship and Civic Education.* London: Citizenship Foundation, 1997.

Crick, Bernard. *Essays on Citizenship.* London: Continuum, 2000.

Crouch, Colin, Klaus Eder, and Damian Tambini, eds. *Citizenship, Markets and the State.* Oxford: Oxford University Press, 2001

Dahl, Robert A. "A Democratic Dilemma: System Effectiveness versus Citizen Participation." *Political Science Quarterly* 109, no. 1 (1994): 23–34.

Danaher, Kevin, and Roger Burbach, eds. *Globalize This! The Battle against the World Trade Organization and Corporate Rule.* Monroe, ME: Common Courage Press, 2000.

Davidson, James Dale, and William Rees-Mogg. *The Sovereign Individual: How to Survive and Thrive during the Collapse of the Welfare State.* New York: Simon & Schuster, 1997.

Debeljak, Aleš. *The Hidden Handshake: National Identity and Europe in the Post-Communist World.* Lanham, MD: Rowman & Littlefield Publishers, 2004.

Delanty, Gerard. *Citizenship in a Global Age: Society, Culture, Politics.* Ballmoor, UK: Open University Press, 2000.

Della Porta, Donatella, and Sidney G. Tarrow, eds. *Transnational Protest and Global Activism*. Lanham, MD: Rowman & Littlefield, 2005.

Dower, Nigel. "The Idea of Global Citizenship—A Sympathetic Assessment." *Global Society* 14 (2000): 553–67.

Dower, Nigel, and John Williams, eds. *Global Citizenship: A Critical Introduction*. London: Routledge, 2002.

Drake, Christine. "Education for Responsible Global Citizenship." *Journal of Geography* 86, no. 6 (1987): 300–306.

Dryzek, John S. "Transnational Democracy." *Journal of Political Philosophy* 7, no. 1 (1999): 30–51.

Edwards, Michael, and John Gaventa, eds. *Global Citizen Action*. Boulder, CO: Lynne Rienner, 2001.

Falk, Richard A. "The Decline of Citizenship in an Era of Globalization." *Citizenship Studies* 4, no. 1 (2000): 3–17.

———. "The Making of Global Citizenship." In van Steenbergen, *The Condition of Citizenship*.

——— *The Declining World Order: America's Imperial Geopolitics*. London, Routledge, 2004.

———. *On Humane Governance: Toward a New Global Politics*. Cambridge: Polity Press, 1995.

Falk, Richard A., and Andrew Strauss. "Toward Global Parliament." *Foreign Affairs* 80, no. 1 (2001): 212–20.

Faulks, Keith. *Citizenship*. London: Routledge, 2000.

Featherstone, Michael, ed. *Global Culture*. London: Sage Publications, 1995.

Ferguson, Yale H., and Richard W. Mansbach. "History's Revenge and Future Shock." In *Approaches to Global Governance Theory*, edited by Martin Hewson and Timothy J. Sinclair. Albany: State University of New York Press, 1999.

Florini, Ann. M. *The Coming Democracy: New Rules for Running a New World*. Washington, DC: Island Press, 2003.

———, ed. *The Third Force: The Rise of Transnational Civil Society*. Washington, DC: Carnegie Endowment for International Peace, 2000.

Frosh, Stephen. "Psychoanalysis, Identity and Citizenship." In *Culture and Citizenship*, edited by Nick Stevenson. London: Sage Publications, 2001.

Gaventa, John. "Global Citizen Action: Lessons and Challenges." In *Global Citizen Action*, edited by Michael Edwards and John Gaventa. Boulder, CO: Lynne Rienner, 2001.

Gladwell, Malcolm. *The Tipping Point: How Little Things Can Make a Big Difference*. Boston: Little, Brown, 2000.

Googins, Bradley. "The Journey towards Corporate Citizenship in the United States: Leader or Laggard?" *Journal of Corporate Citizenship* 5 (2002): 85–101.

Greider, William. *One World, Ready or Not: The Manic Logic of Global Capitalism*. New York: Touchstone, 1997.

Gutmann, Amy. "Democratic Citizenship." In Cohen, *For Love of Country? Debating the Limits of Patriotism*.

Habermas, Jürgen. "Citizenship and National Identity: Some Reflections on the Future of Europe." In Beiner, *Theorizing Citizenship*.

———. *Between Facts and Norms: Contributions to a Discourse Theory of Law and Democracy.* Translated by William Rehg. Cambridge, MA: MIT Press, 1996.

———. *The Divided West.* Oxford: Blackwell, 2006.

———. *The Postnational Constellation.* Cambridge, MA: MIT Press, 2001.

Hahn, Carole L. "Promise and Paradox: Challenges to Global Citizenship." *Social Education* 48, no. 4 (1984): 240–43, 297–99.

Hanagan, Michael, and Charles Tilly, eds. *Extending Citizenship, Reconfiguring States.* Lanham, MD: Rowman & Littlefield, 1999.

Hannerz, Ulf. "Cosmopolitans and Locals in World Culture." In *Global Culture*, edited by Michael Featherstone. London: Sage Publications, 1990.

Harris, Errol E., and James A. Yunker, eds. *Toward Genuine Global Governance: Critical Reactions to "Our Global Neighbourhood."* London: Praeger, 1999.

Hayward, J. E. S. "Solidarity: The Social History of an Idea in 19th Century France." *International Review of Social History* 4 (1959): 270–71.

Heater, Derek. *Citizenship: The Civic Ideal in World History, Politics and Education.* London: Longman, 1990.

———. "Does Cosmopolitan Thinking Have a Future?" *Review of International Studies* 26 (2000): 179–97.

———. *What Is Citizenship?* Cambridge: Polity Press, 1999.

———. *World Citizenship and Government: Cosmopolitan Ideas in the History of Western Political Thought.* New York: St. Martin's Press, 1996.

———. *World Citizenship: Cosmopolitan Thinking and Its Opponents.* London: Continuum, 2002.

Held, David. *Democracy and the Global Order.* Cambridge: Polity Press, 1995.

———. "The Transformation of Political Community: Rethinking Democracy in the Context of Globalization." In *Democracy's Edges*, edited by Ian Shapiro and Casiano Hacker-Cordón. Cambridge: Cambridge University Press, 1999.

Held, David, Anthony McGrew, David Goldblatt, and Jonathan Perraton. *Global Transformations: Politics, Economics and Culture.* Cambridge: Polity Press, 1999.

Hemphill, Thomas A. "Monitoring Global Corporate Citizenship: Industry Self-Regulation at a Crossroads." *Journal of Corporate Citizenship* 14 (2004): 81–96.

Hewson, Martin, and Timothy J. Sinclair, eds. *Approaches to Global Governance Theory.* Albany: State University of New York Press, 1999.

Hirst, Paul, and Grahame Thompson. *Globalization in Question.* 2nd ed. Cambridge: Polity Press, 1999.

Hollenbach, David. *The Common Good and Christian Ethics.* Cambridge: Cambridge University Press, 2002.

Hollinger, David A. *Postethnic America: Beyond Multiculturalism.* New York: Basic Books, 1995.

Honig, Bonnie. *Democracy and the Foreigner.* Princeton, NJ: Princeton University Press, 2001.

Honohan, Iseult. *Civic Republicanism.* London: Routledge, 2002.

Hooghe, Liesbet, ed. *Cohesion Policy and European Integration: Building Multi-Level Governance.* Oxford: Oxford University Press, 1996.

Hurrell, Andrew. "Kant and the Kantian Paradigm in International Relations." *Review of International Studies* 16 (1990): 183–205.

Hutchings, Kimberly, and Roland Dannreuther, eds. *Cosmopolitan Citizenship.* London: Macmillan, 1999.

Ignatieff, Michael. *Blood and Belonging: Journeys into the New Nationalism.* New York: Farrar, Straus and Giroux, 1993.

Isin, Engin F., ed. *Democracy, Citizenship and the Global City.* London: Routledge, 2000.

Jackson, Robert, ed. *International Perspectives on Citizenship, Education and Religious Diversity.* London, Routledge, 2003.

Jacobson, David. *Rights across Borders: Immigration and the Decline of Citizenship.* Baltimore: Johns Hopkins University Press, 1996.

Jelin, Elizabeth. "Toward a Global Environmental Citizenship?" *Citizenship Studies* 4, no. 1 (2000): 47–63.

Jones, Charles. *Global Justice: Defending Cosmopolitanism.* Oxford: Oxford University Press, 1999.

———. "Patriotism, Morality and Global Justice." In Shapiro and Brilmayer, *Global Justice.*

Joppke, Christian, ed. *Challenge to the Nation-State: Immigration in Western Europe and the United States.* Oxford: Oxford University Press, 1998.

———. "Immigration Challenges the Nation-State." In *Challenge to the Nation-State: Immigration in Western Europe and the United States,* edited by Christian Joppke. Oxford: Oxford University Press, 1998.

Kaldor, Mary. "Civilising Globalisation." *Millennium* 29, no. 1 (2000): 105–14.

Kant, Immanuel. "Perpetual Peace: A Philosophical Sketch." Translated by H. B. Nisbet. In *Kant: Political Writings,* edited by Hans Reiss. Cambridge: Cambridge University Press, 1991.

Kaul, Inge, Isabelle Grunberg, and Marc A. Stern, eds. *Global Public Goods: International Cooperation in the 21st Century.* Oxford: Oxford University Press, 1999.

Keck, Margaret E., and Kathryn Sikkink. *Activists beyond Borders: Advocacy Networks in International Politics.* Ithaca, NY: Cornell University Press, 1998.

Kell, Georg. "The Global Compact: Origins, Operations, Progress, Challenges." *Journal of Corporate Citizenship* 11 (2003): 35–50.

Keohane, Robert O. *Power and Governance in a Partially Globalized World.* London: Routledge, 2002.

Kerr, Clark. "International Learning and National Purposes in Higher Education." *American Behavioral Scientist* 35, no. 1 (1991): 17–42.

Kymlicka, Will. *Multicultural Citizenship: A Liberal Theory of Minority Rights.* Oxford: Oxford University Press, 1995.

———. *Politics in the Vernacular: Nationalism, Multiculturalism and Citizenship.* Oxford: Oxford University Press, 2001.

———, ed. *The Rights of Minority Cultures*. Oxford: Oxford University Press, 1995.

Kymlicka, Will, and Wayne Norman. "Return of the Citizen: A Survey of Recent Work in Citizenship Theory." In *Theorizing Citizenship*, edited by Ronald Beiner. Albany: State University of New York Press, 1995.

Lane, Robert E. *Political Man*. New York: Free Press, 1972.

Lasch, Christopher. *The Revolt of the Elites and the Betrayal of Democracy*. New York: W. W. Norton, 1995.

Levitt, Peggy. *The Transnational Villagers*. Berkeley: University of California Press, 2001.

Linklater, Andrew. "Citizenship and Sovereignty in the Post-Westphalian European State." In Archibugi, Held, and Köhler, *Re-imagining Political Community: Studies in Cosmopolitan Democracy*.

———. "Cosmopolitan Citizenship." In Hutchings and Dannreuther, *Cosmopolitan Citizenship*.

Lipschutz, Ronnie, ed. *Globalization, Governmentality and Global Politics: Regulation for the Rest of Us?* London: Routledge, 2005.

Lister, Ian. "Citizenship and Citizenship Education in Britain." In *Citizenship and Citizenship Education in a Changing World*, edited by Orit Ichilov. London: Woburn Press, 1998.

Lu, Catherine. *Just and Unjust Interventions in World Politics: Public and Private*. Basingstoke, UK: Palgrave Macmillan, 2006.

Lu, Catherine. "The One and Many Faces of Cosmopolitanism." *Journal of Political Philosophy* 8, no. 2 (2000): 244–67.

Lynch, Marc. "The Dialogue of Civilisations and International Public Spheres." *Millennium* 29, no. 2 (2000): 307–30.

Machacek, David, and Bryan Wilson. *Global Citizens: The Soka Gakkai Buddhist Movement in the World*. Oxford: Oxford University Press, 2000.

Malcomson, Scott L. "The Varieties of Cosmopolitan Experience." In Cheah and Robbins, *Cosmopolitics: Thinking and Feeling beyond the Nation*.

Marshall, T. H. *Class, Citizenship and Social Class*. Cambridge: Cambridge University Press, 1963.

Maxwell, Joseph A. *Qualitative Research Design: An Interactive Approach*. London: Sage Publications, 1996.

McLuhan, Marshall. *The Global Village: Transformations in World Life and Media in the 21st Century*. Oxford: Oxford University Press, 1989.

Meadows, Donella. *The Global Citizen*. Washington, DC: Island Press, 1991.

———, and others. *The Limits to Growth: A Report for the Club of Rome's Project on the Predicament of Mankind*. London: Earth Island, 1972.

Muetzelfeldt, Michael, and Gary Smith. "Civil Society and Global Governance: The Possibilities for Global Citizenship." *Citizenship Studies* 6, no. 1 (2002): 55–75.

Muldoon, James P., Jr. "The Diplomacy of Business." *Diplomacy and Statecraft* 16, no. 2 (2005): 341–59.

Muirhead, Sophia A., and others. "Corporate Citizenship in the New Century: Accountability, Transparency and Global Stakeholder Engagement." New York: Conference Board, 2002.

Miller, David. "Bounded Citizenship." In Hutchings and Dannreuther, *Cosmopolitan Citizenship*.

———. *Citizenship and National Identity*. Cambridge: Polity Press, 2000.

———. *On Nationality*. Oxford: Oxford University Press, 1995.

Noddings, Nel, ed. *Education for Global Awareness*. New York: Teachers College Press, 2005.

Norris, Pippa. "Global Governance and Cosmopolitan Citizens." In *Governance in a Globalizing World*, edited by Joseph S. Nye Jr. and John D. Donahue. Washington, DC: Brookings Institution Press, 2000.

Notes from Nowhere, ed. *We Are Everywhere*. London: Verso, 2003.

Nussbaum, Martha C. *Cultivating Humanity: A Classical Defense of Reform in Liberal Education*. Cambridge, MA: Harvard University Press, 1997.

———. "Patriotism and Cosmopolitanism." In Cohen, *For Love of Country: Debating the Limits of Patriotism*.

Nye, Joseph S., Jr. *The Paradox of American Power: Why the World's Only Superpower Can't Go It Alone*. Oxford: Oxford University Press, 2003.

———. *Soft Power: The Means to Success in World Politics*. New York: Public Affairs, 2004.

Nye, Joseph S., Jr., and John D. Donahue, eds. *Governance in a Globalizing World*. Washington, DC: Brookings Institution Press, 2000.

O'Brien, Lynne M., and William E. Pulliam. "Media and the Global Citizen." *Social Education* 42, no. 7 (1978): 624–29.

O'Byrne, Darren. *The Dimensions of Global Citizenship: Political Identity beyond the Nation-State*. London: Routledge, 2003.

Oldfield, Adrian. *Citizenship and Community: Civic Republicanism and the Modern World*. London: Routledge, 1990.

O'Neill, Onora. "Justice and Boundaries." In Brown, *Political Restructuring in Europe: Ethical Perspectives*.

———. "Bounded and Cosmopolitan Justice." *Review of International Studies* 26 (2002): 45–60.

Ong, Aihwa. "Flexible Citizenship among Chinese Cosmopolitans." In Cheah and Robbins, *Cosmopolitics: Thinking and Feeling beyond the Nation*.

———. *Flexible Citizenship: The Cultural Logics of Transnationality*. Durham, NC: Duke University Press, 1999.

———. "(Re)Articulations of Citizenship." *PS: Political Science & Politics* 38, no. 4 (2005): 697–99.

Pacheco, Manuel, and Celesino Fernandez. "Knowing No Boundaries: The University as World Citizen." *Educational Record* 73, no. 2 (1992): 23–27.

Parekh, Bhikhu. "Cosmopolitanism and Global Citizenship." *Review of International Studies* 29, no. 1 (2003): 12.

———. "Dilemmas of a Multicultural Theory of Citizenship." *Constellations* 4, no. 1 (1997): 54–62.

———. *Rethinking Multiculturalism: Cultural Diversity and Political Theory.* Cambridge, MA: Harvard University Press, 2000.

Parker, Walter C., Akira Ninomiya, and John Cogan. "Educating World Citizens: Toward Multinational Curriculum Development." *American Educational Research Journal* 36, no. 2 (1999): 117–45.

Pocock, J. G. A. "The Ideal of Citizenship since Classical Times." In Shafir, *The Citizenship Debates.*

———. *The Machiavellian Moment: Florentine Political Thought and the Atlantic Republican Tradition.* Princeton, NJ: Princeton University Press, 1975.

Pogge, Thomas. "Cosmopolitanism and Sovereignty." *Ethics* 103 (1992): 48–75.

———. *World Poverty and Human Rights: Cosmopolitan Responsibilities and Reforms.* Cambridge: Polity Press, 2002.

Post, James E. "Global Corporate Citizenship: Principles to Live and Work By." *Business Ethics Quarterly* 12, no. 2 (2002): 143–53.

Reich, Robert B. *The Work of Nations: Preparing Ourselves for 21st-Century Capitalism.* New York: Knopf, 1991.

Reimers, Fernando. "Citizenship, Identity and Education: Examining the Public Purposes of Schools in an Age of Globalization." *Prospects* 36, no. 3 (2006): 275–94.

Richards, Lyn, and Tom Richards. "From Filing Cabinet to Computer." In *Analyzing Qualitative Data,* edited by Alan Bryman and Robert G. Burgess. London: Routledge, 1994.

Riesenberg, Peter. *Citizenship in the Western Tradition: Plato to Rousseau.* Chapel Hill: University of North Carolina Press, 1992.

Risse, Thomas. "The Power of Norms versus the Norms of Power: Transnational Civil Society and Human Rights." In *The Third Force: The Rise of Transnational Civil Society,* edited by Ann M. Florini. Tokyo and Washington, DC: Japan Center for International Exchange and Carnegie Endowment for International Peace, 2000.

Robbins, Bruce. "Actually Existing Cosmopolitanism." In Cheah and Robbins, *Cosmopolitics: Thinking and Feeling beyond the Nation.*

———. "Comparative Cosmopolitanisms." In Cheah and Robbins, *Cosmopolitics: Thinking and Feeling beyond the Nation.*

———. *Feeling Global: Internationalism in Distress.* New York: New York University Press, 1999.

Roberts, John C. de V. *World Citizenship and Mundialism: A Guide to the Building of a World Community.* Westport, CT: Praeger, 1999.

Robertson, Roland. *Globalization.* London: Sage Publications, 1999.

Robertson, Roland, and Habib Haque Khondker. "Discourses of Globalization: Preliminary Considerations." *International Sociology* 13, no.1 (1998): 25–40.

Rodrik, Dani. *Has Globalization Gone Too Far?* Washington, DC: Institute for International Economics, 1997.

Rorty, Richard. "Justice as a Larger Loyalty." In Cheah and Robbins, Cosmopolitics: Thinking and Feeling beyond the Nation.

Rosenau, James "Citizenship in a Changing Global Order." In Governance without Government: Order and Change in World Politics, edited by James Rosenau and Ernst Otto Czempiel. Cambridge: Cambridge University Press, 1992.

———. Distant Proximities: Dynamics beyond Globalization. Princeton, NJ: Princeton University Press, 2003.

———, and others. On the Cutting Edge of Globalization: An Inquiry into American Elites. Lanham, MD: Rowman & Littlefield, 2008.

Rousseau, Jean-Jacques. Émile. Translated by Allan Bloom. New York: Basic Books, 1979.

Rowe, James K. "Corporate Social Responsibility as a Global Business Strategy." In Globalization, Governmentality and Global Politics: Regulation for the Rest of Us? edited by Ronnie Lipschutz. London: Routledge, 2005.

Rubin, Herbert J., and Irene S. Rubin. Qualitative Interviewing: The Art of Hearing Data. London: Sage Publications, 1995.

Ruggie, John Gerard. Constructing the World Polity: Essays on International Institutionalization. London: Routledge, 1998.

———. "The Theory and Practice of Learning Networks: Corporate Social Responsibility and the Global Compact." Journal of Corporate Citizenship 5 (2003): 27–36.

Sandel, Michael. Democracy's Discontent. Cambridge, MA: Belknap Press of Harvard University, 1996.

Sassen, Saskia. Guests and Aliens. New York: New Press, 1999.

———. Losing Control? Sovereignty in an Age of Globalization. New York: Columbia University Press, 1996.

———. Territory, Authority, Rights: From Medieval to Global Assemblages. Princeton, NJ: Princeton University Press, 2006.

———. The Global City: New York, London, Tokyo. Princeton, NJ: Princeton University Press, 1991.

Schattle, Hans. "Communicating Global Citizenship: Multiple Discourses beyond the Academy." Citizenship Studies 9, no. 2 (2005): 119–33.

Scholte, Jan Aart. Globalization: A Critical Introduction. 2nd ed. Basingstoke, UK: Palgrave Macmillan, 2005.

Schuck, Peter H. Citizens, Strangers and In-Betweens: Essays on Immigration and Citizenship. Boulder, CO: Westview Press, 1998.

Scruton, Roger. The Philosopher on Dover Beach. New York: St. Martin's Press, 1990.

Shafir, Gershon, ed. The Citizenship Debates. Minneapolis: University of Minnesota Press, 1998.

Shapiro, Ian, and Lea Brilmayer. Global Justice, Nomos XLI. New York: New York University Press, 1999.

Shapiro, Ian, and Casiano Hacker-Cordón, eds. Democracy's Edges. Cambridge: Cambridge University Press, 1999.

Shaw, Martin. *Theory of the Global State: Globality as Unfinished Revolution*. Cambridge: Cambridge University Press, 2000.

Shklar, Judith. *American Citizenship: The Quest for Inclusion*. Cambridge, MA: Harvard University Press, 1991.

Shue, Henry. *Basic Rights: Subsistence, Affluence and U.S. Foreign Policy*. 2nd ed. Princeton, NJ: Princeton University Press, 1996.

Slaughter, Anne-Marie. *A New World Order*. Princeton, NJ: Princeton University Press, 2004.

Smith, Anthony D. *Nations and Nationalism in a Global Era*. Cambridge: Polity Press, 1995.

———. "Towards a Global Culture?" In *Global Culture*, edited by Michael Featherstone. London: Sage Publications, 1990.

Somers, Margaret. "Romancing the Market, Reviling the State: Historicizing Liberalism, Privatization, and the Competing Claims to Civil Society." In *Citizenship, Markets and the State*, edited by Colin Crouch, Klaus Eder, and Damian Tambini. Oxford: Oxford University Press, 2001.

Soysal, Yasemin Nuho lu. *The Limits of Citizenship*. Chicago: University of Chicago Press, 1994.

Steger, Manfred. *Globalism: Market Ideology Meets Terrorism*. 2nd ed. Lanham, MD: Rowman & Littlefield, 2005.

Stiglitz, Joseph E. *Globalization and Its Discontents*. New York: W. W. Norton, 2003.

———. *Making Globalization Work*. New York: W. W. Norton, 2006.

Strauss, Andrew, Daniele Archibugi, and others. *Debating Cosmopolitics*. London: Verso, 2003.

Strauss, Anselm L., and Juliet Corbin. *Basics of Qualitative Research: Grounded Theory Procedures and Techniques*. London: Sage Publications, 1990.

Tarrow, Sidney G. *The New Transnational Activism*. Cambridge: Cambridge University Press, 2005.

Thompson, Janna. "Community Identity and World Citizenship." In Archibugi, Held, and Köhler, *Re-imagining Political Community: Studies in Cosmopolitan Democracy*.

Tichy, Noel M., Andrew R. McGill, and Lynda St. Clair, eds. *Corporate Global Citizenship: Doing Business in the Public Eye*. San Francisco: New Lexington Press, 1997.

Tomlinson, John. *Globalization and Culture*. Chicago: University of Chicago Press, 1999.

Turner, Bryan. "Citizenship Studies: A General Theory." *Citizenship Studies* 1, no. 1 (1997): 5–18.

———. "Cosmopolitan Virtue: Loyalty and the City." In *Democracy, Citizenship and the Global City*, edited by Engin F. Isin. London: Routledge, 2000.

———. "Liberal Citizenship and Cosmopolitan Virtue." In *Citizenship and Democracy in a Global Era*, edited by Andrew Vandenberg. New York: St. Martin's Press, 2000.

————. "Postmodern Culture/Modern Citizens." In van Steenbergen, *The Condition of Citizenship*.

Urry, John. *Sociology beyond Societies*. London: Routledge, 2000.

Vandenberg, Andrew, ed. *Citizenship and Democracy in a Global Era*. New York: St. Martin's Press, 2000.

van Gunsteren, Herman. "Four Conceptions of Citizenship." In *The Condition of Citizenship*, edited by Bart van Steenbergen. London: Sage Publications, 1994.

————. *A Theory of Citizenship*. Boulder, CO: Westview Press, 1998.

van Steenbergen, Bart, ed. *The Condition of Citizenship*. London: Sage Publications, 1994.

————. "Toward a Global Ecological Citizen." In *The Condition of Citizenship*, edited by Bart van Steenbergen. London: Sage Publications, 1994.

Vertovec, Steven. "Migrant Transnationalism and Modes of Transformation." *International Migration Review* 38, no. 3 (2004): 970–1001.

Vertovec, Steven, and Robin Cohen, eds. *Conceiving Cosmopolitanism: Theory, Context and Practice*. Oxford: Oxford University Press, 2002.

Waddock, Sandra. *Leading Corporate Citizens: Vision, Values, Value Added*. New York: McGraw-Hill, 2001.

Waddock, Sandra, and Neil Smith. "Relationships: The Real Challenge of Corporate Global Citizenship." *Business and Society Review* 105, no. 1 (2000): 47–62.

Waldron, Jeremy. "Minority Cultures and the Cosmopolitan Alternative." In *The Rights of Minority Cultures*, edited by Will Kymlicka. Oxford: Oxford University Press, 1995.

————. "What Is Cosmopolitan?" *Journal of Political Philosophy* 8, no. 2 (2000): 227–43.

Walzer, Michael. "The Civil Society Argument." In Shafir, *The Citizenship Debates*.

————. "Spheres of Affection." In Cohen, *For Love of Country: Debating the Limits of Patriotism*.

Warren, Meg Little. "Educating for Global Citizenship Through Children's Art." *Educational Leadership* 48, no. 7 (1991): 54–55.

Waters, Malcolm. *Globalization*. 2nd ed. London: Routledge, 2001.

Wheeler, Nicholas J., and Tim Dunne. "Good International Citizenship: A Third Way for British Foreign Policy." *International Affairs* 74, no. 4 (1998): 847–70.

Weinstock, Daniel. "Prospects for Transnational Citizenship and Democracy." *Ethics and International Affairs* 15, no. 2 (2001): 53–66.

Wiener, Antje. "From Special to Specialized Rights: The Politics of Citizenship and Identity in the European Union." In *Extending Citizenship, Reconfiguring States*, edited by Michael Hanagan and Charles Tilly. Lanham, MD: Rowman & Littlefield, 1999.

Will, Don, ed. *The Global Citizen*. 2nd ed. New York: Pearson Custom Publishing, 1999.

Yack, Bernard. "Popular Sovereignty and Nationalism." *Political Theory* 29, no. 4 (2001): 517–36.

Young, Iris Marion. "Polity and Group Difference: A Critique of the Ideal of Universal Citizenship." *Ethics* 99, no. 2 (1989).

Yuval-Davis, Nira. "The 'Multi-Layered Citizen': Citizenship in the Age of 'Glocalization.'" *International Feminist Journal of Politics* 1, no. 1 (1999): 119–36.

Yunker, James A. "Rethinking World Government: A New Approach." Lanham, MD: University Press of America, 2005.

Zachary, G. Pascal. *The Global Me: New Cosmopolitanism and the Competitive Edge: Picking Globalism's Winners and Losers.* New York: Public Affairs, 2000.

Zadek, Simon. "Doing Good and Doing Well: Making the Business Case for Corporate Citizenship." New York: Conference Board, 2000.

Zolo, Danilo. *Cosmopolis: Prospects for World Government.* Translated by David McKie. Cambridge: Polity Press, 1997.

Index

citizenship, 71–75; as fulfilling its duties as a global citizen, 142; Iraq invasion and occupation, 79–80, 137, 139, 142–45; refusal to ratify Kyoto Protocol, 140–41; 2004 presidential election, 145–47; withdrawal from international agreements, 140
United Way of Santa Clara County, 120
Universal Declaration of Human Rights, 33, 122, 154
University of Birmingham, 101
University of Michigan, 23
University of Minnesota, 146
University of Missouri, Kansas City, 8
University of Queensland, 9
University of San Diego, 144
University of Southern California, 148
University of Texas at Austin, 19
University of Washington, 186n51
Urry, John, 65, 179n2
U.S. Army, 146
U.S. Clean Air Act, 141
U.S. Congress, 141
U.S. Declaration of Independence, 157
U.S. Department of Education, 187n53
U.S. Department of State, 19, 152; embassy protection while abroad, 72–73
U.S. Federal Reserve System, 142
U.S. Peace Corps, 17
Ustinov, Sir Peter, 53

Vallade, Courtney, 172n20
Vallade, Susan, 175n80
van Gunsteren, Herman, 56, 175n72
Vancouver, British Columbia, 88, 143
Vasella, Daniel, 124–25, 135, 171n5, 175n64
Vermont, civil union legislation, 72
Visual Artists Guild, 127

Vlaams Belang (formerly Vlaams Blok), 176n5
Voice of America, 146
Voluntary Principles on Security and Human Rights, 152
volunteer work: framed as partnerships with local communities, 86–87; overseas, 9–10, 13–14, 78–87; as transforming the lives of individuals, 80–83, 90, 161

Wachovia Bank, 131
Walzer, Michael, 67
Wardwell, Ruth, 174n59, 176n6
Warwick, Dionne, 53
Warroad, Minnesota, 9
Washington, D.C., 13, 71, 158
Waters, Malcolm, 171n10
Watson, Thomas, 20
Weingart, Liat, 128–30
Weinstock, Daniel, 167n6
West Virginia University, 9
Westhill Religious Education Centre, 101
Westlaw All News Plus, 168n13
Whitson, Sarah Leah, 129–30
Wiesenmayer, Randall, 172n26
Will, Don, 8, 107–9
Willcox, Sarah, 15–17
Withers LLP, 132
Wolfensohn, James D., 69
Wollongong, New South Wales, 51
Woodhead, Chris, 187n59
World Bank, 42, 69–70, 74–75
World Bridges, 79
"world citizen," 38, 58, 71, 75, 90, 94, 134
world citizenship, 94, 105–6, 110, 141, 165–66n1, 169n1, 172n30
World Council of Churches, 42
World Economic Forum, 69, 118, 124
world government: absence of, 2, 27; advocated as essential to global citizenship, 88–89; detached from

About the Author

Hans Schattle teaches political science and international relations at Roger Williams University in Bristol, Rhode Island.